THE RIVEN HOME

THE RIVEN HOME

Narrative Rivalry
in the American Renaissance

Ken Egan Jr.

Selinsgrove: Susquehanna University Press
London: Associated University Presses

Associated University Presses
440 Forsgate Drive
Cranbury, NJ 08512

Associated University Presses
16 Barter Street
London WC1A 2AH, England

Associated University Presses
P.O. Box 338, Port Credit
Mississauga, Ontario
Canada L5G 4L8

The paper used in this publication meets the requirements
of the American National Standard for Permanence of Paper
for Printed Library Materials Z39.48–1984.

Excerpts from INCIDENTS IN THE LIFE OF A SLAVE GIRL, WRITTEN BY HERSELF by Harriet A. Jacobs. Copyright 1978 by the President of Harvard College. Reprinted by permission of Harvard University Press.

Excerpts from HARRIET BEECHER STOWE: THREE NOVELS. Copyright 1982 by Literary Classics of the United States, Inc. Reprinted by permission of Library of America.

Library of Congress Cataloging-in-Publication Data

Egan, Ken, 1956–
    The riven home : narrative rivalry in the American renaissance / Ken Egan, Jr.
      p. cm.
    Includes bibliographical references (p.   ) and index.
    ISBN 1-57591-004-7 (alk. paper)
    1. American fiction—19th century—History and criticism.
2. Domestic fiction, American—History and criticism. 3. United States—Intellectual life—19th century. 4. Narration (Rhetoric)
5. Home in literature. I. Title.
PS377.E35 1997
813'.309355—dc21
                                                96-52298
                                                  CIP

For Terry, Devin, and Brian

Contents

Acknowledgments

How does one trace the complex origins of a book? All acknowledgments seem necessarily partial and incomplete. But let me begin by thanking the teachers who guided me through a much earlier version of this study: Sargent Bush Jr., the late William T. Lenehan, E. N. Feltskog, William L. Andrews, and Paul Boyer. John Carlos Rowe helped me refine key concepts during an NEH Summer Seminar, then provided a scrupulous critique of the full manuscript. Susan V. Donaldson shared thoughtful suggestions and encouragement. Gregory S. Jay and James L. Machor reviewed the manuscript in earlier versions and often saved me from inept phrasing and careless reasoning. Grants from the National Endowment for the Humanities and Rocky Mountain College funded research and writing. This book could not have been completed without the assistance of the staffs at the Huntington Library and the American Antiquarian Society. However, I reserve special thanks for Jan Jelinek and Julie Price of the Paul Adams Library at Rocky Mountain College, who efficiently, kindly, patiently procured the necessary materials, obscure and common. Finally, my regards to Tim Lehman and David Strong, colleagues in History and Philosophy who helped me keep the faith.

THE RIVEN HOME

1

The Uncanny Home: Narrative Rivalry in Antebellum America

> But the true home still remains to us. Not, indeed, the feudal
> castle, not the baronial hall, but the home of the individual man—
> the home of that family of equal rights, which continually separates
> and continually reforms itself in the new world—the republican
> home, built by no robbery of the property of another class, main-
> tained by no infringement of a brother's rights; the beautiful, rural,
> unostentatious, moderate home of the country gentleman, large
> enough to minister to all the wants, necessities, and luxuries of a
> republican, and not too large or too luxurious to warp the life or
> manners of his children.
>
> —Andrew Jackson Downing, 1850

ANTEBELLUM AMERICAN WRITERS CELEBRATED THE HOME AS THE
symbol of "America," the site of nurture and republican fraternity,
the embodiment of equality, affection, and toleration. Andrew Jackson
Downing exemplifies this commitment to a well-nigh sacred symbol,
waxing rhapsodic about "the American home" as contrasting image
to "the feudal castle" or "the baronial hall." Indeed, Downing echoes
the central terminology of this idealization of the home: "equal rights,"
"republican," and "a brother's rights." He reminds us that antebellum
Americans lived in the aftermath of "the revolution against patriarchal authority," the simultaneous decrowning of "the father" and the
affirmation of fraternal political and personal relationships.[1] Alexis de
Tocqueville, that typically canny observer of the American scene, was
himself seduced by this image of the fraternal home: "Democracy also
binds brothers to each other. . . . Under democratic laws, all the children are perfectly equal, and consequently independent: nothing
brings them forcibly together, but nothing keeps them apart; and as
they have the same origin, as they are trained under the same roof,
as they are treated with the same care, and as no peculiar privilege
distinguishes or divides them, the affectionate and frank intimacy of

13

early years easily springs up between them."[2] Pursuing the logic of
the home as symbol of the nation, we would conclude that American
society exemplified egalitarian social, economic, and cultural ideals.

But despite the vigorous mythologizing of Downing's prose, he cannot quite conceal the paradoxes, even contradictions of his idealized
home. We notice, for example, the confusion about "individual" and
"family," as though Downing is not quite sure which term he values
more. Is the American nation committed to individual happiness, or
to a collective identity, best embodied in the intimate family? Even
more tellingly, this encomium to republican domesticity builds toward
praise for "the beautiful, rural, unostentatious, moderate home of the
country gentleman." Downing has unwittingly introduced powerful
class-bound terms into this vision of the egalitarian home. Surely he
must realize at some level that a small minority of Americans could
aspire to the status and financial comforts of "the country gentleman."
Indeed, "in implementing his vision of residential republicanism,
Downing brought to his drawing table an eighteenth-century conception of a hierarchical social order, and he designed different homes for
the different classes he saw represented in a well-ordered American
republic."[3] We begin to sense that "the American home" was more
dream work than reality, more wish fulfillment through fantasy than
transcript of actual social conditions. In fact, historians have shown
that the American home increasingly carried the weight of yearning
for social order in a turbulent, conflicted social scene.[4] In other words,
family ideologists made the home a paradigm precisely because social
reality terrified them. How to bring order to the entrepreneurial striving, class conflict, gender divisions, and racial tensions of the pre-Civil
War nation? Ideologists embraced the home as the site of reform and
control, an institution conveniently located between anarchic individualism and statist domination. But could the home carry such a
burden, as symbol or reality? Could America realize the dream of an
egalitarian, fraternal "family"? If not, what sort of American family
might we discover in the narratives of that culture?

I. SIBLING LOVE

The term "home" carries the double sense of "house" and "family,"
suggesting the necessary interconnection between physical dwelling
and human relationships.[5] In part this usage emerges from the narratives we will examine in depth, for American writers emphasized this
vital bond between place and people, perhaps under the influence of
Puritan typological theology.[6] More importantly, as the example of

Andrew Jackson Downing has already hinted, architectural designs carry immense meaning about how human beings can and should relate to one another. If a house is designed in a rigidly hierarchical style, segregating servants from masters, and parents from children, then predictably that house will compel division and subordination. Conversely, a house (or cabin) lacking such physical barriers, and so affording easy movement from room to room, should encourage re-laxed familiarity and affectionate ties among the members of the household. As we track the contrasting versions of the American home through this study, we will observe precisely this contrast be-tween hierarchical and democratic homes, ranging from Cooper's com-plicated architectural designs to Stowe's idealization of kitchen and cabin to Southworth and Melville's troubling descriptions of an American Gothic home.

But behind these competing architectural and familial designs lay a common ideology of domesticity, emerging with full force in the Jack-sonian era. Cultural historians have come to refer to this ideal as "the middle-class home," underscoring the connection between class and values. Antebellum writers and their recent historians present a multi-layered image of this domestic ideal. As the nation moved rapidly toward entrepreneurial capitalism, it experienced an increasingly trou-bling rift between the site of production and the site of consumption. If the nation affirmed the necessary strife of the marketplace, it could not fully surrender the dream of republican simplicity and individual morality. The middle-class home seemed to offer a way out of this contradiction of desires, for the home could remain "a haven in a heartless world" while capitalist aggression circulated beyond its bounds. The home would provide nurture (spiritual and physical) and emotional comfort.[7]

While this description of the domestic ideal is immediately familiar to scholars of American culture, we have tended to overlook a crucial element of the celebration of home life: its embrace of sibling relation-ships. "The 'leading design' of marriage, wrote William Alcott, was 'to secure a brother or sister . . . to form a brotherhood or sisterhood for life.'"[8] Americans of the first half of the nineteenth century recognized dangers built into the split between home and work, most prominently, the possibility that the male would ruthlessly dominate his wife. Not only did such overt power-mongering run counter to the expressed values of the culture, but women had to deal with childbearing, both its physiological and economic consequences. Sexuality posed a threat to the middle-class matron. Antebellum culture sought to soften this relationship of domination by emphasizing that husband and wife could be as brother and sister. We catch a glimpse of this value in

Poe's relationship with Virginia Clemm, for the writer frequently
referred to his young bride as "Sissy" or "Sis," an apparent attempt
to "spiritualize" his relationship with his cousin.[9] Writers such as
Susan Warner lent credence to this view of marriage, for in The Wide,
Wide World Ellen Montgomery falls in love with "brother" John
Humphreys. Given Warner's evangelical upbringing, it is hardly surprising that she should invoke a religious sense to the brother/sister
relationship. Ellen and John are truly kin in the church of Jesus: "In
other words, to speak intelligibly, Ellen did in no wise disappoint her
brother's wishes, nor he hers. Three or four more years of Scottish
discipline wrought her no ill; they did but serve to temper and beautify
her Christian character; and then, to her unspeakable joy, she went
back to spend her life with the friends and guardians she best loved,
and to be to them, still more than she had been to her Scottish relations, 'the light of the eyes.'"[10] Their marriage will flourish at the
spiritual as well as physical level.

    Indeed, this evangelical tradition profoundly shaped American atti-
tudes toward equality in general and fraternal relations in particular:
"Both the libertarian rhetoric of the American Revolution and the
renewed emphasis on the equality of persons before Christ in the
religious revivals hastened this process. Myriad voluntary associations
in the young republic reaffirmed the decline of deference and its re-
placement by an activist conception of a polity of peers."[11] The celebrated sibling relationships of antebellum America symbolized that
"polity of peers." In fact, that dream of equality largely explains the
attraction to sibling relationships as an alternative to traditional concepts of dominance and control. When we look at same-sex sibling
bonds, we see precisely this desire for affectionate but noncompetitive
relationships; put more strongly, sibling relationships became alternatives to relationships involving conflict over power, such as relationships between men and women, between masters and slaves, between
capitalists and laborers. Thus, "sisterhood" provided women with
comfort and security beyond complex relationships with spouses. Sibling affection flourished among men as well. For example, male abolitionists committed themselves to same-sex love, in part out of
Christian principle, in part out of a need for comfort and safety:
"Affection cemented the Garrisonian community and provided the
emotional support necessary to challenge the social order, tolerate
social ostracism, and endure personal violence. For the most committed members of the group, the language of fraternal love symbolized
a rejection of rigid definitions of gender and reflected a theory of
Christian social androgyny that sought to restructure American society."[12] Of course, the abolitionist "family" finds solidarity through its

conflict with other members of the American nation, implying complex struggles in the larger "family of America," an issue we shall address shortly.

But to bring the ideal of sibling love closer to American writing, we can focus on the friendship between Melville and Hawthorne as they composed several of their major texts. While Hawthorne's side of the relationship will remain forever elusive, Melville's letters reveal an overpowering affection, one that the older writer may have found excessive, even oppressive. (It is difficult to imagine the reticent Hawthorne taking pleasure in Melville's effusions.) These two writers' fraternal bond is especially telling since the younger often linked that relationship to their work as writers. In effect, Melville saw in Hawthorne an ideal reader who would "embrace" his daring prose. In a series of letters composed during the writing of *Moby-Dick*, Melville addresses his reader as "my fellow-man," "my dear fellow-mortal," and, simply, "My dear Hawthorne."[13] Melville clearly feels at ease to disclose his innermost thoughts, his most daring speculations. Hawthorne provides him the security, the fraternity to realize himself through writing. Not surprisingly, then, Melville breaks forth with the language of brotherhood when he receives Hawthorne's letter of praise for "The Whale":

> Whence come you, Hawthorne? By what right do you drink from my flagon of life? And when I put it to my lips—lo, they are yours and not mine. I feel that the Godhead is broken up like the bread at the Supper, and that we are the pieces. Hence this infinite fraternity of feeling.[14]

Even this most daring of "Truth Tellers" invokes Christian imagery when figuring his brotherly relationship with a fellow writer. Indeed, Melville sacrilegiously suggests that he and Hawthorne are Christlike, for they are "the bread at the Supper." Melville also suggests a passionate kiss between the fellow writers when he describes (in rather convoluted language) their sharing the "flagon of life." Besides Walt Whitman, it is difficult to recall an antebellum writer who invested more in sibling love between males.

Melville and Hawthorne both incorporated images of fraternal love into their fictions written during the intense phase of their friendship. In *Moby-Dick*, Ishmael develops a full and fulfilling relationship with Queequeg, a brotherly bond that survives death since the lone survivor reminisces fondly about his South Sea friend. In *The Blithedale Romance*, Coverdale employs the language of brotherhood to describe the utopian experiment in general and his relationship with Hollingsworth in particular. So, for instance, upon his first arrival at Blithedale, the tale-teller remarks, "We all sat down—grisly Silas Foster, his rotund helpmate, and the two bouncing handmaidens, included— and looked at one another in a friendly, but rather awkward way. It was the first practical trial of our theories of equal brotherhood and sisterhood; and we people of superior cultivation and refinement . . . felt as if something were already accomplished towards the millennium of love." If Coverdale's ever-present sarcasm lurks beneath the fine language of "brotherhood and sisterhood," he strikes the reader as far more sincere in discussing his relationship with Hollingsworth. In- deed, the early intimacy between the two males appears the most heartfelt relationship in the entire novel: "Hollingsworth's more than brotherly attendance gave me inexpressible comfort. . . . [T]here was something of the woman moulded into the great, stalwart frame of Hollingsworth; nor was he ashamed of it, as men often are of what is best in them. . . ."[15] This characterization of the androgynous reformer suggests that fraternal relations allowed males and females alike to move beyond constrictive ascribed identities. Not only would sibling love free American citizens from relationships of domination, but they would allow the individual to explore alternative aspects of the self.

But this mutual affection between Coverdale and Hollingsworth, a union of effete poet and hermaphroditic reformer, ultimately unrav- els at the utopian commune. And that very undoing reminds us of another element of sibling relations in antebellum culture, rivalry, often leading to violence: "To be married figuratively to one's sibling was to be safe from outside forces. When those forces caused a person to stray, then the counterforce was visualized as familial, most com- monly an avenging sibling."[16] While the critic refers specifically to Priscilla's punishment of Zenobia, his comment can easily extend to Coverdale's treatment of Hollingsworth, at least to the degree that the writer takes vengeance upon his "brother" through composing the often poisonous narrative.[17] We can further extend this concept of sibling rivalry to such novels as *Ruth Hall*, for "Fanny Fern" exacts a fair measure of vengeance against brother Nathaniel Parker Willis. Thus, while the culture of the American Renaissance celebrated the home, and more precisely its nurturing affection and sibling relation- ships, the narratives of antebellum America point to other currents, other realities.

II. SIBLING RIVALRY

It is difficult to imagine a more important statement of domestic ideology than Catharine Beecher's *Treatise on Domestic Economy*

(1841). As Gillian Brown has commented, "for Beecher, good house-keeping is a political practice and the home a model political province."[18] A century and a half after its publication, we can see clearly enough that Beecher proposed a seemingly impossible combination of independence and submission for American women. In effect, Beecher offered those women sentimental power within the confines of patriarchy. If a modern reader feels inclined to dismiss the ideologue for her blindness, that reader must realize Beecher was often aware of this difficult, if not contradictory position.[19] She even begins her ambitious valorization of the feminized home with a direct statement of apparently self-defeating principles. After asserting that "There are some reasons why American women should feel an interest in the support of the democratic institutions of their Country," specifically, for political and religious reasons, Beecher immediately adds, "But, in order that each individual may pursue and secure the highest degree of happiness within his reach, unimpeded by the selfish interests of others, a system of laws must be established, which sustain [sic] certain relations and dependencies in social and civil life." In case we do not catch the drift of this caveat, Beecher becomes more explicit:

> But who shall take the higher, and who the subordinate, stations in social and civil life? This matter, in the case of parents and children, is decided by the Creator. He has given children to the control of parents, as their superiors, and to them they remain subordinate, to a certain age, or so long as they are members of their household. . . . In most other cases, in a truly democratic state, each individual is allowed to choose for himself, who shall take the position of his superior. No woman is forced to obey any husband but the one she chooses for herself; nor is she obliged to take a husband, if she prefers to remain single. So every domestic, and every artisan or laborer, after passing from parental control, can choose the employer to whom he is to accord obedience, or, if he prefers to relinquish certain advantages, he can remain without taking a subordinate place to any employer.[20]

Despite its egalitarian rhetoric, despite its commitment to sibling love, pre-Civil War culture clearly asserted that some citizens were more equal than others, that some had a right to dominate, to subject, to command. In a rather tortured revisit of the freedom/fate conundrum, Beecher asserts that the subordinate members of the society had a right to *choose* their dominant figure. However, she undermines even this claim when she turns her gaze to foreign-born and black servants: ". . . a woman, who has been accustomed to carry forward her arrangements with well-trained domestics, would meet a thousand trials to her feelings and temper, by the substitution of ignorant foreigners, or shiftless slaves. . . ."[21] At least in the case of these members of "the American family," Beecher shows only contempt, and further implies that when a genteel woman is in the position of superior, she carries the valid right to hire and fire upon performance. So much for the undiminished freedom of workers to choose!

Beecher's unusually honest account of "domestic politics" reveals that the American home was riven, internally divided. Because it balanced individual desires against a drive for social control, the home necessarily produced conflict among its members. The Hawthornes' marriage exposed those strains with unusual clarity. Coming of age during a transition from paternalistic to egalitarian marriage, Sophia and Nathaniel registered all the ambiguities, doubts, and conflicts necessarily arising from such a transformation: "Yet this union of perfect beings was simultaneously a battlefield of souls, marked at times with scenes of cruelty and agony; this ideal model of middle-class normality embraced fierce collisions of opposing psychic, social, and religious forces, and it produced a madwoman, a criminal, and a saint."[22] In this way the Hawthornes' marriage provides a microcosmic image of the larger tensions circulating through antebellum American society. "Fierce collisions of opposing psychic, social, and religious forces" applies as readily to the larger culture as to the relationships among these intense individuals. Transcontinental expansion, increasing urbanization and industrialization, immigration from Europe, intensified debates about gender and racial roles, economic upturns and downturns, and debates over slavery rived the society. These dramatic transformations, imaged in texts as diverse as *The House of the Seven Gables* and *Life in the Iron Mills,* caused painful disparities in wealth and power, differences that led to social conflict.

Social historians have analyzed these inequities and power struggles during the antebellum period. In a study of social structure in five New England towns from 1800 to 1860, one historian reaches this unequivocal conclusion: "Resulting from variations in hierarchical location and economic development, these group configurations produced sharp inequalities and very high rates of geographic mobility. Elite and middle groups owned virtually all the wealth, and members of the young and casualties moved with astounding frequency."[23] And how did participants in the culture cope with perceived gaps? The shoemakers of Lynn, Massachusetts provide a paradigm of political activism that we can extend to other subgroups:

[The shoemakers] defined equal rights according to their interests in society: a general elevation in the moral and material condition of labor and an equalization of the upper and lower ranks of the social order. This

definition also set them apart from others of the same period who pursued
their own versions of equality—Women's Rights advocates, Abolitionists,
and antimonopoly entrepreneurs. The issue of equality confronted all sec-
tors of American society, and apart from its reactionary opponents—commercial nabobs of the Northeast and planter aristocrats of the Southeast—
most groups embraced some form of the idea.[24]

Diverse classes of pre-Civil War society attempted to overcome disparities in status by asserting equal rights in terms applicable to them. If
the workers demanded a more equal distribution of wealth, women
demanded a more equal distribution of constitutional rights to vote
and hold office. Operating within a common ideology of equal rights,
citizens claimed full (fraternal) status through a rhetoric of enfranchisement and inclusion. However, the assertion of rights consistently
involved challenging the claims of others, for citizens of antebellum
society often acted as though they were playing a zero-sum game. For
the worker, or the slave, or the female to gain power within the
economy and politics, necessarily someone else must surrender power.
What began as calls for equality frequently turned into outright assertions of authority and domination.

To understand better the interaction among these subgroups in narrative terms—to make sense of these sibling conflicts—we can initially
turn to Harold Bloom's theory of influence anxiety, for Bloom shows
that writers engaged in conscious and unconscious "misprision" in
order to advocate their texts' "strength" or significance:

> . . . strong poets necessarily are perverse, "necessarily" here meaning as if
> obsessed, as if manifesting repetition compulsion. "Perverse" literally
> means "to be turned the wrong way"; but to be turned the right way in
> regard to the precursor means not to swerve at all, so any bias or inclina-
> tion perforce must be perverse in *relation to the precursor*. . . . If the imagi-
> nation's gift comes necessarily from perversity of the spirit, then the living
> labyrinth of literature is built upon the ruin of every impulse most gener-
> ous in us. . . . The strong imagination comes to its painful birth through
> savagery and misrepresentation.[25]

As many critics of this approach have fairly emphasized, the theory
depends upon a masculinist bias that values Oedipal struggles between
literary fathers and sons over all others. However, feminist critics
have found powerful uses for the paradigm, a revisionary tactic I
hope to employ as well.[26] Most importantly, I would emphasize the
necessary conflicts among sibling writers (male and female, white and
black, Southern and Northern, etc.), as well as the perverse relationship with the precursor. Put differently, antebellum writers engaged

in two obvious revisionary processes, one we might label "vertical," the other "horizontal." Vertical revision refers to the writer's complex relationship with older writers and their preferred genres. As Melville developed his savage satire on the New York aristocrat Pierre, he by necessity challenged the mythologizing of earlier New York writers, especially James Fenimore Cooper in *Satanstoe*. When narratives make claims for the rights of a subgroup, those narratives must explicitly or implicitly challenge the rhetorical power of the literary "fathers." But as I have been at pains to emphasize here, sibling relationships took on added ideological significance in Jacksonian America, and so, not surprisingly, "horizontal" perversity toward contemporaries figured even more prominently than perversity toward the precursors. As Bloom suggests, that anxiety of influence manifests itself "through savagery and misrepresentation," hinting at the role of parody, ridicule, and aggressive misreading in these narrative struggles. So Frederick Douglass will ridicule the authority claims of the Southern slavebreaker by manhandling Covey in his prose; so Harriet Beecher Stowe will demean manhood by subverting Southwestern humor and male adventure narrative.

As another means for comprehending these misapprehensions, we should attend to another text that centers on perversity, Poe's "The Imp of the Perverse." This story is crucial to my analysis both because it reveals the tormented unconscious of Poe's culture and because it demonstrates the literary reserves for speaking the seemingly unspeakable. In other words, Poe's narrative theorizes the means for articulating the power struggles that were often repressed in the culture. The narrative begins quietly enough, for it initially reads like a philosopher's treatise; the style appears technical, precise. The critique neatly marks its target, the *a priori* assumption that the self should act rationally for its own preservation. The persona then urges more careful attention to the evidence of how individuals actually behave, and especially to those "marginal" actions that escape our commonsense notions. To account for such events in our experience, the model must include some element of the uncanny: "Induction, *à posteriori*, would have brought phrenology to admit, as an innate and primitive principle of human action, a paradoxical something, which we may call *perverseness*, for want of a more characteristic term. . . . Through its promptings we act without comprehensible object; or, if this shall be understood as a contradiction in terms, we may so far modify the proposition as to say, that through its promptings we act, for the reason that we should *not*."[27]

However, a careful rereading of the opening paragraphs of "Imp" reveals an altogether different style and persona. We come to recognize intense emotion not fully suppressed by the precise manner. These lapses into the irrational reveal the illogical, even violent personality of the speaker. This discovery in turn leads us to consider how the form of the philosophical treatise could be commandeered by an anar-chic personality. Consider the force of "suffer" in this commentary on perversity: "We have suffered its existence to escape our senses, solely through want of belief—of faith;—whether it be faith in Revelation, or faith in the Kabbala" (826). The term is simply too strong for the sentence, implying more powerful emotions at work beneath the surface. What has the speaker suffered? we inevitably inquire. Such questions are multiplied by the speaker's obsessive repetition of "we" in the opening paragraph, possibly signaling a need to attach personal suffering to a universalized condition, or, more likely, operating as the royal plural in a manic personality's discourse. One also notices how the principle of perversity is introduced with the frantic words, "It would have been wiser, it would have been safer to classify, (if classify we must,) upon the basis of what man usually or occasionally did, and was always occasionally doing, rather than upon the basis of what we took it for granted the Deity intended him to do" (827).

Our suspicions about the speaker are confirmed by the story that follows the formal introduction. The treatise is linked to a narrative form, producing a dialogue of genres that undermines the "serious," "official" form. This philosopher is in fact a murderer facing the death sentence; what began as a rationalist's discourse concludes as a Gothic thriller. Reconsidering the persona's "first principles," we recognize the extremity of his claims for moral nature. We realize that the principle of perversity cannot merely be superadded to the prior sys-tem, but that it requires a destruction of that system, for once we admit the possibility of a death wish superseding Eros, what prevents the entire system from collapsing? If the individual psyche even occa-sionally attacks self-preservation, what prevents us from dismissing altogether the assumption that the self "essentially" acts for "the good" of either itself or the other?

In sum, "The Imp of the Perverse" subverts a dominant ideology of the self by marking a repressed urge toward self-destruction. In this way "The Imp" represents the texts generated by antebellum literary production, perverse texts that turn against orthodox forms in order to create their own political and imaginative spaces. Narratives become stalking doubles for other texts, mocking established conventions and substituting alternative norms. Furthermore, Poe's story demonstrates the primary means used in this struggle for expressive authority: the usurping text incorporates a parodized version of the "official" text. As such, Poe can be seen as an American double for the Soviet theorist

Mikhail Bakhtin, whose theory of narrative illuminates these very qualities of revision.

III. THE CARNIVALIZED HOME

As we have seen, Americans of the pre-Civil War era idealized the home as the place of nurture and egalitarian caring. However, tensions within the actual home and within the larger republic divided the family within. Specifically, economic and political inequities caused writers to describe riven homes, scenes of sibling rivalry and even violence. At the same time, these "children" continued to wrestle with paternal figures, reflecting a nostalgia for the fathers who had originally built the House of America. These ongoing narrative conflicts—both vertical and horizontal—play themselves out through perverse misreadings of each other's narrative forms. To put it simply, writers' visions of "the American home" were reflected in their preferred narrative forms. There is, in other words, a direct correspondence between the writers' domestic and literary structures. Writers who long to sustain the claims of cultural patriarchs are drawn not only to imposing mansions for their settings but to literary forms that idealize hierarchy. Conversely, writers committed to leveling familial relations tend toward narratives featuring humor, parody, and sometimes sentiment. As we observe the ongoing domestic struggles among antebellum writers, then, we must of necessity attend to their media, their narrative structures. Mikhail Bakhtin's dialogic theory of the novel pivots on precisely these competing narrative forms, showing that rivalry is embedded in storytelling itself, especially within the novel. Punning upon the meaning of "novel" as "new" or "innovative," Bakhtin shows that fictions shape reality in diverse ways and that these alternative versions necessarily speak to and against each other.

Bakhtin establishes the novel's special status as social discourse by contrasting it with two other traditional genres, the epic and the lyric. According to the Soviet theorist, epic and lyric are both "monologic" discourses. That is, each genre denies the conflicted, strained, heterogeneous nature of language, asserting instead a definitive language and an authoritarian voice. The epic sustains a unitary, one-to-one correspondence between the utterance and the represented object, the epic hero. This official form persistently represents the epic hero through a one-dimensional style that avoids irony or complexity of motivation. The lyric monologizes by positing a one-to-one correspondence between the utterance and the utterer, the speaking subject.

Bakhtin defines the lyric phenomenologically: the poem is that genre in which the constituting subject turns its gaze inward to reflect upon the internal operations of consciousness. Thus, as the epic is located in the distant, unapproachable past, so the lyric is situated outside chronological time in the internal time consciousness; the lyric bids to escape the time of history for the time of awareness. The novel sets against such monologism and temporal distance its own dialogism and immersion in a concrete present. The novel literally brings social discourse to life by depriviliging sanctioned, authoritarian uses of language, substituting diversity, conflict, and instability: "It is necessary that heteroglossia wash over a culture's awareness of itself and its language, penetrate to its core, relativize the primary language system underlying its ideology and literature and deprive it of its naive absence of conflict."[28] In effect, novel forms operate like the aggressive sibling writers of antebellum America.

The novel's dialogic method is an instance of a more encompassing cultural process, "carnivalization." Bakhtin describes the carnival as the social ritual in which hegemony and authority are temporarily suspended so that the various participants in a society, from whatever class or profession, can interact on a basis of equality. The central symbolic event in the carnival is the mock crowning of the king, a parodic doubling of the official ritual by which social power is instituted. In a similar manner, the novel parodies various "high" genres in order to unmask the arbitrary (conventional) nature of authority and hierarchy in discourse. More than this, the carnival operates by an ambivalent laughter: "Crowning/decrowning is a dualistic ambivalent ritual, expressing the inevitability and at the same time the creative power of the shift-and-renewal, the *joyful relativity* of all structure and order, of all authority and all (hierarchical) position."[29] Similarly, the carnivalizing novel instigates laughter and fear by introducing the uncanny into what appeared to be a stable situation and so unveiling the relativistic basis of monologic discourse. The serious epic world is dragged into the laughing present by parodic duplication; the epic hero, pulled into the contemporary as well, takes on the problematic status of the protagonist in a bildungsroman; the author, unlike the self-authoring, self-present lyric poet, is dialogized as his/her language enters novelistic discourse as only one among multiple languages.

Finally—and this is crucial—the novel is a protean genre. As a dialogic utterance immersed in social life, the novel inevitably shape-shifts. However, given a tendency in social discourse toward a unitary, monologic form (a tendency Bakhtin refers to as "centripetal"), the novel is always striving to stabilize itself, to finish itself, to assume the status of the classic and so hold its own vis-à-vis the other finished

genres. This centripetal tendency results in a struggle among various
subgenres to control the form. One subgenre claims the status of the
epic, as it were, only to be undone by a carnivalizing double in the
form of a competing subgenre: "But it is characteristic that the novel
does not permit any of these various individual manifestations of itself
to stabilize. Throughout its entire history there is a consistent parodying or travestying of dominant or fashionable novels that attempt
to become models for the genre. . . ."[30]

Having come this far with Bakhtin, however, we become aware of
a major crux in the theory: the function of ideology in the novel.
Bakhtin seems anxious to make the novel an open-ended forum for
dialogized heteroglossia, freed from the constraints of a single controlling political stance. The novel would then be a permanent carnival.
However, if the novel is relativized and value-free, then presumably
it has cut loose from the political infighting that would seem to dominate all social discourse. On these grounds Bakhtin has been accused
of a Romantic allegiance to a folk art that would make the reader
forget the political constraints on discourse, for he "makes it very clear
in those texts signed with his own name that dialogism cannot be
confused with dialectics. Dialogism cannot be resolved; it has no teleology. It is unfinalizable and open ended."[31]

It is necessary, then, to supplement Bakhtin's theory with a concept
of the interrelationship between ideology and genre. Fredric Jameson
addresses precisely this problem in The Political Unconscious. We hear
echoes of "dialogism" in his description of textual structure: "The
novel is then not so much an organic unity as a symbolic act that
must reunite or harmonize heterogeneous narrative paradigms which
have their own specific and contradictory ideological meaning." But
Jameson solves the problem of ideology, first, by arguing that a text
does indeed enforce a dominant set of beliefs—does "harmonize" the
various elements—and second, by showing that narrative is fundamentally ideological. To clarify this second point, we must take into
account Jameson's notion of a genre as "ideologeme," emerging at the
conclusion of his critique of Northrop Frye's modal theory of genre:
"The modal approach to genre must be pursued, until, by means of a
radical historicization, the 'essence,' 'spirit,' 'world-view,' in question
is revealed to be an ideologeme, that is, a historically determinate
conceptual or semic complex which can project itself variously in the
form of a 'value system' or 'philosophical concept,' or in the form of
a protonarrative, a private or collective narrative fantasy."[32] Thus
when Jameson refers to a novel as a heterogeneous ideological text,
he has in mind the ways in which a writer has woven together contrasting, even conflicting ideologemes. Jameson is interested in how a

text inscribes and then puts to use various ideologemes in constructing its own narrative ideology. This model has the advantage of assuming complex intratextual relationships while at the same time insisting on a dominant ideological position within the text.[33]

Reapproaching pre-Civil War discourse through Bakhtin's theory, we discover, first, its variable form. Antebellum prose is dominated by polyphonic texts that fuse diverse modes into "informal" unities. In this sense, *Uncle Tom's Cabin* is a much more representative text for the period than *The Scarlet Letter*. The former shifts from the mimetic, to the romantic, to the eschatalogical, fusing layers of reality, as it were. Melville's *Moby-Dick* is another exemplary heterogeneous text, linking the "facts" of cetology, outlandish Shakespearian rant, and Ishmaelian downeast humor in a "chowder" that both delighted and frustrated contemporary reviewers. However, the composite nature of these texts should not conceal their ideological implications. More than being polyphonic texts, antebellum narratives were explicitly rhetorical. This is not to say, simply, that these texts were argumentative. Much more fundamentally, these heteroglossic narratives made claims about the status of the writer and his/her subgroup in antebellum culture. These writers sought political benefits from their discourses. As Jane P. Tompkins has put it, antebellum narratives did *work* in the culture.[34]

Arguably narrative forms functioned to further the social aspirations of various subgroups of society.[35] This claim is confirmed by the emergence of identifiable subclasses of the novel in the pre-Civil War United States. We can infer as much from the fact that reviewers worked with classifying terms such as "domestic novel," "historical novel," and "highly wrought novel." Moreover, these subgenres clearly served the interests of discrete social groups: "If the *first* characteristic of the modern novel was its greater fidelity to everyday life, the *second* was precisely its proliferation and fragmentation into subgenres treating different segments of the social field."[36] Metaphorically speaking, each subgenre projected a competing architectural plan for the house of America. Each described a kind of building, who should be allowed to live within that building, the roles of these respective family members, and the rules of conduct both toward other family members and those excluded. Imagine a multitude of builders constructing an edifice using a blueprint with conflicting instructions. These builders might agree on general principles (equality of expressive opportunity and religious toleration), but beyond these self-evident concepts, their terms, their style, their materials would be strikingly different.

To understand more fully this struggle for expressive and ideological authority, we will find it useful to incorporate two terms familiar to scholarship of the antebellum United States: pastoral and Gothic. These representational modes were central to American domestic art: while the pastoral traditionally summoned an image of the home anchored in a middle landscape, the Gothic suggested a haunted, guilt-ridden house. Viewed through Bakhtin's theory, "pastoralizing" appears a type of monologizing, for it conceals language's sedimentation by insisting on a one-to-one relationship between utterance and represented object. In a pastoralized description, language becomes wholly naturalized as conflict and strain drop away and the scene emerges full-blown as a self-contained, sealed-off world. Pastoralizing is an apt term for describing antebellum narrative because of a long-standing pastoral tradition in New World discourse. Even more importantly, antebellum culture struggled to preserve a definition of the United States as a society that escaped history. Marvin Meyers has pointed out how Jacksonian rhetoric functioned to conceal capitalization behind a Jeffersonian agrarian ideal.[37] Thus pastoralizing is correlative to "normalization," that process of making the uncanny canny, the strange conventional. We observe pastoralizing not only in explicit pastoral passages, but also in those normalizing strategies that texts employ to pull back within the bounds of dominant beliefs.

Gothicizing is the antithesis of pastoralizing, for it is the process of turning the canny into the uncanny. "The Imp of the Perverse" is an excellent case in point, for Poe scrambles antebellum psychology by introducing the inexplicable impulse to act precisely contrary to one's self-interest. That text describes the perverse in terms of a stalking double "that goes within," tracking and ridiculing the manifest intentions of the subject. Moreover, gothicizing is a version of carnivalizing. Whereas the carnivalized moment inspires ambivalent laughter, the gothicized moment inspires fear of the uncanny.[38] If pastoralizing is correlative to "normalizing," gothicizing is correlative to "defamiliarizing." We can point not only to explicit Gothic moments, but to instances in which a text subverts conventions and courts fear in lieu of earnestness. Thus, in this struggle for mastery among texts we will frequently observe a dialectic between pastoralizing and gothicizing within individual texts. Texts generally gothicize, and, more broadly, carnivalize another text only in order to substitute an alternative norm, that is, to pastoralize its own set of values.[39]

IV. Repetition Compulsions

In the following chapters we will examine these dialogic struggles among subgenres competing for hegemony within the antebellum literary arena. In one sense this study provides an overview of important narrative forms within a particular historical period, all the while emphasizing that those narrative practices were grounded in the social realities of the time. In sequence, we will examine the historical novel—along with versions of the American epic and the novel of contemporary life—the plantation novel, the slave narrative, the reform novel—along with the local color sketch, the Southwestern humor tale, and the male adventure story—and highly wrought or melodramatic fiction. We will come to understand the distinguishing characteristics of these subgenres, at the same time highlighting the interaction among these narrative types, that is, their explicit resistance to competing forms. We will also examine the diverse ways in which such dialogic exchanges occurred within the culture. Thus, we will analyze two instances of single authors cannily or uncannily entering the arena of dialogic struggle (Cooper and Stowe), an instance of a complex chain of parody (conflicts over slavery and Southern society in general), and an instance of two writers engaging in direct conflict over their roles in the culture (Southworth and Melville). It is hoped that these representative cases will direct readers toward their own examples. How, for instance, might we explicate Hawthorne's *The House of the Seven Gables* in the context of these generic struggles? How might we read a chain of American autobiographies through the perverse lenses of Bloom, Poe, and Bakhtin, including such narratives as Douglass's *Narrative,* Thoreau's *Walden,* and Barnum's *Struggles and Triumphs?* How might we interpret Lydia Maria Child's *Hobomok* against Cooper's Indian fiction? In short, I offer these perverse readings as incitements to further analysis, analysis that will expand and correct the model offered here.

But we should not think of the individual readings of these subgenres as discrete units, defining contained skirmishes in antebellum culture. Instead, we will discover recurring issues that move across textual boundaries, suggesting repetition compulsions within pre-Civil War culture, obsessive circling-back to dominant concerns. I have in mind here a strict analogy to Freud's concept, which he linked to a death wish in the human psyche:

> But how is the predicate of being "instinctual" related to the compulsion to repeat? At this point we cannot escape a suspicion that we may have come upon the track of a universal attribute of instincts and perhaps of organic life in general which has not hitherto been clearly recognized or at least not explicitly stressed. *It seems, then, that an instinct is an urge inherent in organic life to restore an earlier state of things* which the living entity has been obliged to abandon under the pressure of external dis-

turbing forces; that is, it is a kind of organic elasticity, or, to put it another
way, the expression of the inertia inherent in organic life.[40]

Writers of antebellum America shared instinctual attractions to central issues, believing that such drives would lead toward change or
progress but which in fact reflect a longing for a prior order, an Edenic
home ("America") that would embody their cherished ideals. Ironically, though, as Freud would suggest, these repetition compulsions
actually reflect an urge toward a cessation of action, toward death.
Figuratively at least the repetition compulsions of the American Renaissance led to the Civil War and the death of prewar optimism.

Put in its broadest terms, each writer is attempting to define
"America" in such a way that he/she is empowered within that culture. Inevitably this struggle to define "America" meant that all writers had to engage questions of authority, rights, and inclusion. Put
more simply, Cooper, Kennedy, Douglass, Simms, Jacobs, Stowe,
Hooper, Melville, and Southworth each wrestled with who should
hold political power and what degree of political participation should
be granted to men, women, and various ethnic and racial groups. The
U. S. Constitution was very much up for grabs, undergoing strict and
liberal interpretations as writers confronted immediate social crises in
context of a "founding" political document with glaring inconsisten-
cies or gaps. The compromises, elisions, and lacunas in the foundational text of "America" were exposed and explored by the competing
subgenres, alternative answers were proposed, and few compromises
were found. To underscore these struggles over the meaning of
"America," I have chosen to analyze openly polemical texts, those
that amplify the arguments that are often implied (or repressed) in
other texts by the same writers. Once again, it is hoped that by listening to the most provocative, the most melodramatic, the most politically engaged texts of the period, we will be positioned to discern
these same conflicts within other texts of the time.

As a final means for figuring the social and narrative situation of
the antebellum United States, we can recall that Freud saw repetition
compulsion as the most prominent instance of "the uncanny," defined
as "that class of the terrifying which leads back to something long
known to us, once very familiar." To clarify this principle, he traces
the etymology of the term in German to show that "*heimlich* is a word
the meaning of which develops towards an ambivalence, until it finally
coincides with its opposite, *unheimlich.*" In other words, the "homely"
somehow necessarily involves the "unhomely," that which resists the
home. But how can this be? How does that which most defies our
"homing instincts," our domestic commitments, reside nonetheless in

that very home? Simply because "this uncanny is in reality nothing new or foreign, but something familiar and old-established in the mind that has been estranged only by the process of repression."[41] The official ideology of the American home sought to suppress the conflicted power relations of pre-Civil War society. But sibling writers, suffering that suppression and sensing the repressed truth, uncannily articulated the silenced desires of the American family. In the conclusion to this study, I turn to Poe's "The Fall of the House of Usher," which narrates the homicidal sibling struggle between Madeline and Roderick Usher. Poe's uncanny narrative provides the seemingly inevitable coda to this study of the riven home of America. That fantastic story symbolizes the erotic and murderous relationships among writers of different regions, genders, races, and classes during the antebellum period. "The Fall of the House of Usher" anticipates the Civil War that would rend not only the plantation economy but would seal forever the fate of Cooper's agrarian dream and further complicate women's roles in American culture. That destruction would be the culmination of the violent forces of dissent inscribed in the sibling narratives considered here at length.

2

Home as Lost: Razing Gentry in the Littlepage Trilogy

> In a country whose history has been focused for so long on the
> business of settlement and "development," the issue of how to
> stake out territory, clear it, cultivate it, and build on it has been
> of major economic, political, and psychological consequence. For
> settlers, building on this land meant using native materials on
> "virgin territory" without established architectural context; arriv-
> ing at some compromise between architectural ideas and designs
> imported from Europe and innovative, indigenous forms; and pro-
> ducing rough, hybrid constructions from what was available to
> violent expropriation of land and entering a long struggle over the
> relations between political rights and property ownership.

NO WRITER EXEMPLIFIES THESE GENERALIZATIONS MORE COMPLETELY
than James Fenimore Cooper. His fictions are preoccupied with the
issue of occupation: By what right have we acquired this continent?
What have we made of the opportunity afforded by this "expropria-
tion"? What kind of culture could possibly live up to nature itself?
Early and late, whether in The Pioneers or in The Crater, Cooper
meditated on the responsibilities of the young nation to the place
it had acquired. This questioning often translated into architectural
symbols, for Cooper's prose frequently returns us to troubled descriptions of emerging communities in the wilderness, setting those vexed
beginnings against the finished home of the father, the colonial mansion that hovers as promise and challenge to republican culture. What,
indeed, might the House of America look like? No doubt Cooper's
questioning emerged from his powerful sense of belatedness, of having
arrived too late to participate in the founding of colony or nation. He
lived and wrote on his own "neutral ground," a kind of liminal space
between the founding father and the engaged contemporary. No wonder his prose often vacillates wildly between filiopiety and iconoclasm.
    The tensions within Cooper's sense of himself come clearest in the

Littlepage Trilogy, written in the midst of the Anti-Rent Wars in the 1840s. This political and social crisis focused the issues at the heart of Cooper's ideology, for it pitted the economic levelers against the landlords, traditional bastion of American culture. At a conscious level Cooper clearly staked his claim on the landlords. Thus this "founding father of American fiction" set out to compose an American family chronicle extending from colonial to Jacksonian America, a narrative sequence which would advocate the rights of a landed gentry in the democratic United States. In architectural terms, Cooper aspired to construct a fictional edifice which would serve as a fortress against the anarchic Jacksonian society he had come to distrust, even despise. The writer seems to have been talking himself into a firm belief in the virtue, the relevance of "the American gentleman." But a funny thing happened on the way to this celebration of a natural aristocracy: the three texts show that the distinction between the landed gentry and the capitalist would not hold. The Littlepage Manuscripts trace the arc from self-righteous agrarian elite to a monied class fully immersed in the economic processes of the mid-nineteenth century. In a dramatic act of self-disclosure, Cooper reveals that he as writer and heir to his father's legacy could not escape the web of financial dealings which implicated northern capitalists and Southern plantation owners alike. As we examine the Littlepage Trilogy, then, we will witness the loss of Cooper's most cherished home, the mansion of the American gentleman. In its place these narratives will erect carnivalesque villages and flawed republican houses. Reading this late addition to Cooper's narrative archive, we truly see "home as lost."

This narrative fall occurs by and through genre. As I commented in the previous chapter, domestic and narrative structures tend to mirror each other. It should not come as a surprise, then, if the form of each Littlepage novel should embody contrasting images of the American home. To be more exact, Cooper's rhetorical design virtually required him to reprise generic changes in antebellum narrative, the movement from epic, to complex historical romance, to the novel of contemporary life. But Cooper did not realize that this generic movement worked at odds with his political design. While the landed gentry are an organic element in the colonial social landscape, they appear anachronistic in the contemporary social scene. In effect fictional conventions deconstructed the colonial mansion, replacing it with carnivalesque houses in the early Republic and Jacksonian America. Thus the Littlepage Trilogy provides the literary historian with an overview of important narrative subgenres of the antebellum period, allows insight into the struggle between political design and fictional conventions, and most importantly, signals the demise of that most powerful of precursors, the early American historical novel.[1] In this way Cooper's Trilogy provides us a paradigm of novelistic change in the American Renaissance, setting the stage for later chapters which will invoke the Bakhtinian processes elaborated here. This set of novels will provide a template for interpreting dialogic exchanges between the plantation novel and slave narrative, as well as those between Stowe's major novel and adventure narratives and Melville and Southworth's parodies of paternalistic prose. Perversely, then, we will read Cooper as, indeed, the "father" of antebellum prose, though we will learn from his failures rather than from his triumphs.

I. THE LOST SON

Cooper's writings exemplify the tension between celebrating and ridiculing the father, a division that translates into the strain between epic and novel forms. The impulse toward the epic emerged from cultural anxiety about the status of the new republic: how could this self-made, self-proclaimed political entity justify itself to the world? Inevitably such an apology took the form of labored epics, strained efforts at mythic narratives of origins. Still dominated by neoclassical generic codes, writers such as Timothy Dwight and Joel Barlow assumed that only the heroic poem could legitimize the United States. In this sense the epic represented a desire to celebrate "the rising glory of America," to carry out that traditional task of promising future greatness.[2] But the impulse toward the epic represented more than a desire for cultural sanction, for the post-Revolutionary War generation also wrestled with patricidal guilt. Having destroyed the paternal institutions of British colonial government and established churches, what might the new national culture substitute? The epic offered an imaginative means for repressing patricide by honoring the destroyed colonial system; further, heroic narratives permitted an accounting of debts to earlier generations, thus providing a genealogy, an emotional continuum enabling future action. Along with monumental architecture and statuary, epic narratives manifested the "sacramental" desire discussed by Eric J. Sundquist.[3]

However, Sundquist observes that the sacramental drive was offset by an experimental or revolutionary impulse that celebrated change in and of itself. Even as the culture would build monuments, it would also make fun of that very ambition. In the contest between epic and novel in the new republic we see the Bakhtinian clash between the official, sanctioned version of cultural experience and the carnivalizing alternative. Cathy N. Davidson has emphasized this dialectic between the centripetal official ideology and the centrifugal popular ideology in her analysis of early American picaresque: "The rational Enlighten-ment document of the Constitution—with its rhetoric of fairness and freedom and its cautious regulating of the former and restricting of the latter—disguises the acrimonious debate that preceded its passage and obscures the carnivalization of republican principles enacted in the numerous public displays of the postrevolutionary era—every-thing from rallies and parades to strikes and insurrections."[4] It is pre-cisely the function of the novel to represent these carnival energies, to decrown and destabilize official discourse, to level high and low genres toward a democracy of language. In addition to Brackenridge's *Modern Chivalry* (discussed in depth by Davidson), Charles Brockden Brown's best work creates a literary carnival. *Wieland,* for instance, produces astonishing effects by merging the language of Enlightenment rationality, Crèvecoeur's settlement narrative, a rags-to-respectability story, and, of course, Gothic rhetoric. What better way to depict an unstable, volatile culture, a society uncertain of its place and time, lacking a unitary identity or unifying myth?

Though Cooper does not literally belong to the post-Revolutionary War generation, this protean novelist represents the tension between an epic, sacramental tradition and the novelizing, experimental, carni-valizing tradition. As Howard Mumford Jones has astutely observed, "The writings of this great novelist are haunted by a memory and a dream. The dream is that of his father, Judge William Cooper, a demo-crat in emotion, a federalist by conviction, hardheaded yet philan-thropic, the only landed proprietor in upper New York to escape financial ruin, who proudly declared he had settled more Americans on wilderness land than any other man in the country, and who was murdered by a political opponent. The dream is also a projection of James Fenimore Cooper as gentleman proprietor in succession. . . ."[5] It is hardly surprising that this haunted writer popularized the American historical novel, a form distinctly divided between epic and novelistic intentions. This narrative form can be read as an updated version of the classical epic, for as developed by Scott the historical novel cele-brated a distinctive national culture and recounted its historical past in near mythic terms.[6] However, it is precisely the presence of history, of human error and strife, which undermines that monumentalizing intention. History fractures the monumental past, creating fissures and cracks in the fundament, reminding the reader that epic is always a form of wish-fulfillment.

Cooper's best historical novels balanced epic and novel, simultane-ously placating the memory of the founding father and admitting hu-man foibles and conflict. For this reason *The Pioneers* remains

Cooper's most impressive historical text, for it maintains a balance between the claims of Judge Marmaduke Temple and Natty Bumppo, the former representing "civic," the latter "natural virtue." While Temple's nascent community wins the contest of wills, Natty Bumppo voices the suppressed truth: settlement comes at terrible natural and human costs. Wilderness must be violated; native tribes must be displaced, even eradicated. Furthermore, the narrative sets Judge Temple's elegant theories against the actual carnival appearance of Templeton:

> It consisted of some fifty buildings, including those of every description, chiefly built of wood, and which, in their architecture, bore no great marks of taste, but which also, by the unfinished appearance of most of the dwellings, indicated the hasty manner of their construction. To the eye, they presented a variety of colours. A few were white in both front and rear, but more bore that expensive colour on their fronts only, while their economical but ambitious owners had covered the remaining sides of the edifices, with a dingy red. One or two were slowly assuming the russet of age; while the uncovered beams that were to be seen through the broken windows of their second stories, showed, that either the taste, or the vanity of their proprietors, had led them to undertake a task, which they were unable to accomplish.[7]

Such apparently labored descriptions of the village serve a larger point: to qualify Temple's pious vision. The judge is not named "Temple" for nothing, but the reader is discouraged from naively worshipping at his shrine.

Cooper's vexed return from Europe in 1833 smashed the synthesis achieved in *The Pioneers* and other historical novels of the 1820s, including *The Last of the Mohicans* and *The Wept of Wish-ton-Wish*. Hectored by hostile newspapers, embittered over the seemingly trivial issue of Three Mile Point, distressed at the spectacle of hurly-burly Jacksonian culture, Cooper could no longer consciously novelize the cultural elite. Instead, he produced *The American Democrat*, a political treatise that justifies the role of "the democratic gentleman" in the United States. Apparently the writer believed he was finding a middle ground, advocating a political democracy while acknowledging the rights of a cultivated elite. The text distances itself from European systems, especially the British and French, an evident attempt to celebrate that which is most "American" in the American system. However, because *The American Democrat* is ultimately an apology for Cooper's class, it is difficult for the writer to maintain his equilibrium. His tone becomes that of the superserious advocate, shunning any hint of failure in the gentry:

The democratic gentleman must differ in many essential particulars, from the aristocratical gentleman, though in their ordinary habits and tastes they are virtually identical. Their principles vary; and, to a slight degree, their deportment accordingly. The democrat, recognizing the right of all to participate in power, will be more liberal in his general sentiments, a quality of superiority in itself; but, in conceding this much to his fellow man, he will proudly maintain his own independence of vulgar domina' tion, as indispensable to his personal habits. The same principles and manli' ness that would induce him to depose a royal despot, would induce him to resist a vulgar tyrant.

Cooper's impatience with his "vulgar" culture breaks to the surface here. While the passage begins with an affirmation of democratic politics, by its conclusion the writer has thrown all his weight behind the social superiority of the gentleman. Indeed, Cooper wants to make it clear that there is no intrinsic difference between the *American* and the *European* gentleman. Cooper constructs a wall, a barrier between the social aristocracy and the public, allowing the carnival to swirl around him but beyond the confines of his class. Of particular rele' vance to this study, Cooper stresses that the American gentleman's claim to cultural leadership rests on his possessions, including (presum' ably) his homes: "Property is desirable as the ground work of moral independence, as a means of improving the facilities, and of doing good to others, and as the agent in all that distinguishes the civilized man from the savage."[8]

This division between elite and democratic cultures holds firm in *Home as Found* (1838). Indeed, one critic observes that "in [this novel], Cooper attempts to rewrite America's history and to replace popular sovereignty with a naive notion of benevolent, paternal tyr' anny."[9] Edward Effingham and his daughter Eve represent the refined gentry, and withal, stand above the fray of Templeton politics. Eve serves as a still point in the turning world of Jacksonian chaos, quietly passing judgment on the vulgar behavior of New York and upstate society. In the end she marries Paul Powis, who turns out to be her cousin, an "incestuous" match which assures the preservation of the Effingham hegemony.[10] Characters such as Aristabulus Bragg and Steadfast Dodge represent the coarse, volatile democratic culture at odds with Effingham dignity. Working with gossip mongers upon gull' ible citizens, Dodge the newspaperman incites public anger with the Effinghams over use of a picnic ground. Through Dodge, then, Cooper attacks the fascination with the *new* as opposed to the established and classical. Bragg is a more complex, more likable character, because he demonstrates democratic enterprise and energy. Also, he lacks Dodge's cynical attitude toward fellow human beings. Bragg's problems emerge from his naïveté, his ignorance of social convention and taste. In this sense he poses as large a threat to the democratic gentleman as Dodge, for he stumbles into areas of sentiment that are beyond his comprehension. His marriage to Eve's French maid shocks the American ingenue as an act of gross overreaching. Thus, though by no means an epic in tone or action, this novel of manners reflects Cooper's latter-day commitment to a cultural elite and its founders. His fiction now runs in two tracks, the affirmative, earnest prose devoted to the Effinghams, and the negative, novelistic prose devoted to the surrounding democratic society.

In the mid-1840s the New Yorker's social allegiances were put to an even more severe test by the Anti-Rent Wars on the Hudson River patroonships. Though Cooper had no personal stake in the strife, "nevertheless Anti-Rent aligned all the forces Cooper most detested against all the values he held most dear. . . . Cooper's penchant for enlarging experience led him to a perfectly consistent generalization: the hierarchy of the liberal gentleman presiding over an agrarian society was being inverted by the rabble beneath."[11] His ire aroused, his dismay, even horror at his country peaking, Cooper devised a plan for fictionalizing his interpretation of the debacle:

> "The Family of the Littlepage" will form three complete Tales, each perfectly distinct from the other as regards leading characters, love story &c, but, in this wise connected. I divide the subjects into the "Colony," "Revolution," and "Republic," carrying the same family, the same localities, and same *things* generally through the three different books, but exhibiting the changes produced by time &c. . . . In the "Republic" we shall have the present aspect of things, with an exhibition of the Anti-Rent commotion that now exists among us, and which certainly threatens the destruction of our system—You know I write what I think, in these matters, and I shall not spare "The Republic" in all in which it is faulty and weak, as faulty and weak it has been to a grievous extent in these matters.[12]

Cooper sets out to match narrative to polemic: he will demonstrate the decline of the republic over time, a declension accelerated by "mobocracy." His voice here is stern, judgmental; he clearly falls into the tradition of jeremiad exemplified by Cotton Mather's epic *Magnalia Christi Americana*. And yet, something fascinating happens to the argument when it enters the domain of the novel: the text undermines Cooper's design. This self-subversion (surely unconscious) becomes clear in *The Redskins*, for the final novel of the Trilogy devolves into a carnivalizing text, a decentered, open-ended play of discourses. In the Littlepage Trilogy Cooper's bulwark against democratic culture breaks down, for his hard-won separation of the democratic gentleman from the public dissolves.

II. Epics of New York

In his compelling study of Cooper's pastoral designs, H. Daniel Peck comments that "in every way *Satanstoe* renders the sense of a beginning."[13] In this remark Peck goes a long way toward explaining why this first of the Littlepage Manuscripts reads like an American epic.[14] Bakhtin argues that epic concerns itself precisely with "the world of fathers, of beginnings and peak times."[15] *Satanstoe* (1845) is Cooper's sentimental journey into the founding of New York, his imaginative displacement into the "peak times" of pre-Revolutionary America, when landed gentry held unquestioned authority over the political and cultural fortunes of the community. In the monologic, refined language of Corny Littlepage we hear the tones of a confident class. Furthermore, Corny's adventure story (encompassing his court-ship of Anneke Mourdant) symbolically represents the imperial de-signs of young America as it extends its reach over the wilderness. But before examining setting, character, and action in the novel proper, we should remind ourselves that Cooper composed *Satanstoe* in the con-text of a New York epic tradition which espoused the virtues of Dutch culture and the inevitable decline of American society after the War of Independence. When reading for the political implications of the first Littlepage novel, we must keep in mind that it represents a class of texts espousing a specific ideology.

Washington Irving's texts provide a familiar introduction to the Knickerbocker epic. In its backhanded fashion, Irving's *History of New York* (1809) celebrates the Dutch hegemony which was superseded by British colonization. Despite its hyperbolical, farcical tone, *Knicker-bocker's History* generates a nostalgia for the Dutch past, and, toward the close, even achieves an elegiac dignity:

> Among the numerous events which are each in their turn the most direful and melancholy of all possible occurrences in your interesting and authen-tic history, there is none that occasions such deep and heart-rending grief as the decline and fall of your renowned and mighty empires. . . . King-doms, principalities, and powers have each had their rise, their progress, and their downfall. . . . And thus did it fare with the empire of their High Mightinesses at the Manhattoes under the peaceful reign of Walter the Doubter—the fretful reign of William the Testy—and the chivalric reign of Peter the Headstrong.[16]

"Rip Van Winkle" and "The Legend of Sleepy Hollow" embellish this celebration of the New York past. Though Rip is hardly a heroic figure, his fall from colonial innocence into the complicated new Republic calls into question the benefits of historical progress. In even more dramatic fashion, the intense pastoral opening of "Sleepy Hollow," the quintessential world elsewhere, elevates genial, communalistic Dutch culture above the aggressive, intrusive behavior of the New England interloper, Ichabod Crane. Brom Bones's mock heroic victory over the schoolmaster symbolizes the victory of a stable, traditionalist culture over an insurgent greed.

An even closer literary sibling to *Satanstoe* is James Kirke Paulding's *The Dutchman's Fireside* (1831).[17] Paulding's novel clearly anticipates many of the key events in Cooper's novel. Sybrandt Westbrook, a scholarly, introverted youth, afraid of women and life in equal proportions, is force-fed experience by a journey into the wilderness. As the genial narrator of the tale remarks:

> In the days of which we are speaking, the young men bordering on the frontier were accustomed almost universally to commence the business of this world with a trading voyage among the savages of the borders. Previous to assuming the port and character of manhood, it was considered an almost indispensable obligation to undertake and complete some enterprise of this kind, replete with privations and dangers. The youth went out a boy and returned a man, qualified to take his place among men, and to aspire to the possession of the object of his early love. It was in this way that the character of the patriarchs of this country was formed; and by these means that it exhibited a union of homely simplicity, manly frankness, and daring enterprise, which at length found their reward in the achievement and possession of liberty.[18]

Under the tutelage of Sir William Johnson, living a middle life between civilization and savagery, between city and wilderness, Sybrandt acquires the self-confidence to assume his place as "patriarch" in colonial New York. His initiation into manhood falls into three major stages: his defeat of the debauched Indian Paskingoe, his rescue of Catalina from the vengeful Hans Pipe, and his participation in the French-Indian War. In this way Sybrandt moves from flawed, feeble individual to a character of nearly heroic stature. The text frequently refers to Roman and Greek models, for Paulding wishes to emphasize the heroic dimensions of this colonial story.

But merely to summarize the action of *The Dutchman's Fireside* is to give a misleading impression of its tone, for far from being an adventure-filled, fast-paced text, this novel embodies a pastoral world, and so fully represents the pastoralizing effect discussed in chapter 1.

The very title of the novel hints at this pastoralizing tendency, for what more comforting domestic image can one summon than the hearth? (One need only think of Whittier's "Snow-Bound" to appreciate the power of that image for rural American writing.) Furthermore, "Dutch" is a shorthand term for a simpler, more virtuous historical epoch. As the narrator remarks, ". . . I often catch myself contemplating, with something like sober regret, those days of unostentatious simplicity, easy, unaffected intercourse, and manly independence. Who, indeed, that hath gathered from history and tradition a picture of the manners, modes, and morals of the ancient patriarchs of Albany and its neighborhood, but will be inclined to contrast them dolefully with those of the present times?" (48). This *ubi sunt* theme reminds us again of Irving's treatment of Dutch culture, especially in "The Legend of Sleepy Hollow." Combining material prosperity with an anti-Puritanical sensibility, the Dutch inhabit a special zone of geniality and communality. In Paulding's (and Cooper's) case that pastoral condition depends upon a specific social system: the Dutch patroonships developed along the Hudson River. The pastoralizing function, then, works to idealize the Dutch landed gentry, and presumably it is precisely this connection between Paulding's novel and the Anti-Rent controversy that led Cooper to imitate *The Dutchman's Fireside*. As if to underscore the social system that enables the pastoral condition, Paulding draws an explicit comparison between the defining Dutch house and the Southern plantation: "The mansion-house of the Vancours had ever been open to the footsteps of all respectable strangers, and especially to the military men who frequently sojourned there on their passage from New York to the frontier posts and back again. They came and went as they pleased, and were received and entertained with an easy hospitality, of which we see some remains still lingering in the Southern States, and making head against the silent inroads of heartless and selfish ostentation" (70). As the next chapter will show, this analogy between New York estates and Southern plantation was also utilized by Southern writers such as John Pendleton Kennedy.

Cooper exemplified the pastoralizing, nostalgic drive in Jacksonian America. Marvin Meyers has skillfully analyzed this writer's complicated relationship with the Jacksonian Democrats, a connection made puzzling by the apparent disparities between Cooper's "Tory" sentiments and those of the leveling Democratic Party. Meyers detects the solution to this puzzle in Cooper's attitude toward present and past: "Cooper found his essential party friends among the Jacksonians . . . because he shared with them an angry sense of loss: the First American Republic—the 'Doric' age, to apply his term for Washington's character—was going down before a raw company of the commercial *nouveau riche,* the speculative promoters of paper towns and enterprises, the mock-democrats of the popular press."[19] Shocked by the decadent present, Cooper returns through fantasy to the pastoral, heroic age of the colony, before the fall into time caused, first, by the Revolutionary War, and later by the leveling politics of the 1830s and 40s.

Critics often describe *Satanstoe* as restrained, controlled, and even placid in comparison with such novels as *The Last of the Mohicans.* They rightly attribute this muted tone to the narrator's mild temperament, but the narrative's intense pastoral moments also encourage that reading experience. Indeed, the opening movement of the novel is overwhelmingly bucolic in tone. Cooper dabs on the features of colonial culture, ranging from the Littlepage estate to the more sophisticated (though still provincial) New York City, and so creates a composite portrait of a society superficially disparate but fundamentally unified. This unified society is "pastoral" in the broadest sense of a well-ordered, morally sound society operating at a level of reduced economic needs. "Pastoral" applies in a more specialized sense as well, for the narrative repeatedly presents views of a refined rural landscape in the sentimental mode. Whether describing his own estate, or a trip to Herman Mordaunt's, or New York City itself, Corny stresses the rustic charms of the colonial landscape. Most tellingly, the narrator carefully describes his family home, fetishizing the stones, carpets, and scale of the colonial gentleman's abode:

> The house is generally esteemed one of the best in the colony, with the exception of a few of the new school. It is of only a story and a half in elevation, I admit; but the rooms under the roof are as good as any of that description with which I am acquainted, and their finish is such as would do no discredit to the upper rooms of even a York dwelling. . . . The best room had a carpet, that covered two-thirds of the entire dimensions of the floor, even in my boyhood, and there were oil-cloths in most of the better passages. The buffet in the dining-room, or smallest parlor, was particularly admired; and I question if there be, at this hour, a handsomer in the country. The rooms are well-sized, and of fair dimensions, the larger parlors embracing the whole depth of the house, with proportionate widths, while the ceilings were higher than common, being eleven feet, if we except the places occupied by the larger beams of the chamber floors.[20]

Corny's journey to adulthood begins and ends in the sealed world of this pastoral home, the landscape of reconciliation symbolic of a stratified, stable, and moral social order.

And indeed, the pastoralizing effect of *Satantoe* depends upon a specific social system. Fully the first two-thirds of the novel develops what Harry B. Henderson III terms a "holist" social structure.[21] The colonial society presented in *Satanstoe* demonstrates the virtues of hierarchical social relations in which each member of the society acknowledges his or her role. Cooper goes out of his way to include a cross section of social types precisely to indicate such social accord. The Negro servant Jaap, the Indian guide Susquesus, the Dutch patrician Herman Mordaunt, the English landed gentry represented by the Littlepages, and even the British soldiers all fit into a sound, smooth-functioning social system. The one false note in this well-tuned instrument is Jason Newcombe, the carping schoolmaster from New England who shares few of the values of the other members of colonial New York society. As the Trilogy unfolds, Jason's antipathy to the holist, hierarchical society of New York develops into an outright counter-philosophy of leveling and equality.

Thus far I have emphasized the correspondences between Cooper's colonial narrative and the epic-pastoral texts of Irving and Paulding. However, a closer look at the narrator/protagonist Corny Littlepage forces us to acknowledge crucial differences between *Satanstoe* and *The Dutchman's Fireside*. First, Cooper does not invest all his emotional capital in Dutch culture. While it is true that the novelist sharply contrasts Dutch and New England manners, he also complicates the portrait of New York society by describing Corny as a composite personality. Littlepage stresses his heterogeneous genealogy: while his father has a British family line, his "mother was of Dutch extraction on both sides" (7). Indeed, Corny occupies a middle ground between two extremes, the Dutch exuberance typified by Guert Ten Eyck and the British refinement of Henry Bulstrode. These two supporting characters are reflectors for the key components of Corny's personality, his high-spirited quest for adventure and his strong sense of social responsibility as a member of the landed gentry. As Corny matures, he learns to restrain the excesses of both extremes, the regressive, childlike tendencies of the Dutch character and the licentious, urbane tendencies of the British. By providing Corny a mixed heritage, Cooper is truer to New York social history than Paulding. Further, as we shall see below, this composite social order will cause problems for Cooper's defense of the Dutch patroonships, for it turns out that the leasehold system under attack by Anti-Renters was not the only available option for land development.

However, when we turn to Corny's *story*, we see that Cooper was capable of an even more heroic treatment of character than Paulding. In the former novel Sybrandt's adventure story is cut in half by a digression to New York City, where the reader observes Catalina's temptation by sophisticated culture. By contrast Corny's narrative builds steadily, moving sequentially from the cosmopolitan setting into the wilderness toward the climactic battle at Ravensnest. Littlepage's development follows an inevitable pattern, each phase punctuated by the rescue of Anneke Mordaunt. Following his brief summary of birth and upbringing, Corny describes his journey to New York City, where he rescues Anneke from a lion. In the next phase of development he travels to Albany, a stage of experience climaxed by his rescuing Anneke from the spring breakup of the Hudson River's ice. Next, he journeys north into the primeval wilderness, initially to claim an estate in his father's name, but also to participate in the failed assault on Fort Ticonderoga early in the French/Indian War. Finally, he returns to Mooseridge and Ravensnest, there to defend Anneke against a savage assault by Indians. In overall movement Corny's growing-up story conforms closely to the paradigm of romance elaborated by Northrop Frye. In Frye's terms, Corny must suffer alienation from his home, undergo trials to his valor and moral principles, incorporate knowledge of the darker aspects of himself and the world at large, and ultimately return home, where he is reintegrated into society through his marriage to Anneke Mordaunt. At no point in the narrative do we wonder if the plot might have taken another turn. We might even apply the term "magical realism" to describe Corny's life story, using that term in an idiosyncratic sense to suggest the combined immersion in the folkways of colonial culture and the magical, fated plot line.[22]

But given Cooper's epic form, what of his polemic, his argument in support of the Dutch gentry? As Bakhtin stresses, the epic typically justifies the ways of a social elite to the community at large.[23] Cooper labors mightily to connect Corny Littlepage's heroic tale to the fortunes of the landed gentry. Corny and Herman Mordaunt's journey to the wilderness highlights their determination to create civilized estates out of chaotic frontier. Indeed, the very act of surveying the Ravensnest and Mooseridge estates has an archetypal American appeal, calling to mind that fundamental act of demarcating, dividing, and settling analyzed with such vigor by Marilyn R. Chandler in the passage that introduced this chapter. Furthermore, both Corny and Herman Mordaunt take stage several times to discuss the sheer expense of development, intimating that settling the upstate frontier is an act of civic benevolence: "The clearings of Ravensnest were neither very large nor very inviting. In that day the settlement of new lands was a slow and painful operation, and was generally made at a great outlay to the proprietor" (326). Yet Cooper introduces a distinction between patterns of settlement that proves fatal to his argument for the patroons. Corny observes at several points that while Herman

Mordaunt had decided to lease land, his own father had determined to sell land in parcels. At first this distinction seems to support Cooper's argument, for Corny emphasizes that settlers have a choice between buying or leasing, and so cannot later claim injustice in the face of leases. Further, Cooper is historically accurate, for in contrast to the Dutch patroon system, William Cooper had sold rather than leased land around Cooperstown. However, historical accuracy will later wreak havoc with Cooper's defense of the patroonships, for the lease system encourages careless husbandry, since the tenant has no long-term stake in the quality of the land or its buildings. In *Satanstoe* Cooper idealizes the founding fathers of settlement, combining heroic and pastoral motifs to create an epic of the landed gentry. Unwittingly, perhaps, he has also sown the seeds of the gentry's downfall.

III. The Wavering Hero

The Chainbearer (1845) brings all the force of history to bear against the heroic pastoralism of *Satanstoe*. The scene shifts from the established estates of the landed gentry to the developing estates in upstate New York. In place of the social order of the earlier generation we have the tensions inherent in a nascent social structure in which competing factions struggle for status and control. *Realpolitik* invades the territory of desire. This shift in location diminishes the protagonist's power to control his destiny. Mordaunt is a much more passive character than his father Corny, stumbling into situations from which he must be extricated. For this reason *The Chainbearer* is best read as an American instance of the complex historical novel, complete with the Scott-like "wavering" hero.[24]

In many ways *The Chainbearer* is reminiscent of *The Pioneers*. As commented earlier, the first of the Leatherstocking Tales is Cooper's most impressive historical novel, for it holds in balance the competing claims of epic and novel, the claims of the landed gentry and the anarchic energies of Natty Bumppo. *The Chainbearer* is located in roughly the same historical epoch, the post-Revolutionary War period of transition in upstate New York. Thus, as Cooper had earlier stressed the carnival-like chaos of Templeton, so here he focuses on the crude, heterogeneous appearance of the Ravensnest "home":

> Any one who is familiar with the aspect of things in what is called a "new country," in America, must be well aware it is not very inviting. The lovers of the picturesque can have little satisfaction in looking even on the finest natural scenery at such moments; the labor that has been effected

usually having done so much to mar the beauties of nature, without having yet had time to supply the deficiencies by those of art. Piles of charred or half-burned logs; fields covered with stumps, or ragged with stubs; fences of the rudest sorts, and filled with brambles; buildings of the meanest character; deserted clearings; and all the other signs of a state of things in which there is a manifest and constant struggle between immediate necessity and future expediency, are not calculated to satisfy either the hopes or the tastes.[25]

Surely the reader is meant to contrast this transitional state with the stability, stolidity, and luxury of Corny's colonial mansion. Similar to Marmaduke Temple, Mordaunt seeks to establish permanent social and political hegemony over this transitional world: he journeys to Ravensnest to hammer out leases with the resident farmers. Furthermore, this second Littlepage Manuscript features a sage "natural" man, the Chainbearer, Andries Coejemans, a latter-day surrogate for Leatherstocking. Like Natty Bumppo, the Chainbearer projects the voice of conscience, pulling the narrative out of the everyday world of cause-and-effect into a higher realm of ethical norms. However, despite these apparent similarities between the early and late Cooper novels, the differences are more profound. First, as we shall see, Mordaunt is a diminished patriarch. Secondly, the debate in *The Pioneers* between Temple and Bumppo is completely recast in *The Chainbearer* as a struggle between Coejemans and Aaron Thousandacres. In effect the subversive character (Leatherstocking) has been transformed into the representative of social control. While *The Chainbearer* is relatively novelistic compared to *Satanstoe*, Cooper labors mightily to remain true to the polemical bias of the Trilogy.

Indeed Mordaunt Littlepage has a great deal in common with Scott's protagonist. Throughout *Waverley* the title character is represented as indecisive, immature, driven by circumstance. He stumbles into the Jacobite insurrection, assuming the garb of the Highlander only after he has been charged with treason owing to a series of chance misfortunes. Rather than declaring and enacting his support for Bonnie Prince Charlie, Waverley passively accedes to the role of revolutionist. The mercurial Highland chief Fergus Mac-Ivor takes him to task for his indecisiveness: "'Nay, I cannot tell what to make of you, . . . you are blown about with every wind of doctrine. Here have we gained a victory unparalleled in history, and your behaviour is praised by every living mortal to the skies, and the Prince is eager to thank you in person, and all our beauties of the White Rose are pulling caps for you;—and you, the *preux chevalier* of the day, are stooping on your horse's neck like a butter-woman riding to market, and looking as black as a funeral!'" Waverley's passivity and vacillation are also apparent in the courtship plot, for his affections shift back and forth between the dark lady of romance, Flora Mac-Ivor, the Highland heroine, and Rose Bradwardine, the fair-haired, genteel, Lowland lady. The high-spirited Flora provides yet another apt portrait of Waverley, and at the same time explains why he will inevitably marry Rose: "'But high and perilous enterprise is not Waverley's forte. He would never have been his celebrated ancestor Sir Nigel, but only Sir Nigel's eulogist and poet. I will tell you where he will be at home, my dear, and in his place—in the quiet circle of domestic happiness, lettered indolence, and elegant enjoyments of Waverley-Honour.'"[26] Clearly Edward Waverley is no heroic figure!

Mordaunt Littlepage is a novelistic protagonist in the mold of Waverley. The very tone of *The Chainbearer* suggests this literary kinship. After all, true to the narrator's name, the text is dominated by a mordant or bitter mood. The graceful, tactful, *assured* style of Corny's narrative has fallen away. Mordaunt's polemical tone indicates the changes produced by time in the gentry's condition. In particular Mordaunt assaults two popular American attitudes: a belief that change in and of itself is a good, and the related belief that social leveling will result in progress. The longing for a return to equilibrium, the desire to push through and beyond the transitional stage to a hierarchical stability, emerges throughout the narrative. Early on, Mordaunt acerbically remarks to his sister: "I have seen enough, in my short career, to know there is a spirit up among us, that calls itself by the pretending title of 'the spirit of improvement,' which is likely to overturn more important things than the name of our poor Neck. It is a spirit that assumes the respectable character of a love of liberty; and under that mask it gives play to malice, envy, covetousness, rapacity, and all the lowest passions of our nature" (44–45). The narrator's doubts seem even more ominous for the Republic when we remember that his narrative recounts events immediately following the War of Independence. Like *Wyandotté* (1843), *The Chainbearer* implies that the Revolution was a mixed blessing for British America.

If Mordaunt's querulous tone marks an insecure, late-adolescent personality, his actions even more firmly establish his similarities to Waverley. Upon his arrival at Ravensnest, Mordaunt, though an officer in the just-ended war, refuses to challenge openly the demagoguery of Jason Newcombe. Instead, he conceals his identity and observes how Newcombe manipulates the selection of denomination for the new church. This tactic allows the novelist to narrate in full detail the knavery of the leveler, yet it also casts a shadow over the protagonist's leadership. Why doesn't Mordaunt intervene, declare his role as owner, and put an end to the charade? Here is yet another instance in which novelistic convention competes with polemical design; the writer may gain a dramatic set-piece, but his reputed hero suffers diminished stature. This dilemma is only compounded in *The Red-skins,* in which the Littlepage gentry don motley as itinerant foreigners.

More humbling still is Mordaunt's capture by Aaron Thou-sandacres. This event is triggered by Dus Malbone's seeming rejection of Mordaunt's offer of marriage. The vexed courtship plot provides a synecdoche for larger tensions within post-Revolutionary War America. Whereas Mordaunt's parents and sister would prefer that he marry Pris Bayard, an established member of the landed gentry, he is irresistibly attracted to Ursula (Dus) Malbone, the Chainbearer's niece. In effect Mordaunt is torn between preserving the colonial hegemony and accepting a more complicated new social order. An orphan of reduced means who must work for a living, Dus combines self-sufficiency with a refined sensibility. Indeed, Cooper goes to some extremes to show that despite her apparent coarseness, she has re-ceived the education and social training essential to a cultural matri-arch. In Dus Malbone, Cooper struck upon an effective means for moderating his aristocratic attitudes, for she is a natural aristocrat, a girl of the people who because of her intrinsic abilities deserves higher social status. Predictably, the Chainbearer does not consider his niece a worthy match for Mordaunt, phrasing his objection in terms which remind us of Littlepage's architectural holdings: "No—no—Mortaunt Littlepage, t'e owner of Ravensnest, ant t'e heir of Mooseritge, ant of Satanstoe, ant of Lilacsbush, ant of all t'e find houses ant stores ant farms t'at are in York ant up ant town t'e country, is not a suitaple match for Dus Malbone!" (357).

Dus Malbone is also typical of sentimental heroines of fiction of the 1840s and 50s, calling to mind such characters as Hawthorne's Phoebe Pyncheon and Stowe's Eva St. Clare. It is Dus's piety and devotion to her uncle which cause her to spurn Mordaunt's first advances; she cannot consider abandoning the Chainbearer for a husband. Stunned by this rejection, Mordaunt flees into the forest, and there falls into a deep slumber. Upon waking, he is disoriented, uncertain where he is or which direction to follow. He meets up with Susquesus, the ever-faithful Indian (a diminished version of Chingachgook), and together they discover Thousandacres' illegal mill. Thus this would-be patri-arch falls into the hands of his direst enemy because of a wounded ego: "If I were naught to Ursula Malbone, it mattered little what else became of me" (233). Mordaunt's immaturity and powerlessness are further highlighted when he escapes Thousandacres' prison. In an early version of American farce, Mordaunt is concealed by the love-lorn Lowiny Timberman in a cellar. When he manages to escape his prison, he uses the occasion to court Dus in the woods, a delay which causes him to be recaptured! Perhaps Cooper is straining after a comic effect, seeking a note of levity, but again his protagonist appears a fool.

Thousandacres is without question the centerpiece of the novel. He is in some ways reminiscent of the Highland clans described in *Waverley*, for similar to those figures he inhabits a charmed, mysterious world. Furthermore, Thousandacres (actually named Aaron Timberman) argues vigorously for the rights of his squatter class, defying the law and order of established downstate society. He is a rebel with a cause, for he asserts an ethic of "use" versus the ethic of "law." And yet it would be a misreading of the novel to assume that Thousandacres is entirely *other*, altogether alien to the mainstream culture he opposes, for as Henderson points out, "Aaron Thousandacres represents for Cooper an instance of perverted pastoral, and an instance of great import. . . . These Borderers represent a parody of the existing society, extending the dangerous and rapacious aspects of civilization. . . ."[27] We know that Thousandacres conforms to certain misguided values within the early Republic because he has colluded with Jason Newcombe to harvest, mill, and sell timber illegally. But Thousandacres parodies existing society in more profound and comprehensive senses as well. This semi-mythical figure has much in common with subversive characters out of the Southwestern humor tradition: "[Hooper's Simon] Suggs is the first figure in American literature who fully manipulates Conventional values—piety, discretion, honesty, entrepreneurial shrewdness—for purely selfish ends. The Conventional becomes fully relativized in the world of subversive humor."[28] Similar to Suggs, Thousandacres has a talent for inverting mainstream conventions to suit his immediate needs. For instance, when it comes time to decide Mordaunt's fate, he sets up a mock trial, using the formalities of law to subvert the conventional import of law. Thousandacres also has an excellent ear for language, frequently double-voicing orthodox sentiments as when he remarks to his son: "'W–a–a–l, we've heerd the young man's story, Tobit. I've asked him what he had to say for himself, and he g'in us his tell—tell'd us how he's his own father's son, and that the gin'ral is some sort of a big tenant, instead of being a landlord, and isn't much better than we are ourselves; and it's high time I permitted him to custody'" (261–262). Cooper's villains are especially effective at mimicking the style of their social superiors, thereby dragging the highbrow into the dust of the vernacular.

But Cooper's polemic requires that the New England ethic be defeated, and Andries Coejemans is the man to carry out that duty. He is, first and foremost, Dutch, and so represents continuity with the traditionalist heritage lauded by the Knickerbocker writers. Secondly, he is a laborer, a hard-working measurer of land, the ideal symbol of legal land ownership, and a character who happily accepts his station in a social hierarchy. As mentioned earlier, Andries Coejemans also exhibits Natty Bumppo's passionate intensity toward nature and God: "... Got is in t'e trees, ant on t'e mountains, ant along t'e valleys, ant is to pe hearet in t'e prooks and t'e rifers ..." (355). At first glance this natural theology may seem to contradict his devotion to the landed gentry. However, the Chainbearer argues that there is an organic relationship between an American gentry and natural beauty. If Thousandacres represents purely selfish despoliation, the democratic gentleman represents cultivated, rational land use. Through this phi-losophy the Chainbearer provides a theological sanction for a landed class. Scott Bradfield amplifies this point, and at the same time con-nects Cooper's political stance to his personal crises: "In order to rule the wilderness, pioneers must not establish new laws but recognize old principles already there—such as, presumably, the Cooper family's right to determine who observes the spectacular view from Three Mile Point."[29]

In a melodramatic conclusion, Cooper places the Chainbearer and Thousandacres side-by-side in their death throes. Increasingly the ico-nography of sentimental religion dominates the narrative. The golden-haired Dus prays for Andries Coejemans' redemption; the Chainbearer dies a death "the best calculated to renew the hopes of a Christian" (437). Even more dramatically, upon his death Thousandacres assumes the status of the devil himself:

His eyes were open; ghastly, wandering, hopeless. As the lips contracted with the convulsive twitchings of death, they gave to his grim visage a species of sardonic grin that rendered it doubly terrific. At this moment a sullen calm came over the countenance, and all was still. I knew that the last breath remained to be drawn, and waited for it as the charmed bird gazes at the basilisk-eye of the snake. It came, drawing aside the lips so as to show every tooth, and not one was missing in that iron frame. ... I never before had looked upon so revolting a corpse; and never wish to see its equal again. (432)

Social deviant, frontier humorist, and now devil incarnate, Aaron Thousandacres looms large over this second novel of the Littlepage Trilogy. Unlike Scott's protagonist, Cooper's is never drawn to this alternative value system as Waverley is attracted to the Jacobite cause. For this reason *The Chainbearer* is a static novel compared with *The Pioneers* and *Waverley*. Though there is a clear conflict between two value systems, there is no true suspense since we know which side the protagonist must land on. But by creating a charismatic villain and a wavering narrator, Cooper puts in doubt the American gentleman's claim to cultural leadership.

IV. A NEW YORK CARNIVAL

If Cooper's polemics seem strained in *The Chainbearer,* matter and manner become even more hectic in the final novel of the Trilogy. Set in the 1840s, *The Redskins* (1846) describes cultural and social anarchy in Jacksonian America. In fact, this novel ideally represents the society described so colorfully by David S. Reynolds: "As important as the carnival was in the European culture Bakhtin studies, it was perhaps even more so in democratic America, which was a kind of carnival culture, one that abolished the social distance between people and yoked together the high and low in an atmosphere of jolly relativity."[30] Ironically Cooper wrote to his wife that "Redskins is in great favour with the better classes."[31] Apparently genteel readers sympathized with the contemporaneous Littlepage representatives, Hugh, narrator and grandson of Mordaunt, and his uncle Ro. But the Littlepage heirs participate in and even enable the unstable society described in the third Manuscript.

High and low culture are indeed yoked together in the personalities of Hugh and Ro Littlepage, for they are both mannered and boorish. William Cosgrove presents a convincing summary of their personalities when he comments that "they are the least admirable representatives of the family line because they have replaced the Littlepage love of family, land, and society with self-righteous class pride, love of profit, and contempt for their tenants."[32] As in *The Chainbearer,* the narrator's style provides an immediate clue to the temper of the teller. It is as if Cooper had allowed John Effingham, Eve's insufferable uncle, to narrate *Home as Found:*

And here I wish to say one thing plainly, before I write another line. As for falling into the narrow, self-adulatory, provincial feeling of the American who has never left his mother's apron-string, and which causes him to swallow, open-mouthed, all the nonsense that is uttered to the world in the columns of newspapers, or in the pages of your yearling travellers, who go on "excursions" before they are half instructed in the social usages and the distinctive features of their own country, I hope I shall be just as far removed from such a weakness. . . .[33]

Unfortunately this passage typifies Hugh's prose. He strikes the reader as a snob who is incapable of scrutinizing his own shortcomings. Unconsciously Cooper executes a parody of his own political prose, double-voicing his defense of the landed gentry by overdetermining or exaggerating his position. Whereas Aaron Thousandacres supplied the parody of the Littlepage philosophy in the previous narrative, here the Littlepage representative accomplishes his own undoing. Hugh consistently presents himself as a Europeanized fop who holds little or no claim on the reader's sympathies. Thus *The Redskins,* rather than presenting a straightforward case for the American gentleman, destabilizes that claim in the very moment of its presentation, in the language of narration.

Furthermore, Hugh is materialistic in the extreme, frequently evaluating acquaintances or even potential spouses on the basis of their wealth: "Miss Anne Marston was also an heiress, but on a very diminished scale" (44). Perhaps most discomforting for the reader is Hugh's thorough rejection of his own estate at Ravensnest. Once again Cooper's narrator dwells upon the physical structure representative of his status. However, in this case the overly sophisticated Littlepage representative can feel only scorn for the product of family labor:

> We had been shown into the library, a room that was in the front of the house, and of which the windows all opened on the piazza. I was at first a little overcome, at thus finding myself, and unrecognized, under the paternal roof, and in a dwelling that was my own, after so many years of absence. Shall I confess it! Everything appeared diminutive and mean, after the buildings to which I had been accustomed in the Old World. (166–167)

Not only does this passage further undermine Hugh's claim to our concern, but it calls into question the worth of Ravensnest. If Cooper has designed this fiction to make a case for the patroon system, why present such a disparaging image of the *product* of that system, the settlement at Ravensnest? As I pointed out in the discussion of *Satanstoe, The Redskins* intimates that something's rotten in the system of patroonships, for leaseholders have little incentive to maintain, let alone improve, the land they occupy.

One might fairly ask if the narrator doesn't *develop* in the course of the novel: isn't it possible that like a conventional bildungsroman, *The Redskins* traces Hugh's progress toward greater self-understanding and humility? In two ways the novel does indeed encourage this argument, for Hugh ultimately marries a genteel young lady (Mary Warren) who has no pretensions to wealth, and in the last third of the novel he assumes command for protection of his house.

That is, he sets aside his wearisome diatribe and acts on his principles. However, these seem superficial changes at best, for Hugh's sensibility remains intact. Certainly there is no maturational breakthrough such as Paulding described for Sybrandt Westbrook. Hugh is a static char' acter in outlook and tone, a point emphasized by "the Editor's" con' cluding remark on the narrator's style: "It is the language of a man who feels that he has been grievously injured, and who writes with the ardor of youth increased by the sense of wrong" (505). Hugh weds Mary Warren largely because she and her father (an Episcopalian minister) affirm the rights of property; his defense of the Ravensnest estate is reactive.

Indeed, the narrative resolution depends upon a deus ex machina in which a group of Indian chiefs face down the mock "Injins." The peripatetic chiefs, fresh from a visit to Washington D.C., pause at Ravensnest to honor Susquesus. Literally ageless (no one can tell how old he is), Susquesus represents yet another connection to the old colonial order of Corny Littlepage. In a curious ideological inversion, the dispossessed Indian is called "a true Injin, and a gentleman" (145). Thus the "natural man" becomes one with the social aristocracy, pro' viding yet another moral sanction for the Littlepage hegemony. How' ever, the mock Injins, led by Seneca Newcombe (Jason's grandson), parody the aboriginal virtues of plain speaking, trustworthiness, and courage. They of course also mock the Boston Tea Party, symbolizing once again the declension of American political values. In a hackneyed climax, the Injins approach Ravensnest, threatening arson and may' hem, only to be turned aside by the plain-dealing Indians.

The confrontation between Indians and Injins returns us to the carnival atmosphere of the novel. Hugh and Ro participate in the festival by donning disguises as German organ-grinder and peddler. As with his other peculiar narrative devices in the Trilogy, here Cooper struggles mightily to remain true to the polemical bias of the Manu' scripts. He implicitly argues that events on the patroonships have become so threatening to landholders that they must visit their estates *incognito*. The narrative also links this behavior to the Dutch tradition celebrated in previous texts, for Hugh and Ro are frequently mistaken for Dutch immigrants. By this means Cooper associates their behavior with Andries Coejemans' noble defense of the gentry and Guert Ten Eyck's genial courage. Finally, less flattering to the novelist perhaps, Cooper aims to create a light comic touch reminiscent of Shakespeare's mature comedies. As Viola's disguise allowed her to speak truth to Duke Orsino, so presumably Hugh and Ro's disguises give them li' cense to enunciate "fact" in the face of mob opinion. As with most of his "light" touches (consider David Gamut in *The Last of the Mohi-*

cans), Cooper is not very successful. He mainly succeeds at creating a jarring, discomforting disparity between the tone of levity and the supposedly apocalyptic events brewing on the Ravensnest estate.

The absurdity of Cooper's technique is evident everywhere in the unreadable German dialect of nephew and uncle. In one of his few moments of self-reflection, Hugh describes the bizarre consequences of the disguises during an encounter with the Injins: "'Ve ist two Charmans,' returned uncle Ro, in his most desperate dialect, the absurdity of men who spoke the same language resorting to such similar means of deception tempting me sorely to laugh in the fellows' faces . . ." (218). Hugh raises the central issue: given the characters' asserted commitment to sincerity and law, what is the reader supposed to make of their willful use of deception? Cooper himself had avidly espoused "candor" in *The American Democrat:* "Candor has the high merit of preventing misconceptions, simplifies intercourse, prevents more misunderstandings than equivocation, elevates character, inculcates the habit of sincerity, and has a general tendency to the manly and virtuous qualities."[34] Yet his reputed protagonists conceal their identity not only from the Anti-Renters but from their own family. Furthermore, they use their disguises to sneer at the manners of the leaseholders. In her study of antebellum advice manuals, Karen Halttunen has demonstrated that hypocrisy was treated as the primary threat to virtue: "To Victorian Americans, hypocrisy was not merely a personal sin; it was a social offense that threatened to dissolve the ties of mutual confidence binding men together." Duplicity posed a special threat because "in a theory that may be called the sentimental typology of conduct, [advice writers] asserted that all aspects of manner and appearance were visible outward signs of inner moral qualities." Like *The American Democrat, The Redskins* often reads like an advice manual, for Hugh feels compelled to instruct his readership on proper manners, and manners after all must reflect the inner man. And yet, Hugh and Ro transform themselves into confidence men every bit as devious as the demagogic Seneca Newcombe, even though "confidence men personified the pervasive duplicity of the rising generation."[35] Curiously, then, in this didactic narrative the reputed heroes come to represent exactly those vices against which the advice manual should warn. Mary Warren, the novel's sentimental heroine, exclaims aptly upon Hugh's unmasking, "This is so extraordinary!— so unusual! The whole country appears unsettled! Pray, sir, if you are not the person whom you have represented yourself to be, who are you?" (231).

This conjunction of disguised protagonists, double-voiced narrative, mock "Injins," and peripatetic Indian chiefs forces a comparison between *The Redskins* and P. T. Barnum's American Museum, opened in 1842:

> The transient attractions of the Museum were constantly diversified, and educated dogs, industrious fleas, automatons, jugglers, ventriloquists, living statuary, tableaux, gipsies, Albinoes, fat boys, giants, dwarfs, rope-dancers, live "Yankees," pantomime, instrumental music, singing and dancing in great variety, dioramas, panoramas, models of Niagara, Dublin, Paris, and Jerusalem; Hannington's dioramas of the Creation, the Deluge, Fairy Grotto, Storm at Sea; the first English Punch and Judy in this country, Italian Fantoccini, mechanical figures, fancy glass-blowing, knitting machines and other triumphs in the mechanical arts; dissolving views, American Indians, who enacted their warlike and religious ceremonies on the stage,—these, among others, were all exceedingly successful.[36]

The Redskins is Cooper's American Museum. The narrative begins in Paris, proceeds to New York City and upstate New York (where Hugh and Ro adopt their roles as confidence men), involves "instrumental music" (Hugh after all mimics an organ-grinder), features a live Yankee in Seneca Newcombe, and, of course, describes Indians of various sorts enacting their warlike ceremonies. In a general sense the entire novel presents "dissolving views," for the reader witnesses the dissolution of Cooper's original design, the complete collapse of the epic pretensions to hegemony by the landed gentry. Hugh and Ro mark the terminus of the Littlepage devolution.

V. COOPER: ACCUSER AND ACCUSED

In his introduction to a collection of critical essays on parody, David Roberts has written, "Parody revisited may not be paradise regained. From the perspective of postmodernism parody narrates two versions of the Fall—the endless revisions of the 'authorised' version and the dispersion of the 'original' text. But exile is also liberation. The process of revision is also an act of separation. Parody is necessarily double-faced."[37] Roberts' analysis summarizes both the means and meaning of Cooper's Littlepage Trilogy. *Satanstoe, The Chainbearer,* and *The Redskins* provide a case study in revision, for while narrative technique, setting, and family remain consistent in the three narratives, successive texts revise their predecessors through increasing carnivalization of language and action.[38] The three novels thus mark the fall into time from a pre-Revolutionary War hegemony to the diverse, hectic democratic culture of the 1840s. At the same time, the Manuscripts mark the dispersal of authority, for that carnivalization of action requires a diminished stature for the Littlepage representatives. But in what sense does Cooper's parodic method involve both exile and liberation? To answer that question requires a closer look at the motives behind Cooper's failed polemical design, a task I have deferred to this point.

First, we must understand that the declension from epic to novel is a function of genre, in two crucial senses. The New York epics of Irving, Paulding, and Cooper depend upon a degenerative reading of history. Much of the appeal of "The Legend of Sleepy Hollow," *The Dutchman's Fireside,* and *Satanstoe* emerges from their sense of occupying a special zone of time, set in the distant past, before the incursion of history. Such texts rely upon a "once upon a time" motif. Paulding made this appeal explicit when he incorporated into his prose such stock phrases as "Doric simplicity," establishing a firm contrast between the rural integrity of the past and the urbane decadence of the present. This pastoral-epic treatment of time conformed to a cyclical interpretation of history which was prevalent in the new Republic. We know that Cooper was profoundly influenced by Count Volney's *The Ruins: Or a Survey of the Revolutions of Empire* (1791), which argued that history was cyclical, that the moral condition of a society determined its place in the cycle, and that the pastoral stage is the optimal phase of civilization.[39] This historical vision is graphically represented in Thomas Cole's familiar *The Course of Empire* (1836), which narrates in pictorial terms the movement from wilderness, to pastoral, to city, to destruction and desolation. Thus Cooper's epic pretensions depend upon a downward spiral in the appeal of his Littlepage characters, a difficulty he must not have anticipated when he began the Manuscripts.

This narrative dispersal depends on genre in another important sense. As the Littlepage chronicle approaches the contemporary reader's present, characters enter "a zone of maximally close contact between the represented object and contemporary reality in all its inconclusiveness."[40] Once the Trilogy arrives at 1845, the protagonists operate on the reader's own plane of experience. Hugh and Ro participate in the same public rituals, utilize the same forms of transportation, eat the same food, and speak the same colloquialisms as the reader. Novelization of character is made inevitable by Cooper's progression toward his own present. Furthermore, Cooper is composing at precisely the moment when the novel of contemporary society assumed ascendancy over the historical novel. Both conformist and predecessor, Cooper contributes to a shift in reading habits which popularized such novels as George Lippard's *The Monks of Monk Hall* (1845), Stowe's *Uncle Tom's Cabin* (1852), Hawthorne's *The Blithe-*

dale Romance (1852), and Fanny Fern's *Ruth Hall* (1854). These novels of contemporary society not only mark the factionalization of
literature, but the demise of Cooper's dreamed-for "republican or
democratic novel," a comprehensive genre which would provide a
unified vision of the American polity:

> ... what had happened to the concept of a republican or democratic novel
> by the time of Cooper's death in 1851? It had failed to develop into a
> public institution, into a medium of enlightened discourse in which the
> People individually and collectively defined and redefined themselves, yet
> it had stayed political and national in ambition and scope. It had been
> forced by the dynamics of Jacksonian society to open its definition of The
> People "downwards" according to principles of Christian brotherhood and
> social justice ... and it had responded to the formation of class in a society
> that was egalitarian more in its rhetoric than in its social practice.[41]

Cooper participated grudgingly in this "opening 'downwards,'" approaching the new novel form from the position of the staunch conservative. And yet, as I have tried to show through close reading of key
incidents in his Littlepage Trilogy, his acceptance of the form of the
contemporary novel compromised his defense of the gentry, for his
leading characters frequently appear either fools or guilty parties in
the confidence games of post-Revolutionary War America.

But intellectual history and generic analysis can only take us so
far in understanding Cooper's ambivalent treatment of the Littlepage
progeny. If *The Chainbearer* and *The Redskins* do indeed undermine
the claims of the gentry, to what in Cooper's own biography might
we attribute that subversion? I would suggest that this self-subversion
emerged from Cooper's complex attitudes toward three generations of
his own family, encompassing his father, himself, and his son. Stephen
Railton argues in dramatic fashion that Cooper's intensified piety during the 1840s symbolized his idealization of William Cooper: "In dis-
covering and vesting his faith in God the Father, he was more fully
submitting to the real father. Or, in other words, in the son's unconscious, the stature of William Cooper grew so large, his presence so
commanding, that he underwent an apotheosis: the father became
the Father."[42] This study of the Littlepage Trilogy both confirms and
qualifies Railton's provocative claim. On the one hand, Cooper's idealization of the founding patriarch is evident in *Satanstoe*. It is also easy
to see that the feeble later generations, vacillating and self-interested,
might well be imaginative surrogates for Cooper himself, the son unable to preserve the gentry's authoritarian control of culture and society in the nineteenth century. Cooper's frustration with his class's
social status has already been fully explicated. His financial struggles

during the period he composed the Trilogy further suggest a diminished sense of self-worth. In a letter to Paulding composed shortly
after the publication of *The Redskins,* Cooper remarked,

> I am very sorry to say that my pecuniary benefits, in this country, amount
> to nothing worth naming. I own so much literary property, and so many
> plates, that in the whole they amount to something, though far less than
> you would suppose. The cheap literature has destroyed the value of nearly
> all literary property, and after five and twenty years of hard work, I find
> myself comparatively a poor man. Had I employed the same time in trade,
> or in travelling as an agent for a manufacturer of pins, I do not doubt I
> should have been better off, and my children independent. The fact is,
> this country is not sufficiently advanced for any thing intellectual, and
> the man who expects to rise by any such agency makes a capital mistake,
> unless he sell himself, soul and body, to a faction.[43]

This passage presages the bitter complaints of Hawthorne and Melville concerning the professional writer's marginal status in the
United States. But Cooper's description of his dilemma is more heavily
loaded with the language of economics and political ideology than
that of the two younger writers. Whereas Hawthorne complains of
his country's aesthetic shortcomings and Melville excoriates his readership's failure to realize a "Republic of Letters," Cooper casts an
economist's eye on his literary labors. He metaphorizes his writing as
real estate ("property") that has been devalued by slum-like cheap
literature. Thus the very source of his cultural authority—his literary
property—has been debased by leveling culture. Unlike his powerful
father, James Fenimore Cooper was unable to consolidate his position
of power by mastering the economic processes of American society.
Furthermore, he claims an unwillingness to participate in the immediate political controversies of the 1840s, the turbulent decade of the
Mexican War, abolition, and polarization of classes. Cooper is not
only marginal in a literary, but in a political sense as well. No wonder,
then, that Mordaunt and Hugh Littlepage appear as passive, reactive
main characters, in sharp contrast to the aggressive, progressive behavior of Corny.

But if Cooper felt at times very much the failed son, he could also
appear the disappointed father. If this "father of American fiction"
idealized the patriarchal figure during the 1840s, might he not have
identified himself with paternal authority? During the composition of
The Redskins, Cooper was obsessed with his son Paul's health and
conduct. Clearly fretful that his son would not make a mark on the
world, that he would fall far short of the standard set by grandfather
and father, Cooper writes of Paul in a mixed tone of concern and

disappointment. Here, for instance, he writes to his wife 5 December 1845: "I have now little concern on that head [consumption], and Paul, I can see, is much relieved. Hitherto, he has shown an ingenuity in trying to make out the case against himself. He has confessed to me that he was often stupid from excessive smoking, and that sometimes his hand shook like an old mans [sic]. Tobacco would have killed him, in a year or two, and he is now suffering under the reaction of ceasing to use the stimulant."[44] It is plausible that Hugh Littlepage is a partial portrait of Paul, one which highlights the youthful foibles of a gentleman-about-town.

But Cooper's accession to father-figure entailed not simply a critique of his son's behavior, but a critique of William Cooper's as well. From the perspective of an aging, worldly writer, Cooper was liberated to question his own father's behavior. After all, Mordaunt Littlepage is an almost exact contemporary of William Cooper's; this wavering hero may well be a reexamination of the patriarch's youth, and a far more problematic one than that offered in the character of Marmaduke Temple. And yet, even Temple is an ambiguous figure: "Caught between gentility and speculation—that is, between the polarities of the emergent bourgeoisie—and writing *The Pioneers* even as his entire landed inheritance was being sold to meet family debt, Cooper recreates a two-faced father. The judge may be read as a speculating entrepreneur or as a benevolent member of the gentry, with one or two advanced ideas. Perhaps he is better read both ways."[45] The figure of "the American gentleman" as idealized by Cooper was always a complicated, even contradictory one. In no sense does either William Cooper or the Littlepage clan conform to a model of the landed gentleman who stands entirely outside the processes of an emerging capitalist economy. Herman Mordaunt, General Littlepage (Corny's father), and William Cooper all invest capital in speculative schemes. Thus, Cooper may be said to belong to that group of Jackson supporters who endured the contradiction between capitalist desires and nostalgia:

Many of Jackson's more opportunistic followers enthusiastically endorsed his assault on the "money power," not so much because the B.U.S. threatened their simple way of living but because it served as a restraining influence on their own economic ambitions. . . . But most of the entrepreneurial Jacksonians were not consciously hypocritical. Instead, they were caught in the paradoxical position of unleashing laissez-faire capitalism while at the same time remaining verbally committed to a chaste personal ethic of republican simplicity. They wanted the best of both visions of the good life and were unable to see that they were trying to harmonize dissonant cultural objectives.[46]

In the end, then, the Littlepage Trilogy undermines the binary opposition between American gentleman and materialistic capitalist. The
cancer of speculation infected the landed gentry from within, a disease
that revealed itself as terminal in the final novel of the Trilogy. Ultimately, James Fenimore Cooper stands as accuser and accused in this
family chronicle. As son and struggling writer, he felt the sense of
desolation, of exile, of having been cast out of the Garden of Colony
into the world of the chaotic Republic. But as stern father figure, as
a version of the judge, he castigated his father and his son for demon-
strating the power of capitalist impulses over the Cooper family. It is
not surprising, then, that Cooper would lead the reader through a
series of American homes, from the colonial mansion, to the half-
built early republican home, to the threatened Jacksonian estate at
Ravensnest. This guided tour of American domesticity culminates in
the loss of home, for the would-be gentleman cannot affirm the values
of his own class, nor embrace the Jacksonian culture which swirls
without and within that class. Ironically, this most housebound of
writers ends up homeless.

3

Of Masters and Men: Revising the Patriarchal Institution

As AMERICANS IN GENERAL FIGURED THEIR NATION AS A HOME, SO more specifically did Southerners imagine the plantation household as an extended family. In contrast to the divided spheres of Northern middle-class ideology, Southerners emphasized that the plantation comprised a total economy, incorporating manufacture, agriculture, and domestic relations. The plantation was a microcosmic society unto itself, at least symbolically self-contained and self-sufficient. Within this reputedly unified family the plantation master would be a "father" in multiple senses: father to his children, father to his own wife, and, most crucially, father to his slaves. The white mistress would serve as his surrogate in her dealings with daily chores, a kind of delegated master whose authority always rested on that of the male. Especially within the household itself, the plantation "family" generated both intimacy and strain, for nearness could breed both care and contempt.[1] Be that as it may, Southerners staked a great deal on this patriarchal interpretation of slavery, for it provided a moral justification, a humane (even divine) rationale for a glaringly inequitable social arrangement: "In the minds of slavery apologists, the North failed in its parental responsibilities for its wage laborers; slave labor power offered a more truly familial and stable society than the diffuse, precarious lifestyle produced by the money power of Northern capitalism."[2]

Thus, much as Cooper would advocate a holist social vision, hierarchical in nature and comforting in its stability, so plantation apologists would describe a social system in which whites and blacks could assume appropriate roles. But in the last chapter we examined an act of self-subversion as the Littlepage Trilogy imploded, collapsing upon its approach to the present moment, Cooper's own historical epoch. The novel, both "the new" and the genre, infected the epic intention of the Manuscripts, filling the susceptible form with ironic laughter, causing Cooper's elitist vision to collapse. Here we turn to a similar though more elaborate dialogic struggle, a struggle waged by compet-

ing texts for the representation of the Southern "family." Occupying
the same terrain, slave narratives and plantation novels claim to describe the architecture of the antebellum South. But these are hardly
complementary plans, for the perverse subgenres seek to destroy even
as they double each other. Indeed, the term "sibling rivalry" takes
on added meaning when examining this discursive contest, for slave
narrators were often the children or grandchildren of Southern
whites.

Tracking Southern texts from 1832 to 1861, we observe a sequence
of revisions upon the "originary" plantation novel, Kennedy's *Swallow
Barn*. To appreciate fully the complex political and representational
battles over slavery, then, we must pursue a "signifyin'" chain (to
borrow Henry Louis Gates Jr.'s pun).[3] *Swallow Barn* is a double-
voiced, dialogic account of the Southern plantation, one which surely
elides the horrors of slavery, but one which also satirizes the Virginia
aristocrat as pastoral fool, ignorant of the inevitable progress of history
in the New World. Douglass's 1845 *Narrative* subverts the House of
the Southern Plantation by amplifying the historical dimension of
Kennedy's text, linking the progress of historical time to the liberation
of the slave. In response to Douglass's *Narrative* and Stowe's *Uncle
Tom's Cabin*, white Southerners such as William Gilmore Simms,
John Esten Cooke, and Caroline Lee Hentz monologized the 1832
Swallow Barn, as did the 1851 edition of that novel. That is, these
plantation apologists submerged Kennedy's original criticism beneath
a stream of familial rhetoric, representing the plantation as home
rather than madhouse. But Harriet Ann Jacobs's *Incidents in the Life
of a Slave Girl* (1861) renounces the paternalistic mode of Southern
writing by characterizing the mistreatment of female slaves. In a closing document of antebellum Southern writing, Jacobs not only revises
the prior plantation novels, but signifies upon the male slave narrative
of Douglass. What is at stake in these narratives, then, is the very
image of the plantation as family. While apologists posit the necessity
for paternalism, slave narrators reveal the economic and sexual exploitation within "the master's house." Like Roderick Usher's vengeful
sister, Douglass and Jacobs feel compelled to use their storytelling to
bring down the white master. Cumulatively we will come to see that
Southern home as riven by economic, sexual, and racial conflicts that
are still very much with us.

I. The Defining Plantation Novel

The years 1831–1832 marked the emergence of slavery as an unavoidable political controversy in antebellum culture. On 1 January

1831, William Lloyd Garrison published the first issue of *The Libera-tor,* calling for the immediate emancipation and enfranchisement of slaves. He followed up this incendiary act by forming the New En-gland Anti-Slavery Society in Boston in 1832. On the evening of 31 August 1831, Nat Turner led the bloodiest and most sweeping slave revolt in U.S. history, resulting in the deaths of at least fifty-five whites and the eventual execution of the religiously inspired leader. No doubt responding to these twin threats of abolition and slave revolt, Thomas R. Dew drafted his *Review of the Debates in the Vir-ginia Legislature of 1831 and 1832,* an aggressive defense of slavery as "a positive social and moral good."[4]

It is precisely at this political flash point that John Pendleton Ken-nedy published the first edition of *Swallow Barn.*[5] Scholars have long argued about the ideological import of Kennedy's novel. While one critic avers that "Kennedy implicitly defends slavery as an institution beneficial for both races," another asserts that a progressive historical vision undermines the pastoral defense of slavery.[6] In a seminal analy-sis of Southern plantation literature, Lewis Simpson sees Kennedy's position on slavery as equivocal, for "*Swallow Barn* is an uncertain attempt at a pastoral ratification of slavery."[7] Rather than insisting upon a unitary reading of the 1832 *Swallow Barn,* then, we must allow the text to speak in multiple voices, for this is indeed a highly dialogized narrative. Written at the start of the national debate over slavery, *Swallow Barn* registers the nostalgia, repulsion, and confusion surrounding "the patriarchal institution." This text puts in play com-peting representational strategies in antebellum Southern literature, defining the terms for both slave narratives and later, more epicized plantation novels.

Kennedy was ideally situated to represent those conflicting atti-tudes, for he was both an insider and an outsider on the Virginia plantation, both an emic and an etic observer. While he practiced law in Baltimore and promoted manufactures, Kennedy was tied to the Virginia plantation economy through his mother's family. The fic-tional "Swallow Barn" is explicitly modeled on his cousins' western Virginia plantation, "The Bower." Kennedy also inherited a deeply divided tradition of writing about the plantation. As Jean Fagan Yellin has ably demonstrated, earlier representations of Southern society such as Jefferson's and George Tucker's wavered between defense and criticism. So, for instance, in *The Valley of Shenandoah* (1824), "Tucker incorporates many contradictory elements: a glorification of the Old South and a basic criticism of plantation society; a nostalgic recollection of the vanished past and a didactic analysis of the weak-nesses that have made change necessary and good; a polemic against abolition and an assertion of black humanity."[8] Finally, Kennedy's sporadic compositional efforts assured a certain looseness in the structure and ideology of Swallow Barn, for he took up and set aside the task several times between 1829 and 1832, altering his design as he went. For instance, Kennedy's original plan projected a satiric attack on a decaying Virginia plantation named "Hoppergallop House."[9]

Overall the most striking feature of Swallow Barn upon first encounter is its pastoralizing effect. Kennedy's text creates a literal time-out for reader and narrator, stopping time through a complementary set of narrative tactics.[10] This "sojourn in the Old Dominion" is narrated by a New York aristocrat, Mark Littleton, who visits his Virginia cousins at their plantation on the James River. In his introductory letter to Zachary Huddlestone, Littleton explains that he took the trip South precisely to escape the pressing concerns of life, especially courtship and marriage. Related to such bachelor litterateurs as Geoffrey Crayon, Ik Marvel, and Miles Coverdale, Littleton suffers from an intolerable *ennui* that can be relieved only by a retreat to a rural setting. It is not surprising, then, that the narrator praises the southern setting in these terms: "There is not a by-path in Virginia that will take a gentleman who has time on his hands, in a wrong direction. This I say in honest compliment to a state that is full to the brim of right good fellows."[11] Kennedy's choice of a New York narrator makes sense given James Kirke Paulding's similar structure in *Letters from the South* (1817). Indeed, we should keep in mind the epic characterizations of the American gentleman shared by Knickerbocker and Southern writers of the pre-Civil War period. Much as Cooper asserted the preeminence of the cultivated gentleman in a leveling democracy, so plantation apologists declared the moral and civic superiority of Cavaliers. However, the comparison between the Littlepage Trilogy and *Swallow Barn* would be incomplete if we ignored their subversive subtexts. But more on those qualifications shortly.

True to the Irvingesque tradition, Littleton composes a series of sketches of "domestic" life on the plantation, describing the manners of the plantation master Frank Meriwether, the interior arrangements of his wife Lucretia (Littleton's cousin), the foibles of Ned Hazard (yet another cousin), and the manners of neighboring plantation master Isaac Tracy, a Southern equivalent to Paulding's comic Dutch patroons. *Swallow Barn* generally reads like a series of still paintings, unchanging, charming, saved from time. The sketch form by its nature frustrates forward-moving narrative, for it *spatializes* time. For example, Littleton describes a ruin upon the landscape in stereotypical sentimental fashion: "The ruin of the mill is still to be seen. Its roof has entirely disappeared; a part of the walls are yet standing, and the shaft of the great wheel, with one or two of the pinions attached, still lies across its appropriate bed. The spot is embowered with ancient beech trees, and forms a pleasant and serene picture of woodland quiet" (I, 160). In one sense this passage refers the reader to historical change, but only to convert passing time into a pictorial, spatialized monument. Furthermore, this passage demonstrates the close bond between the sketch form and the pastoralizing mode of nineteenth-century prose. As if to underscore that bond, Littleton goes on to remark, "I, accordingly, frequently go with Ned to this spot; and, as we stretch ourselves out upon the grass, in the silent shade of the beech trees, or wander around the old ruin, the spot becomes peopled to our imaginations with the ancient retainers of Swallow Barn . . ." (I, 162).

In addition to their pastoral qualities, Littleton's sketches of the Old Dominion highlight the stable material condition of the plantation aristocrats. Put simply, Littleton's eye frequently focuses on *things*, palpable, fixed, signifying wealth and social domination. These tangible symbols of political power are wholly naturalized in Littleton's text; that is, the sketchbook technique generally submerges the social implications of these *things*, treating them instead as organic elements of the plantation scene. Similar to Cooper in *The American Democrat*, then, Kennedy accentuates the power of "property." For instance, Littleton emphasizes the sheer material wealth of Swallow Barn by reiterating its sumptuous feasts: ". . . that substantial country meal which it would be altogether inadequate to call by the feeble, but customary name of tea . . ." (I, 251). More tellingly still, the narrator describes Meriwether as horseman in these terms:

> He rides a beautiful full-blooded sorrel; and his pride in all matter that belong to his equitation is particularly conspicuous in the fresh and comfortable character of his housings and house furniture. He has a large new saddle, luxuriously stuffed, and covered with a richly-worked coat of yellow buckskin. The stirrups hang inordinately low, so that it is as much as he can do to get the point of his boot into them. But he sits with a lordly erectness upon his seat, and manages his horse with a bold and dexterous hand. On horseback he is a perfect personification of an opulent, unquestioned squire. . . . (I, 190)

For a moment the narrative borders on self-revelation, for in his obsession with Meriwether's status, symbolized by his "erect" posture upon his horse, Littleton exposes the power of the "unquestioned squire." However, the narrator coyly elides this perception, in the next breath referring to Meriwether as "the very guardian genius of the soil and its prerogatives." In that move from "squire" to "guardian genius,"

Littleton has transformed Meriwether into a Horatian gentleman and Virgilian pastoralist. Thus the fetishized riding accoutrements become "natural" elements in a full-blown vision of pastoral refinement.

Of course, Kennedy's novel does not completely escape narrative movement, for as Littleton comments in his "Preface," "There is a rivulet of a story wandering through a broad meadow of episode" (vii). Commencing with chapter 12, "A Confession," the novel *seems* to embark upon a sequential plot: the courtship between Ned Hazard and Bel Tracy. But this conventional romance unfolds side-by-side with the story of Meriwether and Tracy's attempts to settle a long-standing land dispute. This comic subplot frequently intrudes upon the main plot, thus teasing the reader, withholding the nuptial climax of the story and, once again, slowing time, extending the time-out for narrator and reader. An even more important means for deflecting narrative progress is the narrator's habit of looping back in time to trace the history of the two estates. Littleton expends two full chapters explaining how the previous patriarch at Swallow Barn unsuccessfully attempted to create a dam and mill. These loopbacks deemphasize the conflicted contemporary scene, highlighting instead continuity and tradition. We can also say that this focus on land issues deflects more disturbing issues of property, replacing ownership of slaves with the trivial issue of who, finally, will retain a worthless piece of land. In the long run the controversy is a moot point since we know Ned and Bel will marry and consolidate the landholdings, creating an even more unified elite.

Given Littleton's pervasive avoidance of plantation politics, it is not surprising that the slave quarters are transformed by the sketchbook technique: "These hovels, with their appurtenances, formed an exceedingly picturesque landscape. . . . The rudeness of their construction rather enhanced the attractiveness of the scene" (II, 223). Their homes converted into sentimental cottages, slaves are frequently described as contented participants in the plantation social life. Typically black characters are described in three ways: as subhuman animals (they are referred to as dogs and monkeys, for instance); as happy servants; and as minstrels. The most memorable black character in the narrative is Carey, "the perfect shadow of his master" Meriwether (I, 31). Carey provides a crucial example of a major stereotype in antebellum writing about blacks: "Sambo, combining in his person Uncle Remus, Jim Crow, and Uncle Tom, was the most pervasive and long lasting of the three literary stereotypes. Indolent, faithful, humorous, loyal, dishonest, superstitious, improvident, and musical, Sambo was inevitably a clown and congenitally docile."[12] Carey by turns works diligently to fulfill his master's desires, parodies the political rhetoric of Meriwether, sings a sentimental ballad to the assembled nobility, and leads Ned and Littleton on a "possum" hunt. This slave's primary task, then, is to keep the plantation frolic in full swing, with nary a fret nor an inconvenience.

Given these pastoralizing tactics throughout the 1832 *Swallow Barn*, in what sense can one refer to the dialogic texture of this originary plantation novel? We can begin to appreciate the counterclaims built into this ambivalent text by attending to Simpson's assertion that "Kennedy insinuates the suggestion, whether deliberately or not, that the slaves dominate the life of the plantation."[13] That is, the slaves are the active, energetic, even manipulative participants in plantation life. After all, Carey, though he conforms to the Sambo stereotype, impresses by his range of actions. While the leading white characters perpetually consume and recline, the blacks are up and doing. In a remarkable chapter entitled "Stable Wisdom," devoted to the breeding and care of horses, Carey dominates his master through rhetorical energy and cogent argument. Meriwether is compelled to admit that "rather than disturb the peace, I must submit to his authority" (II, 221).

Such comments hint at failure within the plantation elite, and indeed Littleton (as Kennedy's surrogate) is often unsparing. The first edition of *Swallow Barn* retains traces of its original satiric design, as in this description of Frank Meriwether:

> He has some claim to supremacy in [administering justice]; for during three years of his life he smoked segars in a lawyer's office at Richmond; sometimes looked into Blackstone and the Revised Code; was a member of a debating society that ate oysters once a week during the winter; and wore six cravats and a pair of yellow-topped boots as a blood of the metropolis. Having in this way qualified himself for the pursuits of agriculture, he came to his estate a very model of landed gentleman. (I, 27)

This passage reminds us that Kennedy based Meriwether on his uncle Philip Pendleton, who "was the embodiment of the contrasts and peculiarities of the plantation world with its exaggerated deference and its niceties of conduct. His role as patriarch of the Pendleton clan made him generous and complacent. In his happiest mood he was courtly and charming, but when the spirit of disputation moved him, he could be peevish and arrogant."[14] Given Kennedy's commitment to manufactures, internal improvements, and "progress" in general, he could only have mixed feelings about this plantation host. His doubts about Southern culture are most apparent when Littleton leaves the jovial plantation to observe Virginian culture more widely. For example, upon attending a trial Littleton remarks that various efforts at "improving" courthouses "show that the public functionaries have at times had one or two abortive inspirations of a spirit of improvement, and a transient passion for beauty" (I, 191–92). In other words, the "complacent" temperament of the Southern elite produces shoddy opulence. The writer further critiques the "niceties of conduct" on the plantation by lampooning the "feudal" trappings of Bel Tracy's manners, especially her fondness for falconry. Similar to Twain's later indictment of the aristocratic pretensions of antebellum Southern culture, Kennedy challenges the sham romanticism of the Southern elite.

The 1832 *Swallow Barn* also reflects Kennedy's divided opinion of "the peculiar institution." While Littleton does "not hesitate to pronounce [slaves] a comparatively comfortable and contented race of people" (II, 227), Meriwether provides a more complicated reading of their condition:

> "This topic," said he, "has grown to possess a fearful interest of late. The world has begun to discuss the evils of slavery; and part of the debate has been levelled to the comprehension of our negroes. I believe there is no class of men who may not be persuaded that they suffer wrong in the organization of society;—and, perhaps, it is true; then, how much easier is it to inflame the ignorant minds of these people, especially with a subject so indefensible as slavery? It is theoretically and morally wrong; and, of course, it may be made to appear wrong in all its modifications. But, surely, if these people are consigned to our care, and put upon our commonwealth, without our agency, the only duty that is left to us is to administer wholesome laws for their government, and to make their servitude as tolerable to them as we can." (II, 227–228)

One can imagine no more tortured defense of slavery. At one moment Meriwether confesses that slavery is "morally indefensible," while in the next he accedes to the "white man's burden" view of the race problem.[15] Indeed, there is a strange passivity to his characterization of the institution, for he argues that slavery has been created "without our agency," as though slave masters had no opportunity to abolish slavery or even free individual slaves. It is hardly surprising that Kennedy carefully revised this speech in the 1851 edition to downplay Meriwether's doubts and to affirm the Southerner's right to ameliorate the slave system in his own way, at his own pace.

In addition to satirizing the plantation elite and voicing doubts about slavery, the 1832 *Swallow Barn* incorporates three narratives which run counter to the dominant pastoralizing style. As Yellin has commented, "Each of the three tales Kennedy introduces into the narrative of *Swallow Barn* contrasts dramatically with the easy, familiar tone of the novel. Taken together, they dramatize a darker side of life in the South, undercut the characterization of the black man as happy inferior, and provide a norm against which the quality of plantation life can be measured."[16] In effect the tales of Mike Brown, Abe, and John Smith manifest subversive subtexts. The overlong story of John Smith's exploits in Virginia, which concludes the 1832 edition, provides an epic backdrop to the lassitude of contemporary Virginia. Littleton's final comment on Smith highlights the historical figure's heroic stature: "I closed the Chronicle, and restored it to its shelf in the library with a renewed admiration for the hero of the Old Dominion . . ." (II, 314). In contrast to the epic mode of the Smith story, "Mike Brown" tells the tale of a Revolutionary War hero who resides on the rough margin of "The Brakes" (Tracy's plantation). A blacksmith by trade, Brown carries on a lifelong acquaintance with the Devil, at one point challenging him to a duel, only to be incapacitated for battle when the Devil tricks him into helplessly straddling a muddy canal. As his name would suggest, Mike Brown's story is a Virginian version of "Young Goodman Brown," but written in the Irvingesque comic Gothic mode. Unlike the soulwracking "conversion" experience of the naive Puritan, Brown undergoes a ribtickling introduction to the guile and marital discomforts of "Old Scratch." Indeed, as it borrows from Irving's Gothic technique, so too does "Mike Brown" conform to the Southwest humor tradition, for we learn at the end of the interpolated narrative that Brown indulged in the kind of bragging and talltale telling associated with the ringtailed roarers. But through this humorous talewithinatale Kennedy hints that all is not well in the state of Virginia. As I commented earlier, whenever Littleton's narrative drifts from the immediate plantation scene to describe the marginal life of the Old Dominion, the reader is presented with a less sanguine view of Southern aristocracy. So here Mike Brown, lowerclass white, equally fond of drinking and berating his wife, undermines the idyllic image of the Pendleton regime. Furthermore, in a notsosubtle blow at the selfimage of the Cavalier, at one point the Devil incarnates himself as a gentleman, demanding that Brown acknowledge his subservient place within the social hierarchy. In so many words, Kennedy has compared Meriwether to the Devil!

But the most memorable interpolated story is that of Abe, an example of the stereotypical Nat figure from antebellum culture.[17] The initially rebellious Abe is contrasted with his father, Luke, who serves honorably in the Revolution at the side of his master. In lieu of manumission, Luke accepts as a reward for that service a comfortable cabin at Swallow Barn. He lives out a long, happy life with his wife Lucy, a black version of Wordsworth's pathetic mothers in *Lyrical Ballads*.

By contrast, their youngest son Abe combines evident intelligence with incendiary passion. Rather than serving the revolutionary cause of the master, Abe seems destined to lead his own black revolt. How-ever, his rebellious nature is mastered by Frank Meriwether's thought-ful nurture. In response to the slave's anarchic criminality, Meri-wether sends him to sea as a sailor upon a Chesapeake Bay sloop. Abe matures into a dutiful, even commanding seaman, compelled by hard work and the freedom of the sea. In the climactic episode of his story, he guides a pilot boat toward a foundered clipper in the midst of a violent February storm, only to be killed in the daring rescue attempt. Littleton complacently remarks that Abe had earned the status of chivalric knight through this act of heroism. So it is that Nat is con-verted into a productive slave; so it is that the talented black man can become both loyal slave and Southern hero. Yet Abe's actions cannot be wholly naturalized by the narrator. First, as Lucinda Mac-Kethan has pointed out, Abe's actual heroism forms a telling contrast to the mock heroism of Ned's proposal of marriage.[18] Secondly, Abe's anger has not been completely purged by his reformation and death. As if to emblemize that subversive residue, Littleton dwells upon the passionately grieving mother Lucy, maddened by her loss, awaiting the dead son's return. Certainly Kennedy achieves a picturesque effect through this image of Lucy, but the bereft slave mother signifies more than heroic suffering. She seems the emblem of the riven slave family, the inevitable victim of slave codes which stripped the black family of legal status. We shall revisit Lucy's gothicized cottage with Frederick Douglass in an account that underscores rather than conceals the antislavery implications of a Negro mother's grief.

II. Labor Relations within the Southern Home

In one of those uncanny intertextual moments which recur in ante-bellum representations of slavery, Frederick Douglass describes his wistful view of ships upon Chesapeake Bay, any one of which might have carried Kennedy's Abe:

> Our house stood within a few rods of the Chesapeake Bay, whose broad bosom was ever white with sails from every quarter of the habitable globe. Those beautiful vessels, robed in purest white, so delightful to the eye of freemen, were to me so many shrouded ghosts, to terrify and torment me with thoughts of my wretched condition. I have often, in the deep stillness of a summer's Sabbath, stood all alone upon the lofty banks of that noble bay, and traced, with saddened heart and tearful eye, the countless number of sails moving off to the mighty ocean.[19]

Douglass, confined within the pastoral prison of the plantation, looks upon the free-moving ships as so many ghostly reminders of his condition. And indeed, to turn from *Swallow Barn* to *Narrative of the Life of an American Slave* is to suffer many such shocks of recognition. In place of the pastoral ease of Kennedy's Irvingesque narrative we confront an urgent, terse, tense style, all the more terrifying for its apparent restraint.[20] The time-out from Southern history ends abruptly, for we enter a text dominated by a quest for identity within human time. Reading Douglass's *Narrative* against the plantation tradition is warranted by a "signifyin'" relation between slave narrative and Kennedy's text: "Such hostility signifies the presence of a black discourse both popular and compelling, one which even informed and helped determine the shape of its narrative antithesis, the plantation novel; the two forms seem to have been locked together in a bipolar movement, as it were, or a signifying relationship."[21] We need not assume that Douglass had actually read the plantation novels of the 1830s, for he "read" the institutionalized cultural codes of the plantation in his daily experience as slave. Furthermore, we need not seek a complete break from a text such as *Swallow Barn,* for as asserted earlier, that dialogic novel introduces narrative elements amplified by the polemical autobiography. In effect Douglass's *Narrative* misreads or parodies Kennedy's novel by flattening and distorting it, focusing on select elements of the plantation tradition. Specifically, Douglass's *Narrative* carnivalizes the plantation elite, much as *Swallow Barn* satirizes Meriwether, Ned, and Bel Tracy, and gothicizes slave/master relations, combining the interpolated stories of Mike Brown and Abe.[22]

These narrative tactics depend upon a fall from sacred into profane time. According to Mircea Eliade, "sacred time . . . appears under the paradoxical aspect of a circular time, reversible and recoverable, a sort of eternal mythical present that is periodically reintegrated by means of rites. This attitude in regard to time suffices to distinguish religious from nonreligious man; the former refuses to live solely in what, in modern terms, is called the historical present; he attempts to regain a sacred time that, from one point of view, can be homologized to eternity."[23] Though of course Eliade has in mind religious experience in a strict sense, his terminology describes the time sense of the plantation elite, a temporal sense I have already called "pastoralizing." That is, Bel, Ned, Frank and Mark Littleton occupy "an eternal mythical present," dominated by rituals of courtship and good fellowship. They live outside contingency, outside "the historical present." Furthermore, the concept of "circular time" corresponds to the narrative structure described in the previous section, for *Swallow Barn* evades narrative progression by its still points, sketchbook effect, and loopbacks.

Given the oppressive effects of sacred time on the slave, it makes sense that Douglass would choose to enter profane or secular time. However, to understand this narrative move fully, we need to distinguish between two kinds of secular time, *chronos* and *kairos*:

> All such plotting presupposes and requires that an end will bestow upon the whole duration and meaning. To put it another way, the interval must be purged of simple chronicity, . . . humanly uninteresting successiveness. It is required to be a significant season, *kairos* poised between beginning and end. It has to be . . . an instance of . . . "temporal integration"—our way of bundling together perception of the present, memory of the past, and expectation of the future, in a common organization. Within this organization that which was conceived of as simply successive becomes charged with past and future: what was *chronos* becomes *kairos*.[24]

Douglass's *Narrative* depends upon both these senses of secular time, each subversive of the plantation myth. *Chronos* is an apt term for the slave's sense of time, for the laborer inhabits mere succession, unstructured by beginning or end. As such, *chronos* is a prison-house. On the other hand, the slave gains identity and liberation by achieving *kairos*, a concept of origin and teleology. Put simply, Douglass's *Narrative* tells how the dehumanized slave frees himself by acquiring a plot for his life.

Chronicity oppresses because the slave must work according to a strict work schedule. In the opening chapter Douglass mentions (almost in passing) that his mother visited him only four or five times because "she was a field hand, and a whipping is the penalty of not being in the field at sunrise" (3). Douglass himself experiences this harsh regime when he goes to work for Edward Covey:

> We were worked fully up to the point of endurance. Long before day we were up, our horses fed, and by the first approach of day we were off to the field with our hoes and ploughing teams. Mr. Covey gave us enough to eat, but scarce time to eat it. We were often less than five minutes taking our meals. We were often in the field from the first approach of day till its last lingering ray had left us; and at saving-fodder time, midnight often caught us in the field binding blades. (60)

This regimented time scheme is insidious because it gives the illusion of an organic economy, that is, an economy tied to the rhythms of day and season. It is hardly surprising that Douglass finds himself transformed from a man into a beast by these sweatshop conditions.

Indeed, the slave narrator implicitly challenges the South's defense of slavery as a humane alternative to the northern factory, for the *Narra-tive* demonstrates that plantations and farms are run on principles of time similar to the factory, and with similar results for the laborer.[25] However, plantation control of the slave's time extends beyond the work day, for the slave's year follows a fixed pattern as well. We learn that black laborers traditionally begin new duties upon the first of January, for Douglass refers to this fact at least twice. Though this may seem a relatively minor issue, one cannot forget that the individ-ual slave must take up a new life, a new labor according to the master's calendar. Douglass also reveals much about slave leisure time, pointing to the Christmas holidays as especially disarming: "It was deemed a disgrace not to get drunk at Christmas. . . . These holidays serve as conductors, or safety-valves, to carry off the rebellious spirit of en-slaved humanity" (74). Not only does the plantation system dictate the work schedule, but it systematically releases subversive pressures building within discontented workers. It is apparent, then, that the plantation economy manipulated the slave's sense of time by accultur-ating the worker to well-defined work and rest routines. This time scheme trapped the slave in a constricting historical present, stripping him/her of power because planning becomes virtually impossible: "When in Mr. Gardner's employment, I was kept in such a perpetual whirl of excitement, I could think of nothing, scarcely, but my life; and in thinking of my life, I almost forgot my liberty" (99).

It is only by extending the time sense that the slave can be liberated through secular time. Freedom comes through *kairos*. This is surely what Albert E. Stone has in mind when he writes in moving terms of Douglass's quest for historicity: "Under slavery, man possesses no such historic identity as name, date, place of birth or residence usually provide. Douglass has *achieved* these hallmarks of historicity, has attached himself to time, place, society. Therefore he shows no wish to escape from history."[26] Douglass weaves this theme of time-consciousness through his *Narrative*, beginning with the dramatic as-sertion: "I have no accurate knowledge of my age, never having seen any authentic record containing it. By far the larger part of the slaves know as little of their ages as horses know of theirs . . ." (1). Not only does Douglass lack an origin, but his masters and overseers would deny him a future: ". . . [Master Thomas] advised me to complete thoughtlessness of the future, and taught me to depend solely upon him for happiness" (103). Caught in the wasteland of the isolated present, demarcated by work rhythms dictated by the slave regime, Douglass practically shouts his delight at achieving what we might call "temporal literacy": "I have now reached a period of my life when

I can give dates" (51). This new sense of time allows Douglass to construct his narrative world, a world of cause and effect in which he is an agent of change. Indeed, Douglass's text suggests a strong relationship between this global time sense and narrative itself, which traditionally depends upon a beginning, middle and end. It is only by gaining a sense of origin, a contextualized sense of place, and a teleology that the slave can become an autobiographer, writing about and for himself.

It is partly this profane or secular time sense which motivates Douglass's adoption of the Franklinesque secular autobiography. Critics have often noted Douglass's debt to the Franklin tradition of American autobiography.[27] Key moments in the *Narrative,* such as the persona's entrance into Baltimore, seem uncanny echoes of that archetypal American autobiography. And indeed, despite an obvious debt to the tradition of spiritual autobiography, Douglass's *Narrative* occupies secular rather than sacred time.[28] The secular autobiography narrates the rise from rags to respectability, compressing a complex life story into a formulaic celebration of self and capitalist culture. By careful selection and deletion, the narrator argues that his life could only have followed *this* course, *this* trajectory. As many critics have urged, the secular autobiography was itself an ideological trap for Douglass, one he would later escape through *My Bondage and My Freedom.*[29] By opting for the white, middle-class definition of self, Douglass necessarily turned his back on other possibilities for self-definition in African-American culture. However, as a *first move* toward liberation, the Franklin tradition served Douglass well. After all, it is only when Douglass narrates his life story for the first time to an abolitionist gathering in Nantucket that he finds true freedom: "The truth was, I felt myself a slave, and the idea of speaking to white people weighed me down. I spoke but a few moments, when I felt a degree of freedom, and said what I desired with considerable ease" (117).[30] Thus, though Douglass had claimed earlier that his struggle with Covey marked the decisive shift in his life, we now learn that *narrativity* is at least as important to his liberation. In short, Douglass finds ultimate freedom by transforming his *life* into *narrative,* which in turn depends upon *kairos* or a providential sense of time.

What, then, are the dialogic consequences of this temporal transformation of the literary plantation? Put simply, the plantation economy and its occupants are denaturalized. The plantation can no longer seem an organic family, a natural outgrowth of the Edenic landscape. In Douglass's *Narrative* we see too clearly the human labor and suffering which undergird the leisure time of Meriwether and his merry pranksters. So, for instance, Littleton's grand vision of Meriwether seated upon his horse undergoes a shocking diminution. The slave narrator dwells upon the uncertain fate of the master's two groomsmen, old and young Barney:

> . . . in nothing was Colonel Lloyd more particular than in the management of his horses. The slightest inattention to these was unpardonable, and was visited upon those, under whose care they were placed, with the severest punishment; no excuse could shield them, if the colonel only suspected any want of attention to his horses—a supposition which he frequently indulged, and one which, of course, made the office of old and young Barney a very trying one. They never knew when they were safe from punishment. They were frequently whipped when least deserving, and escaped whipping when most deserving it. (16–17)

Lloyd becomes the apotheosis of Kennedy's "opulent, unquestioned squire," the unvarnished thing itself, stripped of the sentimentalizing representation of master as paternalistic caretaker. Furthermore, this passage focuses our attention upon the arbitrary nature of plantation law, a shortcoming highlighted by Douglass's clever use of chiasmus in the final sentence above. As Keith Byerman has pointed out, the capricious conduct of the master virtually required the slave to adopt trickster behavior. That is, given the "systemic disorder" of master culture, trickery becomes vital for survival.[31]

Douglass thematizes trickster behavior by discussing the slaves' refusal to share their actual feelings with whites. Once again Colonel Lloyd becomes the allegorical figure of white deceit, selling off a discontented slave who has the poor luck to confess his unhappiness to the master he does not recognize. More subtly, the text itself employs trickster rhetoric, that is, subtle irony. Douglass's deadpan style proffers the illusion of earnestness, a straightforward, unvarnished account. And yet, many "flat" statements are loaded with implied invective. For example, after describing Mr. Severe's brutal tactics as overseer, Douglass concludes, "He whipped, but seemed to take no pleasure in it. He was called by the slaves a good overseer" (12). That is all the more we hear about Mr. Severe. Douglass does not overstate his case, nor does he explain his final comment. He sets it on the page, a time bomb ready to explode, to remind the reader both of the brutality of a system which could characterize Severe as a "good" overseer and the ignorance of the slaves who could accede to such a view. Indeed, much of the *Narrative*'s irony is directed at the earlier "Douglass," the slave who was within the circle of mastery and unable to critique it. While such irony may seem condescending toward blacks, we have to remember that Douglass has taken pains to deconstruct the social system that makes the ignorant slave. That is, Douglass's barbed irony is not aimed at the individual slave but at the socially conditioned "nigger" who has been trapped by *chronos*.

Douglass's subtle ironies are closely linked to two other carnivaliz-ing tactics, double-voicing and comic inversion. Douglass is the model of Bakhtinian double-voicing, for he has a marked talent for parody. In a subtle but crucial example, Douglass revoices Hugh Auld's injunc-tions to his wife not to teach a slave to read, for "If you give a nigger an inch, he will take an ell" (33). In the following chapter Douglass, in the midst of describing his quest for literacy, pauses to remark, "Mistress, in teaching me the alphabet, had given me the *inch*, and no precaution could prevent me from taking the *ell*" (38). Douglass adds the italics to emphasize his revoicing of Auld's racist comment. This is a brilliant rhetorical tactic by the slave narrator, for in a curious sense he can be said to demonstrate the master's perspicacity, that is, he has simply lived up to the master's expectation of him as a human being, thereby exposing the fallacy of slave as child or subhu-man dependent. More fundamentally, such double-voicing allows the slave to occupy the site of the master's discourse, evacuating the mas-ter's power and substituting his own.[32] Put more simply, the slave has reclaimed the master's language to express his own achievement of literacy. And of course, by the verbal flair of this performance, Doug-lass demonstrates just how far he has come with that inch provided him by Sophia Auld. A less subtle but more famous parody appears in the "Appendix" to Douglass's *Narrative,* which features the mock Christian hymn:

> Come, saints and sinners, hear me tell
> How pious priests whip Jack and Nell,
> And women buy and children sell,
> And preach all sinners down to hell,
> And sing of heavenly union.
>
> (123)

Here Douglass revoices an entire genre, the hymn, by substituting overt language of mastery for traditional religious rhetoric. In effect Douglass allows the subtext of racist discourse to speak in the form of worship, suggesting which deity the plantation culture actually serves.

Given the severity of the slave regime, it may seem bizarre to find comic modes in Douglass's *Narrative,* and yet, as Butterfield has ob-served, "To respond to tyranny with laughter is also a control on the feeling of helpless anger, a way of belittling the tyrant at times when it is not possible to overthrow him."[33] Such "belittling" occurs in the Covey episode, probably the most memorable set of events in the

Narrative. Douglass tells us that he was sent to Covey to be broken, to be turned into a suitable slave. However, the narrator immediately begins a process of subverting Covey's authority by combining a comic mode of representation with the horrific. The Covey episode generally has the feel of a folktale, with its simplicity, near-allegorical characters, and battle of wits. Indeed, Covey is converted into a snake by the wily narrator, symbolizing the slave-breaker's cunning and deceit. In a sense Douglass must kill the snake to gain his freedom.

The opening scenes of the Covey episode suggest the comic mode, for Douglass begins by telling of his battle with the recalcitrant oxen. True, in the elaborate story of Douglass's near-death we witness Covey's attempt to humiliate the slave. And Covey does after all use Douglass's ineptitude as an excuse to whip the slave, much as Colonel Lloyd had arbitrarily whipped his groomsmen. However, the story has a curiously comic tone, for we witness the unpracticed city boy dragged hither and yon by the dumb beasts. Perhaps the story slyly hints that Douglass is after all beyond this kind of mindless labor, that he is indeed "urbane" in an affirmative sense. Later in the same chapter, Douglass describes his game of hide-and-seek in a cornfield with the inept Covey. One begins to think that it is Covey who is the inexperienced "handler."

Even the most dramatic section of the Covey episode, the fierce battle between white and black for psychological mastery, has a humorous cast to it. The simple fact of hand-to-hand combat between the two figures literally puts Douglass and Covey on equal footing. (It seems impossible to imagine Colonel Lloyd wrestling a slave.) Both slave and overseer become grunting, awkward, tired, desperate *men.* After two hours of struggle, Covey appears the broken breaker:

> Covey at length let me go, puffing and blowing at a great rate, saying that if I had not resisted, he would not have whipped me half so much. The truth was, that he had not whipped me at all. I considered him as getting entirely the worst end of the bargain. . . . The whole six months afterwards . . . [Covey] never laid the weight of his finger upon me in anger. He would occasionally say, he didn't want to get hold of me again, "No," thought I, "you need not; for you will come off worse than you did before." (72)

Not only does Covey look foolish "puffing and blowing," but once again the supposed slave takes over the language of the master class, here giving Covey's statement of authority a new accent or significance, one not altogether flattering to Covey. The laughter originates in the ironic distance between Covey's claimed authority and his actual powerlessness. More fundamentally, the reader observes the

disparity between the slave's *assumed* and *actual* status; while Covey
assumes Douglass's slavery, Douglass demonstrates his independence.

The Covey episode recalls the comic characterization of Meriwether as absent-minded "master," for Carey seems the real host at
Swallow Barn. The *Narrative* also incorporates gothicized scenes that
recall "Mike Brown" and "A Slave Mother." As I commented in the
first chapter to this study, we can perceive a close relationship between
carnivalizing and gothicizing tactics, for both originate in the uncanny
but move toward different reader responses: the carnivalizing mode
depends upon ironic laughter, while the gothicizing mode depends
upon fear. If Douglass's carnival tactics would reduce the master class
to laughable fools, his Gothic tactics would transform that same class
into demonic villains. Thus, as the plantation master metamorphosed
into the Devil himself in "Mike Brown," so the overseer Plummer is
demonized by liquor and jealousy: "The louder [Aunt Hester]
screamed, the harder he whipped; and where the blood ran fastest,
there he whipped longest. He would whip her to make her scream,
and whip her to make her hush; and not until overcome by fatigue,
would he cease to swing the blood-clotted cowskin" (6). This passage,
famous for Douglass's relentless repetition of "whip," marks "the
blood-stained gate, the entrance to the hell of slavery, through which
I was about to pass" (6). As we shall see, Douglass's characterization
of female slaves as victims was another trap for the male slave narrator.
Harriet Ann Jacobs will revise his portrait of the female slave to
downplay the woman as mere object of violence and desire. Nonetheless, as a tactic for appealing to readers in a sentimentalized culture,
this passage has a striking rhetorical power. Plummer's demonization
anticipates the degeneration of two other important white figures in
Douglass's life, Gore and Sophia Auld. The aptly named Gore becomes
the apotheosis of the overseer as Gothic villain: "He was, of all the
overseers, the most dreaded by the slaves. His presence was painful;
his eye flashed confusion; and seldom was his sharp, shrill voice heard,
without producing horror and trembling in their ranks" (22). Emphasizing Gore's trickery and indifference to suffering (qualities he shares
with Covey), Douglass once again characterizes the plantation as a
scene of chaos, the very figure of Miltonic hell. Gore lives up to his
role as Gothic villain when he coolly murders a slave at point-blank
range, an act for which he suffers neither pangs of remorse nor legal
punishment.

Douglass's characterization of Sophia Auld is more moving because
it is apparent the writer cared more about her than the overseers he
masters through discourse. There seems a genuine sorrow (despite the

conventional religious rhetoric) in the following description of Sophia's transformation:

> But, alas! this kind heart had but a short time to remain such. The fatal
> poison of irresponsible power was already in her hands, and soon com-
> menced its infernal work. That cheerful eye, under the influence of slavery,
> soon became red with rage; that voice, made all of sweet accord, changed
> to one of harsh and horrid discord; and that angelic face gave place to
> that of a demon. (32–33)

Thus Sophia Auld is reduced from the slaveholding mistress, the
Southern lady, to the dark villainess of romance. The passage is strikingly similar to Clara Wieland's shocked description of her "transformed" brother in Charles Brockden Brown's *Wieland, or, The
Transformation* (1798), typically referred to as the first American
Gothic novel. Theodore Wieland, that paragon of Enlightenment rationality, is destroyed by religious delusion, made over into parricide
by mania and Carwin's trickery. Douglass's representational strategy
is similar to Brown's not only in its style but in its ultimate purpose:
as Brown would unmask the psycho-social causes of madness, so also
would Douglass. One might say that the religious mania of slavery
misshapes Sophia, who now spends her days obsessively spying on
Frederick, making sure he does not violate the prohibition against
literacy.

Douglass's *Narrative* returns to the characters and plot of Kennedy's "A Slave Mother" in the narrator's charged descriptions of his
grandmother. We recall that Kennedy partially converted Lucy's grief
into the "romantic" suffering of a mother for her lost heroic slave
child. That is, the black mother's grief becomes picturesque, of a piece
with the description of slaves as colorful participants in plantation
life. However, Douglass signifies upon Kennedy's story by foregrounding the injustice causing the slave mother's grief. Here he describes the matriarch's loneliness, rhetorically transforming his
grandmother into a Gothic victim: "The hearth is desolate. The children, the unconscious children, who once sang and danced in her
presence, are gone. She gropes her way, in the darkness of age, for a
drink of water. Instead of the voices of her children, she hears by day
the moans of the dove, and by night the screams of the hideous owl.
All is gloom. The grave is at the door" (49). The narratorial eye moves
from the master's big house to the slave's shattered home. While
Douglass's immediate goal is to arouse pity for the lonely female figure,
he drives toward the larger objective achieved in his characterization
of masters as Gothic villains: to underscore the social causes of the

Gothic nightmare. Douglass has earlier explained *why* his grandmother suffers loneliness: her children have been sold off one by one by ungrateful masters. Furthermore, despite years of service, including nurturing her master, she has been denied her freedom. As Douglass is riveted to the shore in his revery on Chesapeake Bay, so the grandmother is bound to this spot of oppression. She is literally haunted by memories of lost children. If Lucy mourns her dead son, Douglass's grandmother mourns three generations of enslaved progeny. Douglass's grandmother is the tragic symbol of slavery's human cost. Unlike the male slave narrator, who has found freedom through *kairos,* the grandmother is enslaved by an eternal present of loss.

III. Reconstructing the Southern Estate

If the slave narrative dominated the 1840s, the 1850s can be said to belong to plantation apologists. Goaded into discourse by the controversy surrounding the Fugitive Slave Law, the slave narratives themselves, and most prominently, Stowe's *Uncle Tom's Cabin* (discussed in the next chapter), white Southerners attempted the seemingly impossible: putting Humpty Dumpty (the familial South) back together again. These revisionary plantation novels tended to monologize Kennedy's multivocal text by excising the problematic and so converting fiction into propaganda every bit as barbed as Douglass's *Narrative.* More than rewriting *Swallow Barn,* then, these texts often directly refute the slave narratives, casting aspersion upon rebellious slaves, propounding theories of racial inferiority, and representing the Northern manufacturing economy as the ultimate form of slavery.

These revisionary tactics are evident in the 1851 edition of *Swallow Barn.* Perhaps it should not be surprising that a revised edition of Kennedy's novel appeared at the second flashpoint of antebellum political conflict over slavery. As the 1832 edition had focused on opposing attitudes toward the plantation, so the 1851 edition softened Kennedy's depiction. One crucial means for simplifying the text is to push events into a sealed-off past; Swallow Barn's inhabitants are now characterized as quaint, charming ancestors, inhabitants of a simpler prior time:

> Swallow Barn exhibits a picture of country life in Virginia, as it existed in the first quarter of the present century. . . . The mellow, bland, and sunny luxuriance of her old-time society—its good fellowship, its hearty and constitutional *companionableness,* the thriftless gayety of the people, their dogged but amiable invincibility of opinion, and that overflowing

hospitality which knew no ebb,—these traits, though far from being impaired, are modified at the present day by circumstances which have been gradually attaining a marked influence over social life as well as political relation.[34]

Once again we observe a play with time in the dialogic struggles over slavery. As Douglass would return the reader to history, so Kennedy would draw the audience toward the epicized past embodied in the master's home. No doubt Kennedy aspires to the kind of nostalgic glow suffusing Cooper's *Satanstoe*. Immersed in the conflicted present, Kennedy perhaps longed for a simpler political past. But the narrative time shift has clear ideological consequences as well. By converting the plantation into a distant artifact, the 1851 *Swallow Barn* effectively prevents political censure of the Meriwether regime. We are disarmed by the epic effect, for who would call into question cultural fathers and mothers? This monologizing tactic is employed by both Cooke and Simms later in the same decade.

The novel is further "spatialized" by the twenty sketches incorporated into the text. The iconographic significance of these sketches warrants a separate article, for the sketches are revealing of the political designs for reissuing *Swallow Barn*. One notices, for instance, that of the twenty sketches, fully twelve focus on blacks. These iconic slaves are consistently represented as happy, intimate with whites, and bucolic in a quite literal sense. For instance, the second sketch shows a black girl pulled along by a playful cow (30). The artist also uses contrasting sketches to represent Abe's transformation from the rebellious Nat into the heroic slave. In one sketch (following 468) Abe is shown in consort with three other rebellious blacks in a swamp setting, having just committed a theft of livestock. Here Abe is positioned in the background, merely one of four accomplices. In the foreground we see cards, a liquor bottle, and a knife, obvious symbols of the decadent criminal life. By contrast, in the preceding sketch (464) Abe is centered in the foreground, the very figure of heroic leadership. His white shirt, dashing hat, and posture of command distinguish him from his shadowed shipmates. In yet another sketch the artist depicts Abe's mother Lucy in a picturesque pose, a cat in the background suggesting a domestic scene that downplays the Negro mother's grief. Perhaps it is not surprising that the artist devoted four sketches in total to this single interpolated tale, for it is not only the most dramatic sequence in the novel, but as discussed in the first section of this chapter, it provides apparent justification for the slave system. These four sketches constitute a reading of the tale which drains away the subversive implications developed by Douglass.

In addition to the twelve portraits of slaves, the 1851 sketches include two landscape sketches and five images of whites. The opening sketch provides a synoptic view of the plantation, merging a picturesque "Swallow Barn," an amused gentleman and lady, well-dressed, histrionic blacks, and slave children chasing pigs. In the background we glimpse the plantation house itself, dominating the landscape from its perch upon a hill. Thus the artist visually reinforces the hierarchical image of the Old South. The portraits of white characters are in the main comical, though one sketch does portray Meriwether and his friends on horseback (once again we are called back to the primal scene of master and horse). More typical are sketches of Bel and Ned playing at falconry, and, in the least flattering portrait, Ned and his friends at cards late at night. Both by their static form and their ideological import, the sketches reinforce the affirmative view of the plantation as cultivated playground for master and slave alike.

Finally, as briefly discussed in the first section, Kennedy deletes the John Smith tale and revises Meriwether's commentary on slavery in the 1851 edition. Presumably Kennedy decided that the interpolated story of Smith's exploits added little to the main narrative. One can also speculate that by excising that earlier historical epoch, Kennedy further urges the concept that events described in Swallow Barn are themselves "ancient" or sealed off from the contemporary. Kennedy also reinforces the sense of "the Old Dominion" as self-contained artifact by revising Meriwether's discussion of slavery. Specifically Kennedy downplays the moral ambiguity of the patriarchal institution and emphasizes the concept of states rights. In the 1832 version Meriwether commented "how much easier is it to inflame the ignorant minds of these people, especially with a subject so indefensible as slavery? It is theoretically and morally wrong; and, of course, it may be made to appear wrong in all its modifications" (II, 227). That same passage appears in this form in the 1851 edition:

> Ingenious men, some of them not very honest, have found in these topics themes for agitation and popular appeal in all ages. How likely are they to find, in this question of slavery, a theme for the highest excitement; and especially, how easy is it to inflame the passions of these untutored and unreckoning people, our black population, with this subject! For slavery, as an original question, is wholly without justification or defense. It is theoretically and morally wrong—and fanatical and one-sided thinkers will call its continuance, even for a day, a wrong, under any modification of it. (455)

Kennedy's subtle revisions modify our view of slavery in at least three ways. First, the passage implicitly attacks the intelligence of blacks, for Meriwether questions the rationality of slaves in dealing with any issue, least of all that of chattel slavery. Secondly, Kennedy establishes a distinction between "theoretical" and practical slavery. That is, his character acknowledges that "as an original question," that is, in the abstract, slavery has no moral ground, but given the historical reality of slavery in Virginia, a case can be made for its continuation. Basically that defense follows from the racist assumption that blacks are inferiors who are unable to assume "adult" roles in the republic. Finally, the passage registers the increasing sectional tension of the 1850s, for Kennedy refers directly to abolitionists, "fanatical and one-sided thinkers," who demand immediate emancipation. Overall the passage characterizes the slave master as a rational, thoughtful, concerned citizen, who must keep in check the irrational passions of both the ignorant slave and the Northerner.

Two other male fictions of the 1850s pursue many of the tactics set forth by the revised *Swallow Barn*. John Esten Cooke's *The Virginia Comedians* (1854) and William Gilmore Simms's *Woodcraft* (1852) can be read as a sequential history of the Southern plantation from ten years prior to the Revolutionary War to its immediate aftermath. Much as Kennedy had displaced Mark Littleton's narrative thirty years into the past, so Cooke and Simms revert to the South at the height of its national prestige. This return to the historical novel marks the writers' ideological crisis. As Cooper's Littlepage Trilogy revealed, the historical novel had become a suspect genre by the 1840s. Arguably, historical fiction had done its popular "work" by legitimating American culture and society. Readers turned toward the contemporary novel for commentary on and even critique of the American present. It seems apparent, then, that for these Southern writers the American achievement had *not* been ratified or consolidated, for prior celebrations of "America" had excluded plantation culture. In a retrograde gesture, then, Cooke and Kennedy take up historical narrative in the effort to rewrite the American legacy, affirming the crucial role of Southern society and its peculiar institution in that legacy.

Despite the ideological implications of his generic choice, Cooke wrote a friend that *The Virginia Comedians* "is profoundly democratic, and American—the aristocracy whom I don't like, getting the worst of it."[35] However, as Watson observes, "Cooke's romances of the Old Dominion reflect a historical perspective which accepts as essentially true Virginia's cherished notions of its aristocratic past."[36] How can we reconcile these conflicting perspectives on Cooke's novel? Our perplexity is partly laid to rest by attending to the chaotic form of the novel. Part seduction novel, part sentimental novel in the mode of *Uncle Tom's Cabin*, part comedy of manners in the school of Austen, part plantation romance, Cooke's text simultaneously runs in several ideological directions. The novel is most conveniently read as a moralized version of "the rake's progress," for the action focuses on the moral reformation of a young Cavalier, Champ Effingham. Set during the ten years following the Stamp Act controversy, *The Virginia Comedians* devotes an entire volume to Champ's immoral attempts to win the love of a beautiful actress, Beatrice Hallam. This seduction plot climaxes with Champ's failed try at murdering his rival, Charles Waters. When the action recommences in Volume Two, Champ appears an older and wiser Cavalier, prepared to atone for his earlier sins by marrying an acceptably aristocratic mate, Clare Lee. Indeed, the second volume seems a friendly double for Ned and Bel's courtship plot. The novel concludes with the inevitable nuptial frenzy as four couples, ranging from the aristocratic to the servant classes, join in wedlock. So it is that Cooke's "anti-aristocratic" novel affirms the social hierarchy dear to Frank Meriwether. As one would expect, blacks play only an incidental role in the action, such as in this descriptive passage: "We must leave to fancy, too, the crowd of bright-faced Africans, who jostled each other at the door. . . ."[37] Once again slaves are simply a *given* in the plantation scene. Cooke's characterization of blacks becomes even more politically loaded when one realizes that the novel climaxes with the onset of the Revolutionary War. Cooke does not explore the gap between the rhetoric of freedom and the reality of chattel slavery. Indeed, in a lengthy interlude, Patrick Henry propounds his utopian vision for America and never once suggests the elimination of slavery.[38] Whatever the writer's asserted motives for composing *The Virginia Comedians,* the text has the dual effect of glamorizing the Virginian elite and naturalizing slavery in the Old Dominion.

A novel that Simpson calls one of the two crucial Southern novels of the antebellum era,[39] Simms's *Woodcraft* picks up the action after the Revolutionary War, for it narrates the reconstruction of a South Carolina plantation destroyed by British partisans during the war. The novel's two main characters are the comic plantation master, Captain Porgy, and his aggressive, utilitarian overseer, Millhouse. Porgy and Millhouse engage in frequent mock debates on the master's fiscal irresponsibility and ineptitude in courtship. In a sense Simms has reintroduced Kennedy's critique of the plantation elite as regressive and impractical. *Woodcraft* allows for that criticism but puts it to comic use, suggesting that the successful plantation requires a combination of the overseer's pragmatism and the master's gentility. The action proper follows two plots: the eventual discovery and arrest of the slave-stealing M'Kewn and the reconstruction of Glen-Eberley.

The thematic link between the two plots is transparent, for even as Porgy must clear his fields to produce cash crops, so he must morally purify South Carolina to prepare the way for a new republic. Further-more, the specific target of M'Kewn's criminal activities—slaves—is thematically significant; not only does the text assume that blacks are a form of property, but it strongly implies that to steal slaves is to strike at the very heart of South Carolinian society.

But what, more specifically, can we make of Simms's attitude to-ward his black characters? As Yellin observes, ". . . perhaps because his theories of racial inferiority did not permit him to conceive that slaves could threaten Southern society, or perhaps because he wanted to show that society as monolithic—Simms does not even hint at the possibility of black terror in his romance. Throughout [Woodcraft], the black man is consistently seen as a passive inferior."[40] Simms firmly believed in the racist theory that blacks are innately inferior beings who must be cared for in a structured, stratified social system. In an archetypal scene of master/slave relations, eighteen slaves who had fled to the swamp to escape British capture return to take up their field work: "The negroes, glad once more to find themselves in possession of a homestead, certain provisions, and the protection of a white man, have worked with a hearty will and cheerfulness which amply made up for lost time."[41] Here indeed we are meant to see the plantation as extended family. Though Simms described Woodcraft as an ideal response to Uncle Tom's Cabin,[42] in only one passage does he directly attack abolitionists, linking their ancestors to the corrupt M'Kewn: "[M'Kewn] had bought, at moderate prices, a lot of new negroes, from the coast of Guinea, from a virtuous puritan captain, of Rhode Island, who had gleaned wonderfully from the gold coast, and whose great grandson, by-the-way, has since shown himself a virtuous abolitionist in the senate of the United States, breathing hate and horror toward the descendants of the very people to whom his philanthropic grand-sire sold the stolen negroes."[43] Generally Simms prefers to defend slav-ery in less overt terms, such as characterizing Millhouse as a reason-able overseer (in contrast to Douglass's and Stowe's) and representing the master/slave relationship as one of respect and affection. The major black character in Woodcraft is Porgy's cook Tom, who expresses an-guish at the prospect of leaving his master's service in order to pay off an outstanding debt. Tom also reinforces the Sambo stereotype by arguing that blacks innately prefer to mix fun with work: "'De ser-geant [Millhouse] is too cussed foolish! He don't comprehend nigger nater 't all! He's always a-talking 'bout wuk, as ef der's no play in de worl'. . . .'"[44]

Caroline Lee Hentz's The Planter's Northern Bride (1854) prefers a more direct polemical approach to the relative subtleties of Cooke's and Simms's historical novels. Indeed, Hentz's text should be read as an exact double for Douglass's *Narrative*. If Douglass argues that blacks are converted into subservient laborers by an oppressive social system, Hentz replies that blacks are innately dependent. If Douglass asserts that the industrializing North provides a "heavenly" alternative to the hellish South, Hentz counters that northern wage slavery is "hellish" by comparison with slavery. If the slave narrator characterizes the plantation master as barbaric and arbitrary, the female novelist characterizes him as the benevolent patriarch. In sum, Hentz's novel is the apotheosis of the epicized plantation novel, one that fully monologizes slave ideology by silencing mocking counterclaims. If Kennedy, Cooke, and Simms allow for a degree of the humorous to color their descriptions of the Southern elite, Hentz will permit nothing to break the superserious tone of her apology for the slave system.

What makes Hentz's epic text even more dramatic is its contemporaneity. Here there is no pretending that the slave South could only be idealized in a distant past. Instead, Hentz participates with verve in the "sentimentalization" of antebellum writing, focusing on contemporary characters confronting immediate political issues. Philip Fisher has eloquently argued that Harriet Beecher Stowe's sentimental tactics enabled her to persuade the reader of a radical political position, an effect he labels "making familiar."[45] *The Planter's Northern Bride* provides a clear instance of a popular writer utilizing similar conventions to *affirm* rather than deny dominant ideology. That is, Hentz employs the sentimental iconography of domestic fiction to legitimate the existing social system. Her text, then, is an instance of Wolfgang Iser's assertion that "history . . . is full of situations in which the balancing powers of literature have been used to support prevailing systems. Often such works tend to be of a more trivial nature, as they affirm specific norms with a view to training the reader according to the moral or social code of the day. . . ."[46] While Iser rather too easily dismisses popular writing as "trivial," he reminds us that we cannot mindlessly elevate popular art without considering its negative ideological effects. Popular art (or any art, for that matter) can coopt the reader by pleasure, a process all too apparent in contemporary mass media.

Hentz sentimentalizes slavery through the relationship between Russell Moreland, a refined plantation master, and his "northern bride," Eulalia Hastings. Moreland (the surname is curiously revealing of the character's imperialist attitudes) journeys to New England, yet another antebellum literary bachelor in search of a spouse. In effect he reverses Mark Littleton's less successful journey to Virginia. Accompanied by his devoted slave Albert, Moreland confronts a series of challenges to slavery, mastering them all through his charm, elo- quence, and benevolence. In addition to defeating the blustering Has- tings in personal and public debates, Moreland helps a consumptive factory operative, Nancy, the very type of Northern wage slavery. Contemplating Nancy's dire condition, Moreland "turned his thoughts homeward, to the enslaved children of Africa, and, taking them as a *class,* as a *distinct race* of beings, he came to the irresistible conclusion, that they were the happiest *subservient* race that were found on the face of the globe."[47] In addition to winning this battle of conscience, Moreland wins the hand of Eulalia, a pious New En- glander who is converted by the Southerner's passionate defense of his homeland. In the course of the novel virtually all her doubts about slavery are laid to rest by firsthand experience.

This conversion process reaches its emotional climax upon Eula's first sight of her husband's relationship with his plantation slaves:

> More like a father welcomed by his children than a king greeted by his subjects, he stood, the centre of the sable ring. Eulalia thought she had never seen him look so handsome, so noble, so good. She had never felt so proud of being his wife. An impression of his power, gently used, but still manifest, produced in her that feeling of awe, softened by tenderness, so delicious to the loving, trusting heart of woman. He appeared to her in a new character. She had known him as the fond, devoted bridegroom; now he was invested with the authority and responsibility of a master. And she must share that responsibility, assist him in his duties, and make the welfare, comfort, and happiness of these dependent beings the great object of her life. (332)

We have returned to Meriwether upon his horse, the apotheosis of "the unquestioned squire," but here there is no concealing the power behind this posture. Indeed the passage explicitly praises, even aesthet- icizes that power. Furthermore, similar to Simms, Hentz explicitly compares Moreland's role to that of a father to his family, transforming the plantation into an extended domestic sphere. In this expanded home, Moreland is the "masterful" father, Eula the feeling helpmate, and the "sable" slaves the children. As suggested at the beginning of this chapter, this domestic allegory had some basis in historical fact, for Eugene Genovese points out (citing the work of Anne Firor Scott), "women, children, and slaves were expected to accept subordination and obey the head of the white family."[48] We have also returned to the hierarchical social system of Cooper's *Satanstoe,* in which white and nonwhite members tacitly acknowledged specific roles. But again, unlike Cooper, Hentz has felt no need to displace this ideal society into the past, but claims the present-day Southern plantation fulfills that very dream.

If Hentz appeals to the domestic ideology of the 1850s, she also exploits the by-now-inevitable religious iconography of the rhetorical struggle over slavery. Whereas Douglass characterizes the plantation as a kind of Gothic nightmare, Hentz counters that the plantation remains a pastoral retreat. Indeed, Moreland appears a kind of Adam in his New World Garden, Eula his New Eve, and the slaves his "dependent beings." Miltonic chaos only enters the Garden when abolitionism seduces the slaves into rebellion: "Shall we dwell in its beautiful bowers and see the canker-worm eating into the heart of its blossoms, without reaching out a hand to rescue their bloom from the destroyer? Shall we breathe its bland, delicious climate, and know that the noxious miasma is rising and spreading, without endeavouring to disperse its exhalations, or trying to counteract its deadly influence?" (578–79). "The canker-worm eating into the heart of its blossoms" is of course abolitionism, or more precisely, its compromised advocates. Hentz delights in exposing the hypocrisy of Northern characters such as Hastings, who himself depends upon the "wage slavery" of a servant, and Brainard, the abolitionist minister who "snakes" his way into Moreland's confidence, only to plot a slave rebellion. Hentz unloads her most charged religious rhetoric on this abolitionist villain, "an agent of the powers of darkness, . . . one who had served so long an apprenticeship to its Satanic Prince" (460). Only Moreland's patriarchal sensitivity to his slaves' growing restiveness uncovers the plot. The snake is expelled from the Southern Garden on *this* occasion. However, that victory appears short-lived, for the narrator proffers an apocalyptic vision of America's future:

> Supposing, for one moment, the full triumph of fanaticism, how fearful would be the result! The emancipation of brute force; the reign of animal passion and power; the wisdom of eighteen centuries buried under waves of barbarism, rolling back upon the world; the beautiful cotton-fields of the South left neglected and overgrown with weeds; the looms of the North idle for want of the downy fleece, and England, in all her pride and might, bleeding from the wound her own hands had inflicted. (511)

The racist premises behind this passage are so transparent as to require little comment. Hentz assumes that blacks are different in kind rather than degree from their white masters. Put more bluntly, blacks are dependent *animals* who will destroy American civilization if given full license. The text refers often to the "disastrous" consequences of the slave revolt on Santo Domingo and, at least by implication, to Nat Turner's still haunting rebellion of 1831. Indeed, the text incorporates the figure of rebellious Nat to emphasize the folly of liberating blacks. Nat the Giant is a runaway slave who plays upon the gullibility of Northerners. This violent fugitive even takes advantage of Has-tings, living "high off the hog" in the abolitionist's home, only to come to a gruesome end. Not only does this character parody the fugitive slave, but he typifies the sorry lot of blacks in America, for the reader is implored to "let the free negroes, congregated in the suburbs of some of our modern Babylons, lured from their *homes* by hopes based on sand, without forethought, experience, or employment, without sympathy, influence, or caste, let them also tell" (27, emphasis mine).

The female slave Crissy provides a final exemplar of woe. Personal slave to Moreland's sister Illdegerte, Crissy journeys to "a Western city" (presumably Cincinnati) where her mistress's husband seeks a cure for his consumption. As the male character declines in health, Crissy undergoes a seduction by two unfeeling abolitionists, Mr. and Mrs. Softly. In the climactic episode of this subplot, the female slave chooses "freedom" just as Ildegerte's husband passes away, leaving the Southern mistress bereft of support at the very moment of her greatest need. Afterward Crissy comes to know the sorry lot of fugitive slaves living in the North, for she suffers economic and personal degradation. Now converted into "a wage slave," she sorely misses "the protection of a white man" (to quote *Woodcraft*). Only when she returns to Moreland's Southern home does Crissy recover happiness, a heavy-handed moral for the would-be runaway. Thus, *The Planter's North-ern Bride* demonstrates both the personal and public apocalypses that follow from abolitionist fanaticism. In the process Hentz reconstructs the sentimental Southern home, reinforcing the holist social vision that locates slaves in the role of children. However, her rebuilding effort would not go unanswered, for another slave narrator would step forward both to expose this familial ideal and to propose an alternative family model.

IV. Imagining an Alternative Family in *Incidents*

By 1854 discourse over slavery had become locked into binary oppo-sitions between "heaven" and "hell," "good" and "evil," "sincerity" and "hypocrisy." Pro- and anti-slavery writers simply reversed the hierarchies, the former arguing that the plantation is a kind of pasto-ralized home, the latter arguing that the plantation is a Gothic man-sion. One can reasonably ask where the representation of slavery could go beyond this impasse. Given the high political stakes, what kind of text could crack the frame of this thirty-year-old struggle for discursive mastery? One answer is provided by the novelized narrative of Harriet Ann Jacobs,[49] a text that rests uncomfortably among these melodramatic stereotypes. Indeed, Jacobs's *Incidents in the Life of a Slave Girl* is a sophisticated revision of the plantation novel, the sentimental novel, and the male slave narrative. Published in 1861, encompassing Nat Turner's Rebellion and the Fugitive Slave Law, this text provides an appropriate point of closure for this analysis of antebellum Southern representations of slavery.

Before discussing the innovative qualities of this subversive text, I should state the obvious: *Incidents in the Life of a Slave Girl* does often read like an abolitionist tract. Even as Jacobs experiments with dialogized narrative, complete with fictionalized characters, she remains true to her political bias. Indeed, as Hentz had systematically refuted Douglass, so Jacobs consciously knocks out the ideological props from beneath pro-slavery advocates. One by one she assaults apologists' claims that slaves are a relatively comfortable laboring class, northern brides are contented living in the South, fugitive slaves fare poorly in the North, the northern visitor gains an "objective" view of slavery, the Southern lady is a sentimental heroine, and, most importantly, the Southern gentleman is a noble parent and husband (the characterizations of Doctor Flint and Mr. Sands).[50]

Furthermore, Jacobs incorporates the male slave narrative into her text. In a chapter entitled "The Slave Who Dared to Feel Like a Man," Brent narrates her uncle's quest for freedom. Benjamin, ". . . a tall, handsome lad, strongly and gracefully made, and with a spirit too bold and daring for a slave" (17), engages his master in hand-to-hand combat when he refuses to obey an order. Similar to Douglass's encounter with Covey, Benjamin comes out victorious, only to face public whipping and personal humiliation. Brent's uncle chooses flight instead, but he is recaptured, imprisoned, and sold. However, before arriving at his new "master's," Benjamin is able to escape once again, this time successfully. The chapter reprises several key motifs of Douglass's *Narrative,* including the romantic image of the proud fugitive, free-moving ships on Chesapeake Bay, and the primal victory of manly slave over would-be master. However, the interpolated story ends on a somber note: "[Benjamin and his brother] parted with moistened eyes; and as Benjamin turned away, he said, 'Phil, I part with all my kindred.' And so it proved. We never heard from him again" (26). If Douglass leaves the reader with the impression that he has found "home" among the abolitionists of Nantucket, Jacobs's version reflects the reality that flight means divorce from home, loss of identity, and grief for those left behind. In this subtle variation on the male narrative Jacobs marks a difference between female and male representations of slavery, for with the former, again and again we return to issues of familial relations and the domestic price of slavery.[51] In sum, Jacobs assaults the metaphor of the plantation as family by substituting a fuller, more compelling sense of home experienced through her grandmother, parents, and children.[52]

In contrast to the teleological, linear urgency of Douglass's *Narra-tive*, Jacobs prefers an episodic reconstruction of crucial moments in the slave's life before and after escape. Indeed, despite its calculated abolitionist polemics, *Incidents* makes its case for abolition much more powerfully through its "texture." Thus, this text would seem to be more closely linked to the oral storytelling traditions of African-Americans than the male narrative. In her study of contemporary black women writers, Susan Willis argues that oral narratives conform to a "four-page formula," that is, they are "compiled out of short pieces of writing."[53] Willis further remarks that the "four-page formula," echoing the conversational rhythms of daily life, welcomes an array of representational modes. Jacobs's "incidents" seem ideal instances of this narrative technique, for they are brief, self-contained anecdotes which occupy diverse representational worlds.

Among these diverse modes, we note the complete absence of the melodramatic Gothic/pastoral dichotomy familiar in earlier texts. Ja-cobs prefers domestic and mimetic representational modes, for her text generally alternates between sentimentalized descriptions of her familial relations and character analysis in the female realist tradition discussed by Alfred Habegger.[54] She also incorporates black dialect, a tactic that distinguishes her text both from Douglass's (which virtu-ally excludes vernacular) and the plantation novel (which quotes dia-lect for condescending comic effect). For instance, Aggie, a friend of Brent's family, comforts Linda's grandmother, bemoaning the loss of her grandson William: "He's in free parts; and dat's de right place. Don't murmur at de Lord's doings, but git down on your knees and tank him for his goodness" (135). As many critics have pointed out, Jacobs does seem "mastered" by conventions of the seduction novel when characterizing her sexual history, and yet even on this issue she injects a dose of psychological realism: "So much attention from a superior person was, of course, flattering; for human nature is the same in all. I also felt grateful for his sympathy, and encouraged by his kind words. . . . Revenge, and calculations of interest, were added to flattered vanity and sincere gratitude for kindness" (54–55).

This complex weave or texture marks a more open-ended narrati-vity than Douglass's. "Linda Brent" is a more tolerant tale-teller than "Frederick Douglass," granting space to personalities other than her-self, greeting diverse voices, black and white, genteel and uneducated, loving and harsh. But what *authorizes* Jacobs's radical recreation of the slave narrative genre? Willis points to the importance of matriarchal traditions for black women writers: "For black women, history is a bridge defined along motherlines."[55] Toni Morrison has testified to the importance of mothers and grandmothers for her own writing: "Of course my great-grandmother could not read, but she was a midwife, and people from all over the state came to her for advice and for her to deliver babies. . . . Yes, I feel the authority of those women more than I do my own."[56] Similarly, Jacobs's narrative begins and ends with paeans to her grandmother. These powerful female presences contrast not only with the white patriarch but with the one-dimensional, iconographic black females uncovered in the earlier representations of slavery. The dominant black female figure in *Swallow Barn* is Lucy, both heroic slave mother and romantic "madwoman." When recollecting Douglass's *Narrative*, our minds return to Aunt Hester, victim of Plummer's frustrated lust, and the grandmother, lonely, abandoned, essentially helpless. Both female figures represent victimized femininity.[57] Simms's only memorable black female character is Sappho, Captain Porgy's aging nurse, who leads the hiding slaves back to Glen-Eberley to resume their plantation labors after the war. And finally, Hentz focuses upon a single prominent black female, Crissy, the unfortunate runaway who achieves happiness only when she returns to the patriarchal protection of Moreland's plantation.

By contrast, *Incidents in the Life of a Slave Girl* focuses on three complex female characters, representative of three generations: Brent's grandmother Aunt Marthy, Brent herself, and her daughter Ellen.[58] This familial continuity is itself important, for previous texts presented female characters in virtual isolation. Similar to Stowe in *Uncle Tom's Cabin* (alluded to in *Incidents*), Jacobs places special emphasis on slavery's assault on the black family. If this priority seems at first puzzling, it begins to make more sense when considered in context of women's moral development as analyzed by Carol Gilligan. This psychological theorist argues that women typically value relationships more than individuation, and thus will choose "care" before personal success. Within this value system, family amounts to much more than a support network or convenient socioeconomic resting place. Quoting the work of Jean Baker Miller, Gilligan asserts that "women stay with, build on, and develop in a context of attachment and affiliation with others," that "women's sense of self becomes very much organized around being able to make, and then maintain, affiliations and relationships," and that "eventually, for many women, the threat of disruption of an affiliation is perceived not just as a loss of a relationship but as something closer to a total loss of self."[59] Whatever the methodological difficulties of interpreting a nineteenth-century slave narrative through a contemporary psychological model, Gilligan's analysis articulates the value system of Jacobs and her female characters. It also helps us explain the difference in narrative form between Jacobs's and Douglass's texts, for the decentered structure of *Incidents* gives priority to affiliations, while Douglass's powerful sense of *kairos* reveals his commitment to individuation.

Aunt Marthy is, besides Linda herself, the most complex character in the text. Bought out of slavery by a sympathetic white woman, she makes a living as a baker in her North Carolina town. Her stature is such that she can take Dr. Flint to task for mistreating her granddaughter. Like Morrison's great-grandmother, Aunt Marthy is a powerful voice of comfort and authority. And yet, despite her own independence, she has at best ambivalent feelings toward her children's and grandchildren's quests for freedom. I have already noted her sorrowful response to her grandson William's escape. She also dreads Linda's concealment, fearful that if caught her granddaughter will suffer the humiliation and pain inflicted on Benjamin upon his recapture. Above all else, it seems, Aunt Marthy wishes to preserve her family. So it is that Jacobs turns the tables on Hentz's sentimental defense of slavery, for *Incidents* reveals that the "patriarchal" master is himself the primary threat to the black family. Not surprisingly, then, the matriarchal grandmother is also sternly judgmental about Linda's sexual conduct. As the narrator explains, "Humble as were [my relatives'] circumstances, they had pride in my good character" (56). One of the emotional climaxes of *Incidents* occurs when Linda must reveal her liaison with Mr. Sands to her grandmother:

> I knelt before her, and told her the things that had poisoned my life; how long I had been persecuted; that I saw no way of escape; and in an hour of extremity I had become desperate. She listened in silence. . . . She did not say, "I forgive you;" but she looked at me lovingly, with her eyes full of tears. She laid her old hand gently on my head, and murmured, "Poor child! Poor child!" (57)

This passage summarizes not only Aunt Marthy's character, but the narrative force of *Incidents*. We see the grandmother's toughness, her convictions, her authority, and also her love. While she does not sacrifice her principles, through an act of compassion she psychologically rescues Linda. It is this complexity of motivation, this textual density, which sets Jacobs's narrative apart from earlier representations of slavery. Aunt Marthy cannot be reduced to pious formulas or iconographic simplicity.

Certainly the same can be said for the narrator. As Yellin has commented, "In and through her creation of Linda Brent, who yokes her success story as a heroic slave mother to her confession as a woman who mourns that she is not a storybook heroine, Jacobs articulates her struggle to assert her womanhood and projects a new kind of female hero."[60] Though the text initially calls attention to Brent's sexual misfortunes, once "the slave girl" has become a mother, the tenor of the characterization changes. All of Brent's energies are directed toward saving her children from slavery. Similar to Sethe in Morrison's *Beloved,* Brent would wish death upon her children rather than life within the slave regime. Not only does Brent endure painful concealment, but she risks recapture by leaving her hiding place to urge Sands to free his children. After her flight north, Linda continues to assert authority over her children's lives, with particular attention to her daughter Ellen. Offended that her daughter has neither been freed nor educated, Brent arranges for Ellen to attend school, though this necessitates a painful separation between daughter and mother: "It required a great effort for me to consent to part with her, for I had few near ties, and it was her presence that made my two little rooms seem *home-like*" (188, emphasis mine).

Brent also gains complexity by her bluntness concerning Northern racism and her own frustrated quest for acceptance on abolitionist soil. In the last of her major struggles of will, Brent yearns to surrender, to give up the fight for freedom, to simply give in to the pressures of her pursuing master after the passage of the Fugitive Slave Law: "Mrs. Bruce came to me and entreated me to leave the city the next morning. . . . I was weary of flying from pillar to post. I had been chased during half my life, and it seemed as if the chase was never to end" (198). The text is leavened with statements such as this, remarks that provide a moving inside view of the fugitive slave's experience. These passages "humanize" the protagonist, preventing the reader's expectation of "heroic" or larger-than-life behavior. Perhaps this is why when readers complete *Incidents* they are inclined to downplay both Brent's sexual conduct and the incredible seven-year stay in her grandmother's storehouse. These potentially discrediting acts are diminished by the overall sincerity of the narrator.

And what of Ellen, daughter and granddaughter, yet another "slave girl"? Hers is a submerged narrative, available to us only through glimpses, snapshots, isolated incidents. Here Jacobs's first-person point of view creates a kind of suspense, for the reader is very much in the position of Linda Brent, catching sight of the daughter only as chance would allow. In a sense, then, the reader occupies that crawlspace with the narrator, feeling the frustration of limited perspective. The narrative provides three crucial sightings of the daughter: the occasion of her journey North to work as servant; the mother's first meeting with her daughter in New York City; and the final interview concerning Ellen's paternity. Based on these fragmentary sightings, Ellen appears a canny, often lonely young woman, trained by slavery to conceal compromising information, endure suffering without complaint, and repress desire. In her mature comments about Mr. Sands, Ellen reveals both her dispossession and her pride, her alienation and her love:

> "I know all about it, mother," she replied; "I am nothing to my father, and he is nothing to me. . . . I was with him five months in Washington, and he never cared for me. He never spoke to me as he did to his little Fanny. . . . I used to wish he would take me in his arms and kiss me, as he did Fanny; or that he would sometimes smile at me, as he did at her. I thought if he was my own father, he ought to love me. . . . But now I never think anything about my father. All my love is for you." (189)

So it is that Brent's daughter renounces the patriarchal figure, reincarnated in Sands, Moreland, Porgy, Effingham, Lloyd, and Meriwether, embracing the mother and the matriarchal tradition she embodies.

Paradoxically, *Incidents in the Life of a Slave Girl* presents both a more "human" and more terrifying image of the slave regime than earlier texts. Perhaps its depiction is more frightening precisely *because* it is more complexly realized. White characters frequently surprise by their unexpected kindness to Brent and her family. Most notably, a genteel townswoman temporarily conceals Linda in her attic, though she runs the risk of public censure, even social banishment by doing so. We witness many such acts of apparently random kindness on the part of white characters. Brent's grandmother is bought out of slavery by Dr. Flint's concerned aunt; Linda's uncle Benjamin is saved from capture in Baltimore when a white townsman warns him of impending capture; Brent adopts the desperate plan to conceal herself when a white gentleman reveals Flint's plan to "break" her children and herself on his son's plantation. As I discussed earlier, Brent's grandmother, though born a slave, commands the respect of her community, both white and black. Furthermore, Brent expresses pity for white characters, as when she first sees the bride of Dr. Flint's son: "She was a handsome, delicate-looking girl, and her face flushed with emotion at sight of her new home. I thought it likely that visions of a happy future were rising before her. It made me sad; for I knew how soon clouds would come over her sunshine" (92). Such passages mark an intimacy, even empathy between the races in the South dur

ing the antebellum period which belies Douglass's and plantation novelists' assumption of mental segregation between the races.

But such empathy only highlights the terrible nature of the slave
regime, for the Flints' abuse of Linda and Sands's denial of paternity
become all the more horrific when we realize the emotional bonds
among characters. Sands's complex relationship with Ellen and Benny
displays with special clarity the foundational contradiction of Southern slavery: masters could claim in the abstract that blacks were innately inferior and so "beneath them," and yet individual slaves,
through their intelligence and affections, argued quite the contrary.
Of course Douglass compels Covey to acknowledge his manhood, but
only through armed struggle. Jacobs's narrative demonstrates the
slaves' humanity through the more subtle means of human relationships. However, despite its comparative paucity of physical violence,
Incidents in the Life of a Slave Girl provides a fuller portrait of the
slave regime as *police state*. Brent describes the brutal search of black
homes following Nat Turner's Rebellion, the constant harassment of
blacks by "patrols," and the intimidating presence of the constable:
"If he found any slave out after nine o'clock, he could whip him as
much as he liked; and that was a privilege to be coveted" (120). Brent
allows the modern reader to see the slave regime as a *system* of en-
forced labor, insidious, all-encompassing, and violent. No doubt this
effect stems from the "four-step" form of Jacobs's narrative, for that
style deemphasizes the individual slave while foregrounding a community of blacks. If Douglass's struggles and triumphs seem the experiences of a uniquely gifted, even heroic individual, Brent's seem
representative of the tightly woven Southern community in which
she was raised. Even her flight to freedom has a strong communal
element, for she flees along with a black acquaintance, both aided by
a generous slave named Peter and an unusually sympathetic white
ship captain.

Thus, in *Incidents in the Life of a Slave Girl* both success and failure
are products of a community of whites and blacks, chained together
by the peculiar links of slavery. Because of this social and psychological
complexity, Jacobs's narrative seems the most accessible and most
meaningful reproduction of slavery handed to us from the antebellum
period. As a preeminent misreading of the twinned traditions of plantation novel and slave narrative, Jacobs's *Incidents* provides a fitting
last word for the antebellum tradition of representing slavery. After
all, Linda Brent's narrative signifies upon the plantation stereotypes
enunciated by Kennedy's *Swallow Barn,* recasting the Meriwethers
and Tracys as troubled, often abusive participants in a contradictory
social system. Her story also incorporates images of the fugitive slave,

both reaffirming Douglass's heroic self-characterization and tallying the familial costs of escape from the far-reaching slave regime. Jacobs reminds us, then, that the Southern family was indeed an ideological fiction. The plantation family was internally divided by race, gender, and economics. The sibling rivalry among these Southern texts suggests why that plantation myth (and its accompanying reality) would necessarily fall in time. But having participated in the rhetorical destruction of the figurative Southern family, Jacobs remains herself homeless: "The dream of my life is not yet realized. I do not sit with my children in a home of my own. I still long for a hearthstone of my own, however humble" (201). The deracinated slave woman cannot realize the promise of American domesticity, in part because of a continued threat against her children's freedom, in part because of racism, in part because of the economics of the mother's situation. In this radical homelessness Jacobs represents the paradox of emancipation: freedom does not, in and of itself, bring a sense of inclusion, a sense of belonging, a sense of familial connection to the wider American society.

4

At Home in Kitchen and Cabin: Carnivalizing Manhood in *Uncle Tom's Cabin*

UNCLE TOM'S CABIN; OR, LIFE AMONG THE LOWLY HAS GATHERED TO itself an astonishing array of critical responses. Whether we think of James's "wonderful 'leaping' fish," or Baldwin's critique of Stowe's theological terror, or Tompkins' now canonical reading of the novel as woman's fiction, we are made aware of a density and diversity of commentary which puzzles. How can a single text generate so many "swerves" or interpretations, so *much* analysis? As Hortense J. Spillers remarks in her witty, controversial assessment of the text, "The 1852 work, in its startling history of publication . . . apparently has no precedent in its endless powers of proliferation. . . ."[1] Indeed, Stowe's is a novel that will not stop producing readers and responses. But why? What about this text gives it such fecundity, such powers of reproduction?

We can begin to answer this question by attending to the diverse houses which populate this transnational narrative. As Marilyn R. Chandler has commented, "Stowe's [novel] deliberately uses dwellings as tropes for social categories, and her book intensifies the debate about the nature of the American home."[2] Shifting from the Shelbys' genteel Kentucky home, to the cabin of the title, to the Birds' Ohio home, to the Quaker settlement, to the St. Clare plantation, to Ophelia's New England local color domain, and concluding (melodramatically) with Simon Legree's truly uncanny plantation, *Uncle Tom's Cabin* takes us on a guided tour of the domestic possibilities of antebellum America. As I have observed throughout this study, literary images of the home are necessarily linked to genre, a pattern we have already examined in the diverse representational styles of Cooper's New York novels and Southern narratives. Similarly, Stowe's fecundity of domiciles should be connected to the generic diversity of the text. What, exactly, *is* this "novel" called *Uncle Tom's Cabin*? One critical position asserts that this is a protest novel, written in the tradition of reform literature prominent in the antebellum era.[3] Another, perhaps more familiar answer holds that Stowe's is an ideal instance of the sentimental novel, focused upon female characters, the home, and reform through feeling.[4] Yet another answer maintains that *Uncle Tom's Cabin* is an instance, even the ultimate example, of Southern Gothic fiction.[5] As a final sample response, we note the recurring analysis of the novel as typological narrative in the tradition of the New England jeremiad.[6] Though of course these terms are not mutually exclusive, and can in fact be imagined to reinforce each other, the sheer *number* of designations suggests that this novel does not lend itself easily to generic categorization. Apparently this is a text with multiple faces, multiple voices. Indeed, *Uncle Tom's Cabin* is pangeneric, a repository of antebellum narrative subgenres brought into dialogic exchange on pre-Civil War art and politics. This 1852 novel produces so much analysis and so many views precisely because critics respond to select elements of the text, isolating those features and asserting the preeminence of that thematic strand.

Rather than a static, "totalized" text, then, *Uncle Tom's Cabin* emerges as a polyphonic, heterogeneous, often funny book.[7] We discover not a neat, balanced double-plotted novel, but a Victorian multiplot novel, related by structure and tone to the major British novelists discussed by Peter K. Garrett in a book subtitled "studies in dialogical form."[8] Indeed, we find a much more literary text, a novel loaded with cross-references to contemporary British and American writers, one stuffed with dialects, competing modes, and varied emotional pitches. In part no doubt because it was published serially, the novel releases energies not entirely under the narrator's control.[9] In other words, my reading of *Uncle Tom's Cabin* refers us back to the observations of Kenneth Lynn: "Those critics who label *Uncle Tom's Cabin* good propaganda but bad art simply cannot have given sufficient time to the novel to meet its inhabitants. If they should ever linger over it long enough to take in the shrewdness, the energy, the truly Balzacian variousness of Mrs. Stowe's characterizations, they would surely cease to perpetuate one of the most unjust clichés in all of American criticism."[10]

This chapter takes as its beginning point, then, the carnivalizing texture of Stowe's seemingly somber novel. I do not pretend that this reading escapes what Wolfgang Iser calls the drive for "consistency building."[11] Similar to the readings summarized above, my analysis establishes order out of apparent chaos, or locates a center in an unstable text. But this interpretation has the advantage of synopsis, for I synthesize the recurring preoccupations of Stowe's readers (women's rights and attitudes toward blacks) while uncovering the literary *means* for Stowe's participation in these antebellum controversies. I will examine the ways the text puts other antebellum discourses to work in a play of differences or parodic misapprehension. Specifically, *Uncle Tom's Cabin* parodies white male pro-slavery discourse, the Southwestern humor tradition, and adventure narrative. These carnivalizing strategies not only subvert the male forms, but they clear imaginative space for Stowe's preferred subgenres, the revivalist homily and the local color sketch.[12] Through these narrative strategies, *Uncle Tom's Cabin* advocates both "domestic feminism" and an unselfconscious racism. In effect, Stowe's novelizing tactics discredit or even raze competing versions of the American home, undermining such structures as the Shelbys' seemingly compassionate household and Legree's deranged plantation. Standing at the end, with full ideological commitment from writer and (presumably) reader, are such homes as the Quaker settlement, Ophelia's New England domicile, and that ultimate home, heaven. What also remains, however, is Stowe's colonizing desire to claim all of America for her cherished domestic spaces, an imperialist ambition that blinds her to romantic racialism.

I. SENTIMENT AND SATIRE, OR FUNNY WOMEN

It has been easy to take *Uncle Tom's Cabin* altogether too seriously.[13] Hanging over the reader's head is Lincoln's famous dictum, "'So this is the little lady who made this big war.'"[14] Surely a novel with such dire political consequences could not be "funny." Furthermore, Stowe herself frequently referred to the text's divine inspiration, urging her readers to take the book as a religious document: "But I am utterly incredulous of all that is said,—it passes by me like a dream. I can only see, that when a Higher Being has purposes to be accomplished, he can make even 'a grain of mustard-seed' the means. . . ."[15] Finally, the recent scholarly rehabilitation of Stowe has emphasized her political "power," her proto-feminist "work." While I am sympathetic toward this analysis, it understates the sharp satire which pulses through *Uncle Tom's Cabin*.

A blindness to Stowe's humor is part of a more pervasive pattern of ignoring humor in women's writing of the nineteenth century. There remains something askew about contemporary views of antebellum women's culture. Fixated by a negative impression of sentimentalism, scholars such as Ann Douglas ignore other resonances, other voices within that subculture. For example, James D. Hart writes of Fanny Fern's magazine sketches: "Compounding sentiment and satire, pathos and puns in a strangely personal blend, they conjured up a feeling, told a brief anecdote, sketched the vignette of a romantic landscape, outlined a quaint character, or served simply to set forth an animated moral. She was almost the only member of the generation's sorority of sentimentalists who had a sense of humor."[16] Though considerable scholarly work has been done to counter this condescending reading of sentimental culture, the predominant image remains one of a superserious, revivalist coterie that provided few counterpoints to Melville's Rabelaisian humor. In his important reexamination of sentimental art, Philip Fisher returns to Rousseau as spiritual father of British and American sentimentalism. Through this strategy he uncovers the importance of compassion, the phenomenology of suffering, and marginalized subgroups in sentimental writing. However, Fisher excludes from view the importance given humor in the sentimental tradition.

If we reexamine one of Rousseau's predecessors, Anthony, Earl of Shaftesbury, we discover an enthusiastic embrace of wit. As Stanley Grean observes,

> The concept of humor plays an important part throughout Shaftesbury's discussion of religion. Humor is not only a method of attack upon all forms of narrow-mindedness, intolerance, and bigotry, but in a more fundamental sense it characterizes the state of mind in which truth is best apprehended. Humor is a means of liberation from patterns of action or thought that are life-destroying rather than life-giving.[17]

Humor becomes an important means for testing authority claims by people and laws. It complements moral sentiment by clearing the ethical arena of false assertions and by relaxing the mind for contemplation. As Shaftesbury states this argument in *Characteristics of Men, Manners, Opinions, Times*, "Truth, 'tis suppos'd, may bear *all* Lights: and *one* of those principal Lights or natural Mediums, by which Things are to be view'd, in order to a thorow Recognition, is *Ridicule* it-self, or that Manner of Proof by which we discern whatever is liable to just Raillery in any subject." Shaftesbury is sensitive to the charge that humor can degenerate into crude or savage mockery, a charge he counters, first, by drawing an analogy between wit and gentility: "To describe true *Raillery* wou'd be as hard a matter, and perhaps as little to the purpose, as to define *Good Breeding*." The British essayist further recognizes the need to train wit, for "'Tis in reality a serious Study, to learn to temper and regulate that *Humour* which Nature has given us, as a more lenitive Remedy against Vice, and a kind of Specifick against Superstition and melancholy Delusion." If humor is to serve its function as litmus test for truth, it must be a refined, artful humor that does not savage pointlessly. In other words, wit itself must function according to compassion. But given these checks on an innate disposition to humor, Shaftesbury asserts, "I know not . . . why others may not be allow'd to *ridicule* Folly, and recommend Wisdom and Virtue (if possibly they can) in a way of Pleasantry and Mirth."[18] As we shall see, this is precisely Stowe's sentimental technique in *Uncle Tom's Cabin.*

If Shaftesbury seems a remote ancestor to the sentimentalists of the 1850s, one need only turn to Catharine Beecher for a contemporary advocate of ameliorative humor. As discussed in chapter 1, Beecher was widely seen as the foremost advocate of women's "sentimental power," and in fiction and formal essays she promoted wit as the woman's ally in her work as cultural mother.[19] Beecher presented this argument explicitly in her *Treatise on Domestic Economy* (1841). In addition to advocating good manners, patience, and sobriety for domestic women, Beecher asserts,

> All medical men unite in declaring, that nothing is more beneficial to health than hearty laughter; and surely our benevolent Creator would not have provided risibles, and made it a source of health and enjoyment to use them, and then have made it a sin so to do. There has been a tendency toward asceticism, on this subject, which needs to be removed. . . . [J]okes, laughter, and sports, when used in such a degree as tends only to promote fealty, social feelings, and happiness, are neither vain, foolish, nor "not convenient." It is the excess of these things, and not the moderate use of them, that Scripture forbids.[20]

Like Shaftesbury, Beecher advocates humor for its power to relax or open the mind, but only when "risibles" are used in moderation. But Beecher emphasizes another aspect of humor which is only implicit in Shaftesbury's apology: its social function. Humor provides a bridge between individuals, establishes a rapport between speaker and listener. Humor creates an informal intimacy which promotes fellow-feeling. Once again, Stowe's text follows this formula, for she often cajoles the implied female reader with wit, creating an assumed commonality of feelings between narrator and reader.

Indeed, despite the inhibitions about and prohibitions upon female humor, antebellum writers *did* utilize wit toward the ends advocated by the Earl of Shaftesbury and Catharine Beecher. As Nancy Walker has written, "Women writers from Frances Whicher to Marietta Holley had parodied the behavior of women they felt to be a discredit to their gender: tendencies to gossip, to social climbing, to dependence on men, to sentimentality and weakness. Such humor, though it frequently made use of the same devices as men's humor—e.g., dialect, hyperbole, the figure of the *eiron*—contained a protest against the restrictions on women's status in American society that differentiates it from the dominant tradition."[21] Much as Jane Austen had employed satire to deflate destructive female behavior and boorish male conduct, so Stowe and her contemporaries used satire to disarm ideologically dangerous behavior. We can begin to appreciate the complementary relationship between satire and sentiment in this fiction, then, for we recognize that satire could discredit harmful ideologies while sentimentalism could credit empowering ideologies. Put in terms of reader response, women's humor could free *desire* from entrapment by inappropriate objects, while sentiment could rechannel the libido toward politically appropriate objects.[22] Furthermore, this channeling of desire fits into the larger commitment to reform on the part of antebellum women writers. Emily Toth argues that in contrast to male humorists, female humorists "do not satirize what cannot be helped."[23] Though our contemporary female comics such as Joan Rivers challenge this generalization, it seems accurate for nineteenth-century female humor. Humor does not become a tool for pointless dominance, but for evenhanded criticism and change. In short, humor serves the end of *correction* or *amelioration*.

Two important contemporaries of Stowe's, Fanny Fern and E. D. E. N. Southworth, demonstrate the political possibilities of women's humor. Fern (Sara Willis Parton) was one of the preeminent female humorists of the 1850s. In her newspaper articles and her novel *Ruth Hall* (1854), she persistently attacked the psychological and financial abuses of women, and she largely did so through "risibles." Even more than Stowe, Fern demonstrates a Dickensian talent for the devastating character sketch, as in this hilarious description of the ineffectual caretaker of Ruth Hall's first baby:

> Ruth's nurse, Mrs. Jiff, was fat, elephantine, and unctuous. Nursing agreed with her. She had "tasted" too many bowls of wine-whey on the stairs, tipped up too many bottles of porter in the closet, slid down too many slippery oysters before handing them to "her lady," not to do credit to her pantry devotions. . . . Her shoes were new, thick, and creaky, and she had a wheezy, dilapidated-bellowsy way of breathing, consequent upon the consumption of the above-mentioned port and oysters, which was intensely crucifying to a sick ear.

This passage's use of repetition, exaggeration, and comic detail marks a talented caricaturist. Fern expends similar comic energy on Ruth's greedy, Calvinistic parents-in-law and, even more pointedly, on her dandyish brother Hyacinth. In a classic instance of female double-voicing, the narrator reproduces the brother's egotistical monologue upon the occasion of Ruth's marriage: "Really, love is a great beauti-

fier. Ruth looked quite handsome to-night. Lord bless me! how im-
mensely tiresome it must be to sit opposite the same face three times
a day, three hundred and sixty-five days in a year! I should weary of
Venus herself. I'm glad my handsome brother-in-law is in such good
circumstances. Duns *are* a bore." The writer allows the character to
condemn himself through his implicit vanity and selfishness. Operating on the basis of this vanity, Hyacinth later refuses to help his sister
following her husband's premature death. Thus, the male egotism satirized in the early passage becomes an all-consuming philosophy of life
which denies Ruth emotional and financial support at her most trying
time. However, Fern does not leave the reader with an unsatisfied
rage toward such conduct, for in the end Ruth *does* triumph through
her writing, establishing a domestic retreat for herself and her two
daughters. In this case satire and sentiment clearly work together to
espouse a circumscribed form of female power.[24]

Though she uses satire less than Fern, Southworth too could turn
to the comic effect in order to critique female and male foibles. To
provide an example virtually contemporaneous with *Uncle Tom's
Cabin,* in *The Curse of Clifton* Southworth first asserts and then
deflates a heroic image of her male protagonist. The novel's parodic
intent is obvious from the beginning. It opens by introducing the two
central male characters, Archer Clifton and Frank Fairfax, described
in romantic fashion as attractive, socially sophisticated soldiers jour-
neying to Clifton's ancestral home. Here, for instance, is the description of Archer:

> His form is of middle size, strongly built, yet elegantly proportioned. His
> complexion is dark and bronzed as by exposure; his features are Roman;
> his hair and whiskers trimly cut, are of the darkest chestnut. . . . His eyes
> are singularly beautiful and brilliant, combining all those dark, shifting,
> scintillating, prismatic hues, that would drive an artist mad, for want of
> colors to portray. . . .

This breathless, erotic portrait of Clifton prepares the reader for heroic
conduct in the Harlequin romance tradition. However, before we have
an opportunity to take this male character seriously, he and Frank are
caught in a thunderstorm. Not only does Clifton evince real terror
and incompetence in the face of this natural disaster, but he is rescued
by the ultimate anti-heroic female character: "At length the attention
of the travellers was attracted by the faint tingling of a bell—then by
the bleating of sheep—and then from the deep clouded glen at their
right, sprung up into their path a bell-wether followed by two—five—
ten—a whole flock of sheep; and driven by a girl on a pony; a little

coarse, sun-burned girl, in a boy's coarse straw hat and a homespun gown, riding on a little rough-coated, wiry, mountain pony." Kate Kavanaugh, the novel's female protagonist, inhabits an entirely different narrative world from that of Archer and Fairfax. She is described in a realistic mode that calls attention to her physical and social ungainliness. And yet it is this "mountain girl" who rescues Archer and Fairfax from the storm. In a sense Southworth wants to have it both ways: on the one hand, she provides the presumably female reader with a dashing romantic hero, but on the other she takes him down a notch or two by making him subject to Kate's help. In effect this early incident is a microcosm of the entire novel, for *The Curse of Clifton* narrates Clifton's gradual humbling and Kate's gradual ascension to power. In the end, these two strikingly different characters do in fact wed, but only when Archer has given up his aristocratic, sexist pretensions.[25]

From the beginning of her career as a professional writer, Stowe also used a combination of satire and sentiment to critique false ideals and affirm moral behavior. No doubt Stowe's respect for wit emerged (as did Catharine's) from her childhood experience: "One of my most decided impressions of the family as it was in my childish days was of a great household inspired by a spirit of cheerfulness and hilarity. . . ."[26] In her first published story, "Uncle Lot" (originally titled "Uncle Tim"), Stowe articulates the values and techniques which would later serve her in *Uncle Tom's Cabin*. The narrator begins by disavowing romantic motifs, declaring ". . . these are all too old—too romance-like—too obviously picturesque for me. No, let me turn to my own land—my own New England. . . ."[27] Having deflated high romance, she in turn deflates her own embrace of the local, mocking her "little introductory breeze of patriotism" (31). In general the story makes fun of overheated rhetoric, preferring the concrete, the domestic, and the regional to the abstract, public, and cosmic. With her tongue firmly planted in cheek, the narrator addresses the matter at hand: the courtship between James Benton and Grace Griswold. The narrative has an improvisatory air, for the reader can sense Stowe's fabricating as she goes. No doubt this air of insouciance emerges from the nature of her authorship, which she often described as a haphazard activity squeezed in among her domestic duties.[28] Writing under time pressure and with little concern for revision, Stowe seems to be culling available character types from magazine fiction of the 1830s, generating an amusing, ultimately didactic story out of the couple's maturation.

The narrator's witty characterization of James typifies the general tone of the first half of the story: "There was a saucy frankness of countenance, a knowing roguery of eye, a joviality and prankishness of demeanor, that was wonderfully captivating, especially to the ladies" (33). This light, almost slangy style, bordering on a full-blown New England vernacular dialect, will reappear in Stowe's treatment of males in *Uncle Tom's Cabin*. In contrast to *Ruth Hall* and *The Curse of Clifton*, however, the narrator does not dwell upon the moral weaknesses of the male figure, but proceeds to narrate his development into a dedicated minister. Through the mentoring of George Griswold, a young minister who dies in the course of the story, James leaves behind the thoughtless, carefree manner and adopts the role of husband and community leader: "The calmness, the settled purpose, the mild devotion of his friend, formed a just alloy to the energetic and reckless buoyancy of James's character, and awakened in him a set of feelings without which the most vigorous mind must be incomplete" (48). As in her masterwork, Stowe depicts the taming of the energetic but self-directed male, much as Hawthorne would do in his characterization of Holgrave in *The House of the Seven Gables*. Grace, presumably a partial portrait of the writer, begins with qualities similar to James, though she is more pious. "Pleasant," "lively," "chatty," and "good-humored," Grace plainly possesses the wit to carry on a vivacious courtship with James (37). The association between wit and independence is crucial, for that merriness both expresses and protects the young woman, serving as foil to the wills of male figures, including James and her father, Uncle Lot. But Grace does not remain the vivid, independent young woman, for in tandem with James she grows toward a more settled, controlled happiness: "'Yes,' said James; 'and let us only take it as we should, and this life will be cheerfulness, and the next fulness of joy'" (55). This archetypal New England couple, similar to Hawthorne's Edgar and Edith in "The Maypole of Merry Mount," suffers a fortunate fall into adult roles, but with this notable difference: while James and Grace must set aside the anarchic passion of youth, they need not sacrifice a good-spirited if quiet pleasure. In contrast to Hawthorne's dour vision of the demoralized new Adam and Eve, Stowe offers a less apocalyptic, more "sentimental" vision of the middle-class antebellum marriage, anticipating the easy familiarity of couples' interactions in *Uncle Tom's Cabin*.

And what of the title character, Uncle Lot? He functions as the signature character in the story, the apotheosis of the New England type. Craggy, angular, but withal sweet-tempered, Uncle Lot is the embodiment of the New England personality. He provides a regional anchor for what is after all a fairly conventional tale of courtship (though Stowe downplays the erotic elements of the plot). Speaking in dialect, Uncle Lot expresses his opinion in pointed fashion, ever the figure of honest disclosure. In a strikingly realistic episode, Lot reacts to George's premature death by turning bitterly, despairingly upon his wife: "'Be still a' contradicting me; I won't be contradicted all the time by nobody. The short of the case is, that George is goin' to *die* just as we've got him ready to be a minister and all; and I wish to pity I was in my grave myself, and so—' said Uncle Lot, as he plunged out of the door, and shut it after him" (51). By the end of the story Lot has resigned himself to his son's death, accepting James as a surrogate son, the character who fulfills the promise of the intellectual George's life. Along with the young couple, Uncle Lot learns the lessons of resignation and faith: "'There's a great deal that's worth having in this 'ere life after all,' said Uncle Lot, as he sat by the coals of the bright evening fire of that day; 'that is, if we'd only take it when the Lord lays it in our way'" (55).

Appropriately Josephine Donovan has placed Stowe's early fiction "among the first authentic American pieces of local color literature."[29] Combining an eye for regional peculiarities with an understated New England wit, Stowe not only anticipates her major work, but the work of postbellum local color writers. Crucially, Stowe's talent for evoking "the customs of the country" go hand-in-hand with her wit, for as I have already suggested, her satire upon male forms of expression and narrative archetypes prepares the way for idealized or reformed local color settings. As in the cases of Fern and Southworth, Stowe's humor works in tandem with sentimental ideals to assert cultural power. Her satiric designs in *Uncle Tom's Cabin* are most apparent in her treatment of male defenders of slavery, to which we now turn.

II. MAKING FOOLS OF THE OPPRESSORS: FEMALE AND BLACK HUMOR

In the last chapter we saw how Frederick Douglass double-voiced the language of his "masters" in order to generate a psychological freedom. *Uncle Tom's Cabin* is loaded with similar uses of double-voicing as the overtly female narrator repeatedly revoices language of male oppressors, thereby infecting the monologic authoritarian language with ironic laughter. Black characters also frequently undermine the authority of white males through verbal wit and practical jokes. But before tracing specific cases of these novelizing tactics, I want to be more precise about Stowe's *kind* of humor. Given the general *effect* of her wit (to critique destructive ideologies), can we be more exact about that narrative voice? Constance Rourke's classic study of American humor provides an initial if problematic framework for dis-

tinguishing among the comic qualities of the narrator, her black characters, and her male characters. Rourke argues that three predominant
humorous traditions emerged during the early nineteenth century:
the New England "downeast" tradition, the Southwestern tall-tale
tradition, and the minstrel tradition.[30] The first is characterized by an
understated ironic tone which subtly undermines the pretensions of
characters who take themselves too seriously. By contrast, the Southwestern tall tale focuses upon the outlandish, larger-than-life exploits
of frontier males. Thus, if the New England tradition emphasizes the
eiron, the Southwestern tradition develops the *alazon.* Indeed, according to Northrop Frye, the conflict between the ironist and the
boaster is fundamental to all comedy, a generalization borne out by
Uncle Tom's Cabin.[31] Finally, the minstrel tradition presented white
actors in black face who used the disguise to satirize contemporary
political events and sentimentalize black figures. Stowe's novel clearly
employs all three of these comic traditions, for the narrator generally
conforms to the *eiron,* male characters such as Dan Haley and Tom
Loker represent the *alazon,* and black characters such as Sam and
Andy are archetypal minstrel figures.

However, Rourke's framework is incomplete and must be handled
with caution. Specifically, she understates the contributions of female
writers to the humorous tradition and is not critical of the racist
premises behind the minstrel tradition. She all but excludes female
humorists from her taxonomy, a point made with considerable bite by
Walker: ". . . by omitting from consideration the substantial contributions of women writers to American humorous literature, Rourke's
book succeeds only partly in achieving its purpose. Although it is true
that American humor as traditionally perceived by editors and scholars grows, as Rourke contends, out of the restless dreams and fantasies
of a young and brawny nation . . . women's comic sense, present from
the beginning, complicates and enriches that tradition."[32] Walker argues for an alternative tradition of women's humor, one focused upon
the preoccupations of females who often dwell within a separate
sphere from men. While female humor typically employs the *eiron,* it
cannot be said to conform exactly to the New England tradition, for
codes of gentility prevented women writers from composing in dialect.
(Frances Whitcher's Widow Bedott is a crucial exception to this
rule.) Indeed, in "Uncle Lot" Stowe generated humor by contrasting
the polite if sometimes slangy narrator with the full-blown dialect
character. This narrative gap holds in *Uncle Tom's Cabin,* for ". . .
Stowe's diction . . . linguistically leaves the ideals of her refined, Christian lady readers snugly in place." Yet, as this critic goes on to observe,

"even diction becomes a polemical resource" in Stowe's attack on mainstream American culture.[33]

But how can we reconcile these two views of Stowe as genteel in the extreme and ironic even at the level of language? Shaftesbury has already shown us that the two need not follow separate paths. But we gain even clearer insight into the conjunction between gentility and satire by attending to a powerful comic contemporary of Stowe's, Emily Dickinson. While Stowe's narrator is far more loquacious than Dickinson's personae, and while that narrator presents herself as a mother rather than a Dickinsonian child, narrator and personae share the ability of "transcending convention and expectation by rendering them laughable."[34] Their gentility serves them as a comic resource, for housed within a refined, educated English, these female speakers wear a convenient mask for their subtle barbs. If humor has been the domain of males, and if humor is seen as an aggressive act, then surely respectable New England women could not openly embrace antiestablishment wit. Instead, Dickinson and Stowe's speakers present themselves as very much "at home" in their domestic world, experienced, aware of people as individuals, sensitive to the gap between assertion and reality, amused by the foibles of a culture and its citizens, and withal protected by that genteel status. One of Dickinson's better-known assaults on female manners demonstrates the satiric power of her elevated New England comic voice:

> What Soft—Cherubic Creatures—
> These Gentlewomen are—
> One would as soon assault a Plush—
> Or violate a Star—
>
> Such Dimity Convictions—
> A Horror so refined
> Of freckled Human Nature—
> Of Deity—ashamed—
>
> It's such a common—Glory—
> A Fisherman's—Degree—
> Redemption—Brittle Lady—
> Be so—ashamed of Thee—[35]

This poem is at one and the same time an attack on squeamish gentility and an ultra-sophisticated literary performance. The speaker satirizes a social class which prefers its religion (and its people) sanitized, cleansed, socially appropriate. Implicitly, of course, such a socioreligious attitude rejects Jesus, the carpenter-savior. But once one grasps the thematic significance of the poem, one begins to recognize the linguistic skill of the presentation. The speaker employs clever, com-plex imagery such as "plush" and "Dimity," culled from the very do-mestic sphere that the poem seems to attack. That is, the speaker clearly enunciates from within the context of a culture shared with the victims of satire. Indeed, the refined wit of "Dimity," combining an image of soft, gauzy cloth with a pun upon "dim," marks a genteel woman at work with language. Thus, this poetic persona affirms a religion of human experience while confirming her place within a privileged social class. Put differently, "What Soft—Cherubic Crea-tures" is both radical and conservative, for while it takes genteel be-lievers to task for false religion, it reasserts the moral and intellectual superiority of a class of speakers.

This is precisely Stowe's tactic in her characterizations of Marie St. Clare and Ophelia, who can be said to combine the false values of Dickinson's "cherubic creatures." By way of introducing the Southern mistress, the narrator sardonically remarks, "she consisted of a fine figure, a pair of splendid eyes, and a hundred thousand dollars; and none of these items were precisely the ones to minister to a mind diseased."[36] Petted and selfish, Marie represents the strict class sense that converts her black slaves into "things" (to cite the original title of the novel). Ophelia, while outwardly more liberal than Marie in her attitudes toward blacks, suffers from the puritanical equation of cleanliness with godliness. In Dickinson's terms, she is plagued by "a Horror so refined / Of freckled Human Nature," revealed and gradu-ally healed through her relationship with Topsy.

Thus, Stowe performs the traditional humorous task of critiquing false ideals of female conduct discussed by Walker above. However, she is even more effective at satirizing male conduct, specifically by contrasting the heartless *public* conduct of males with the caring *pri-vate* conduct of females. Joan D. Hedrick has argued that Stowe devel-oped a radical political alternative to patriarchal politics by reversing a hierarchy of "high" and "low" in antebellum America: "In contrast to the mutuality and fluidity of women's culture, the hierarchical institutions Stowe attacked depended on separations between the pub-lic and the private, head and heart, the system-makers and the victims of systems. In *Uncle Tom's Cabin* and *The Minister's Wooing*, Stowe simultaneously invokes these separations and undercuts them through satiric juxtaposition of 'high' and 'low' culture designed to reveal the arrogance, posturing, and mendacity of such disjunctions."[37] Hedrick aptly cites Stowe's characterization of Senator Bird as a paradigmatic instance of such mockery. Indeed, the following passage is a case study in double-voicing the discourse of the oppressor: "Our good senator in his native state had not been exceeded by any of his brethren at Washington, in the sort of eloquence which has won for them immortal renown! How sublimely he had sat with his hands in his pockets, and scouted all sentimental weakness of those who would put the welfare of a few miserable fugitives before great state interests!" (110). The narrator employs indirect discourse to paraphrase with a difference the politics of Bird. By removing "welfare of a few miserable fugitives" from the Senator's quotation marks and giving that phrase a new accent, the narrator highlights the harshness and inhumanity of the language. Furthermore, as Hedrick ably demonstrates, the Senator is caught between his public and private values, between the legal code and the law of the heart, a disparity which becomes so intolerable that he agrees to help the fleeing Eliza and Harry.[38] Thus, if Stowe critiques female conduct from within the sphere of true womanhood, revealing a lack of sincere compassion on the part of Marie and Ophelia, she more poignantly assaults public figures who would work outside her frame of reference, beyond the appeals of domestic sentiment.

Stowe was fond of reproducing character speech with a heavy narrative overlay, a technique that both exposes the character's values and guides the reader's response to those values. The novel systematically assaults white male ideology in its various guises as political, social, and religious discourse. The irony runs thickest when the narrator casts her eye on Dan Haley, the slave trader who precipitates the action by forcing Shelby to sell Uncle Tom and little Harry. Here, for instance, the narrator represents Haley's complacent thoughts aboard the riverboat just after he has sold off a slave woman's baby:

> The trader had arrived at that stage of Christian and political perfection which has been recommended by some preachers and politicians of the north, lately, in which he had completely overcome every humane weakness and prejudice. His heart was exactly where yours, sir, and mine could be brought, with proper effort and cultivation. The wild look of anguish and utter despair that the woman cast on him might have disturbed one less practised; but he was used to it. He had seen that same look hundreds of times. You can get used to such things, too, my friend; and it is the great object of recent efforts to make our whole northern community used to them, for the glory of the Union. (157)

In a mock celebratory style, the narrator contrasts the imputed dignity of the slave trader with his actual inhumanity. The passage incorporates such stock phrases of justification as "for the glory of the Union," but by placing this phrase at the end of the sentence, as a weak tag, the narrator highlights its inanity.

Thus the female wit of *Uncle Tom's Cabin* generally conforms to the downeast tradition, but with a difference caused by gender. Stowe's narrator wheedles, satirizes, and subtly condemns through the under-stated New England voice, but generally remains true to the codes of genteel manners. The narrator also allows black characters to dialogize the language and behavior of the master class. In the surprisingly comic scenes which surround Eliza's flight and Tom's exile from the Shelby home, the narrator shows slave and female humor acting in collusion. Sam, an obsequious trickster who sees Tom's misfortune as his potential fortune, frustrates Haley's attempts to track Eliza, for he knows that Mrs. Shelby would prefer this course of action. Sam thus plants a nut under the saddle of Haley's horse, causing the horse to throw the slavetrader. Stowe's narrator delights in recording the di-verse reactions to this event: "Haley ran up and down, and cursed and swore and stamped miscellaneously. Mr. Shelby in vain tried to shout directions from the balcony, and Mrs. Shelby from her chamber window alternately laughed and wondered,—not without some in-kling of what lay at the bottom of all this confusion" (64–65). We might call this the primal comic scene in *Uncle Tom's Cabin,* for it reveals in archetypal fashion women and blacks besting males through guile. Sam continues his comic function, first, by leading Haley down a false road, and second, by parodying the discourse of white politi-cians. In these ways, and in his general garrulous manner, Sam con-forms to the minstrel stereotype analyzed by Rourke.[39] But Stowe also develops willful trickster figures who go beyond the minstrel tradition, though these comic tactics also carry racist implications.[40] That is, consciously or not, Stowe incorporated representations of the "the signifyin' monkey" discussed by Henry Louis Gates Jr.[41] Mulatto fig-ures such as George Harris and Cassy shrewdly analyze their predica-ments, then take calculated action to liberate themselves. Indeed, the male and female characters can be read as Stowe's highly melodramatic reproductions of narratives by Frederick Douglass and Harriet Ann Jacobs.[42] George Harris employs the disguise of a Spanish gentleman to flee his abusive master, a man who would break Harris much as Covey attempted to break Douglass. Harris's tactic is appropriate in a text dominated by disguise, for, as we shall discover shortly, Haley has already appeared under the cover of a gentleman and "a man of humanity." The difference between Harris's and Haley's disguises is that while the former's costume expresses his actual personality, the latter's provides a cloak of hypocrisy. In an important sense, then, *Uncle Tom's Cabin* develops a similar critique of American culture to Cooper's in the last of his Littlepage novels, *The Redskins.* As we saw in chapter 2, Cooper characterizes his would-be protagonists as frauds who live a life of masquerade, using their disguises to heap scorn upon their opponents and bring dishonor upon themselves. Several years prior to Melville's brilliant deployment of "the masquerade," both Stowe and Cooper had analyzed the apocalyptic threat facing a society living behind masks.

If George Harris's tale-within-a-tale recalls elements of Douglass's *Narrative*, Cassy's "stratagem" (the narrator's term for her elaborate practical joke on Legree) provides an uncanny echo for Jacobs's experiences in *Incidents in the Life of a Slave Girl*. Similar to "Linda Brent," Cassy chooses confinement in an enclosed space with her surrogate daughter Emmeline rather than continued psychological enslavement by the transplanted northerner. However, Stowe casts her female trickster in the stereotype of the tragic mulatto, cutting against the realistic grain of Jacobs's fictionalized autobiography. For example, Cassy exploits Gothic conventions to achieve her freedom: "It had suddenly occurred to Cassy to make use of the superstitious excitability, which was so great in Legree, for the purpose of her liberation, and that of her fellow-sufferer" (465).[43] Aware that Legree had confined and murdered a black woman in the attic "some few years before" (464), Cassy creates her own Gothic drama complete with sound effects. In Cassy's act of vengeance, then, Stowe conflates carnivalizing and gothicizing tactics by the oppressed against the oppressor. The tragic mulatto both laughs at the perplexed "master" *and* provokes madness in a male character who has literally murdered womanhood. Cassy becomes the avenging angel for all womanhood against the pornographic actions of Legree, the melodramatic icon of male antisocial values. The narrator joins in this comic-gothic destruction by reducing Legree to a humiliated coward: "Legree's knees knocked together; his face grew white with fear" (469).

So far, then, we have examined Stowe's use of humor by the oppressed to invert the hierarchies of male/female and white/black within antebellum America. To appreciate these strategies of humor we have had to revise Rourke's schema of humorous traditions by attending to a distinctive tradition of women's humor and the trickster tradition represented by antebellum slave narratives. To comprehend the political tactics of this pangeneric novel more fully, we turn now to a subgenre and a literary mode that provide narrative structure to dominant male values. In chapter 1 I referred the reader to Fredric Jameson's analysis of narrative as ideological construct. We have already seen the "historically determinate conceptual or semic complex" of white male dominance enunciated in the revoiced language of Senator Bird and Haley. We now turn to two proto-narratives or collective fantasies that project this same value system, the Southwestern humor tale and the male adventure narrative.

III. Puttin' on the Good Ol' Boys: Stowe and the Southwestern Humor Tradition

We have seen that the confrontation between the *eiron* and the *alazon*, between the ironist and the braggart, is fundamental to com-edy. Stowe stages such an encounter by pitting her feminized New England wit against the unequivocally male tradition of Southwestern humor.[44] This is no simple clash of styles, however, for women's humor and the Southwestern tradition often inhabit mutually exclusive moral universes. As Walter Blair and Hamlin Hill have written of the latter tradition:

> . . . occasionally, at least, the conviction is unshakable that there is more than just a note of desperation to the values lying beneath subversive humor: might does indeed make right, it is vital to be shifty in *any* country, and the best defense is to be as offensive as possible. Survival itself depends on brutality and victimization. Logical and moral precepts just do not work in a world where the good are punished and the hell-raisers go scot free.[45]

If Stowe's humor depends upon moral sentiments, and if she gathers humorous authority from her place within a cultivated domestic sphere, the writer could only feel revulsion toward the moral system implicit in antebellum male humor. Though Blair and Hill refer to this tradition as "subversive," it seems just as appropriate to describe Stowe's humor with this term, for the ethos of "brutality and victim-ization" seems the entrenched orthodoxy of pre-Civil War public life. More precisely, then, both female and male humor are subversive of their discursive counterparts.

Johnson Jones Hooper's *Adventures of Captain Simon Suggs, late of the Tallapoosa Volunteers* (1845) is a revealing instance of the ante-bellum Southwestern tradition.[46] Suggs's famous motto reads, "IT IS GOOD TO BE SHIFTY IN A NEW COUNTRY."[47] The erstwhile "volunteer" remains true to this motto throughout his long, varied career as con man on the margins of civilization. He is yet another instance of the "masquerade" American culture had become by the 1840s.[48] Frequently, similar to Stowe's Sam, he simply takes advantage of the greed or vanity of another character. So, for instance, Suggs allows a would-be bank director to believe that he is an influential politician, and thus he gladly accepts the fool's bribes. Just as often, however, Suggs exploits sentimentality. Like his latter-day surrogates, Twain's Duke and Dauphin, Suggs will let tears fly if necessary to seal a con. Whether addressing a court of law or a supposed relative,

Suggs will shamelessly don the guise of a man of sorrows to convince his victims of his "sound heart." This manipulation of sentiment originates in the character's misogyny; Suggs loses few opportunities to insult or berate female characters. Indeed, one of his first "comic" acts in this parodic campaign biography is to fill his mother's pipe with gunpowder! In another sequence, he fires at, wounds, and courtmartials the hapless Widow Haycock, the very embodiment of all that Suggs despises in woman. The "captain" completes this particular confidence game by relenting on his decision to execute the widow: "Tears came into Suggs' eyes at this appeal [for mercy], and the sternness of the officer was lost in the sensibility of the man" (101). As a result of this "sentimental" moment, Suggs allows the Widow Haycock to pay a fine rather than face execution! Thus, Suggs's con games represent an anarchic, amoral universe in which knaves exploit fools. His colorful Southwestern dialect mirrors this anarchy, for he violates every imaginable rule of grammar and decorum.

The most famous episode in Suggs's picaresque tale, "The Captain Attends a Camp-Meeting," summarizes the predominant ideology of the Southwestern tradition and highlights its opposition to Stowe's politics. The revival meeting was the distinctive site of women's religion during the first half of the nineteenth century. Frances Trollope, in her acerbic look at antebellum culture, observed revival meetings in Cincinnati. Though her attitude echoes Suggs's cynicism, her observations reveal just how central this social event could be to women's lives. Noting that "I never saw, or read, of any country where religion had so strong a hold upon the women, or a slighter hold upon the men," Trollope describes the climactic moment of a revival in these terms:

> It was a frightful sight to behold innocent young creatures, in the gay morning of existence, thus seized upon, horror struck, and rendered feeble and enervated for ever. . . .
> Did the men of America value their women as men ought to value their wives and daughters, would such scenes be permitted among them?
> It is hardly necessary to say that all who obeyed the call to place themselves on the "anxious benches" were women, and by far the greater number, very young women.[49]

The historian Nancy F. Cott conveys a similar impression for New England revivalism when she remarks that "[f]emale converts in the New England Great Awakening between 1798 and 1826 . . . outnumbered males by three to two."[50] While Trollope and Cott describe middle-class revivals rather than camp meetings, based on Hooper's account we can assume a similar proportion between female and male converts at frontier revivals. And there is yet another telling feature to this woman-centered revivalism: its covert aggression toward males. In his social history of revivals in Rochester, New York, between 1815 and 1837, Paul E. Johnson calls attention to a kind of underground network of conversion among female converts: "While Finney led morning prayer meetings, pious women visited families. . . . Visitors paid special attention to the homes of sinners who had Christian wives, and they arrived in the morning hours when husbands were at work."[51] When Simon Suggs manipulates the camp meeting for his personal ends, he is returning aggression for aggression, for he is countering an ideology of Christian conversion that would undermine his Hobbesian behavior.

Suggs's revivalist con is set in motion by the Captain's rueful realization that he is out of money, a cause for sorrow because "to a man like the Captain, of intense domestic affections, this state of destitution was most distressing" (111). The passage is of course sarcastic, for as we know, Suggs feels at best indifferent toward "domestic" values. Nonetheless, the broke captain journeys twenty miles to a camp meeting, where Hooper uses the male character to attack evangelical religion. Observing the caressing of young women and the gyrations of "niggers," Suggs takes a cool, calculating approach to the meeting: "Amid all this confusion and excitement Suggs stood unmoved. He viewed the whole affair as a grand deception—a sort of 'opposition line' running against his own, and looked on with a sort of professional jealousy" (115). Never one to remain passive in the face of opportunity, a perverse version of Emerson's self-reliant individual, Suggs proceeds to convince the revivalist preachers and their adherents that he is experiencing a conversion. In phrasing crucial to this analysis, the Captain is "altogether unmanned, and bathed in tears" (117). Clearly the conversion experience is "feminine" in its sentimentalism. However, the reader (addressed as a male throughout *Adventures*) knows all along that Suggs has simply adopted another disguise. Suggs concludes this escapade by announcing he "would take up a collection to found a church in his own neighbourhood" (123). So it is that Suggs, propelled by "intense" domestic affections, manipulates one of the central experiences of antebellum women's lives, the revival meeting, for his personal gain.

Significantly, Shelby tells Haley that Uncle Tom "got religion at a camp-meeting, four years ago" (12). Furthermore, the novel's most famous icon, Little Eva, is virtually an evangelist in the cause of abolition. Coming out of her father's revivalist tradition, it is hardly surprising that Harriet Beecher Stowe directly countered the misogynistic, anti-conversion values of Southwestern humor. Dan Haley is an obvious parody of the Southwestern male,[52] for like Suggs he adopts various disguises, mainly rhetorical and sartorial, to carry on his slave trade. In effect Haley's "business" is one large scam at the expense of blacks and their families. By implication, then, the entire slave trade is a male practical joke with dire consequences for the American re-public. Stowe's aggression toward Haley has already been seen in Sam's antics and the double-voicing of the trader's complacent thoughts aboard *La Belle Riviere*. But careful attention to the opening chapter reveals that her critique of the Southwestern male is present from the start. She begins by carefully distinguishing between the mannered if misguided Shelby and the sham gentleman who is his guest:

> He was a short, thick-set man, with coarse, commonplace features, and that swaggering air of pretension which marks a low man who is trying to elbow his way upward in the world. He was much over-dressed, in a gaudy vest of many colors, a blue neckerchief, bedropped gayly with yellow spots, and arranged with a flaunting tie, quite in keeping with the general air of the man. . . . His conversation was in free and easy defiance of Murray's Grammar, and was garnished at convenient intervals with vari-ous profane expressions, which not even the desire to be graphic in our account shall induce us to transcribe. (11)

Haley's "profane" voice often functions to gloss his capitalist motives for carrying on the trade: "Now, they say . . . that this kind o'trade is hardening to the feelings; but I never found it so. Fact is, I never could do things up the way some fellers manage the business. . . . It's always best to do the humane thing, sir; that's been *my* experience" (15–16). Stowe specifically relates this hypocrisy to Haley's attitude toward women, for he confides, "It is mighty onpleasant getting on with women, sometimes. I al'ays hates these yer screachin', screamin' times" (15). Similar to Suggs's treatment of the Widow Haycock, Haley either circumvents or abuses women. Indeed, in the riverboat episode already referred to, Haley acts counter to his own advice by arrogantly selling a black child, causing the mother to commit suicide. And yet, Haley does not entirely offend the reader, perhaps because there is an element of self-deception in him. It is true that even master con artists such as Suggs dupe themselves, believing they are more clever or powerful than they in fact are, leading to disastrous setbacks. Certainly there is no shortage of hubris among the Southwestern male characters. However, Haley's self-deception is unusually audacious, for he seems to have convinced himself that he can conduct a slave trade and achieve salvation as well: "I don't care, now, who hears me say it,—and I think a cussed sight on it,—so I may as well come out with it. I b'lieve in religion, and one of these days, when I've got matters tight and snug, I calculates to tend to my soul and them ar matters; and so what's the use of doin' any more wickedness than's re'lly necessary?—it don't seem to me it's 't all prudent" (85). Haley could well be one of those "sinners" Charles Finney and his female coworkers approached, for he recognizes the need for religion but cannot surrender his materialist values. All events are still "calcu- lated" with the scales of commerce. But of course there is no "Chris- tian wife" to convert Haley and so he must remain an unregenerate sinner, doomed to hellfire.

If the reader can only anticipate Haley's final punishment, in the case of Tom Loker, Stowe narrates a full-blown conversion experience. Indeed, Loker's "death and resurrection" describes the ethical rehabili- tation of an entire ideology of male violence toward women and blacks. While Haley conforms to the confidence man archetype of Southwestern humor, Loker embodies another persona: the ring-tailed roarer. As his business partner says of him, "Now, Tom's a roarer when there's any thumping or fighting to be done . . ." (87). "A brawny, muscular man, full six feet in height, and broad in proportion" (81), the normally taciturn Loker becomes a bragging ball of fire when prodded by whiskey and the promise of a big payoff: "Ye know that . . . I don't pretend none of your snivelling ways, but I won't lie in my 'counts with the devil himself. What I ses I'll do, I will do,—you know *that*, Dan Haley" (88). However, as Suggs punishes the Widow Haycock, so the novel punishes the violent Loker. In the climactic scene of the George-Eliza plot, Loker charges up a chasm to capture the fugitive slaves, only to be pushed over the edge by Phineas Fletcher, there to suffer a rhetorical thrashing by the narrator: "Down he fell into the chasm, crackling down among trees, bushes, logs, loose stones, till he lay, bruised and groaning, thirty feet below. The fall might have killed him, had it not been broken and moderated by his clothes catching in the branches of a large tree; but he came down with some force, however,—more than was at all agreeable or conve- nient" (236). In a nearly allegorical account of spiritual humiliation, Loker tumbles down the hill of his vanity, only to be saved by the Quaker community: ". . . having lain three weeks at the Quaker dwell- ing, sick with a rheumatic fever, which set in, in company with his other afflictions, Tom arose from his bed a somewhat sadder and wiser man; and, in place of slave-catching, betook himself to life in one of the new settlements, where his talents developed themselves more happily in trapping bears, wolves, and other inhabitants of the forest" (447). Though Loker denies that he has been converted by the Quakers, he has rechanneled his anarchic male energy into socially useful action, a sign of victory for the feminine ethos.[53]

As if to underline her reconstruction of American masculinity, Stowe incorporates two Southwestern male characters who attack slavery. The first appears in chapter 11, "In Which Property Gets into an Improper State of Mind," focused on George's escape. Stowe opens the chapter with a genre painting of Southwestern masculinity:

> In the bar-room [Mr. Wilson] found assembled quite a miscellaneous company, whom stress of weather had driven to harbor, and the place presented the usual scenery of such reunions. Great, tall, raw-boned Kentuckians, attired in hunting-shirts, and trailing their loose joints over a vast extent of territory, with the easy lounge peculiar to the race,—rifles stacked away in the corner, shot-pouches, game-bags, hunting-dogs, and little negroes, all rolled together in the corners,—were the characteristic features in the picture. At each end of the fireplace sat a long-legged gentleman, with his chair tipped back, his hat on his head, and the heels of his muddy boots reposing sublimely on the mantel-piece,—a position, we will inform our readers, decidedly favorable to the turn of reflection incident to western taverns, where travellers exhibit a decided preference for this particular mode of elevating their understandings. (127)

If "this loafing ruffianism was associated with laughing groups of men, and women's fiction often glanced in fear and disgust at such groups,"[54] Stowe's passage should be seen as an instance of a female writer substituting bemused, even condescending observation for fear and loathing. Stowe "colonizes" the male domain, reworking the terrain with her uncanny eye for detail and a sarcastic irreverence ("this particular mode of elevating their understandings"). However, this opening scene does more than introduce yet another local color sketch into the national novel, for one of those "free-spirited" Kentuckians pointedly challenges slavery. In response to a poster offering a reward for the capture of George Harris, one of the reclining "gentlemen" opines, "Any man that owns a boy like that, and can't find any better way o' treating on him, *deserves* to lose him. Such papers as these is a shame to Kentucky; that's my mind right out, if anybody wants to know!" (130). The same "honest drover" who double-voices the minister's defense of slavery on *La Belle Riviere* here argues for treatment of "niggers" as "men" rather than "dogs." What makes this vignette even more effective is that Stowe does not avoid the implicit racism in the drover's position. He clearly sees the "nigger" as an "other" species, different in kind and not just degree from himself. But despite that incipient racism, he asserts the blacks' right to freedom. In this

way Stowe combines an acute eye for social realism with her polemical thrust.

Phineas Fletcher provides an even more dramatic instance of the
"converted" male, for he is the prototypical backwoodsman-turned-
abolitionist: "To tell the truth, Phineas had been a hearty, two-fisted
backwoodsman, a vigorous hunter, and a dead shot at a buck; but,
having wooed a pretty Quakeress, had been moved by the power of
her charms to join the society in his neighborhood; and though he
was an honest, sober, and efficient member, and nothing particular
could be alleged against him, yet the more spiritual among them could
not but discern an exceeding lack of savor in his developments" (224).
Fletcher uses his frontier skills to bring George and Eliza to safety at
the rocky precipice, then confidently guides George in his self-defense.
Indeed, Fletcher strongly recalls Cooper's Natty Bumppo, for Stowe's
backwoodsman combines a natural piety with the desire to defend the
persecuted. Fletcher also duplicates the manners and language of Jim
Doggett, the protagonist of T. B. Thorpe's well-known "The Big Bear
of Arkansas." Doggett is a benign version of the ring-tailed roarer, for
his boastfulness does not involve the acquisitive, even destructive
values of Suggs and Loker. Instead he narrates the moving story of
his quest for "the creation bear" and his rueful response to his victory:
"Perhaps, he had heard of my preparations to hunt him the next day,
so he just come in, like Capt. Scott's coon, to save his wind to grunt
with in dying. But that ain't likely. My private opinion is, that the
bear was an *unhuntable bear, and died when his time come.*"[55] Doggett
has come face-to-face with the mythical, the numinous, the supernatu-
ral, and he is awed by its presence. Indeed, he is humbled by his
Pyrrhic victory, for he feels as though he has been part of a process
much larger than himself. Unlike the egotistical male of frontier tradition, Doggett has a sense of proportion, a perspective on his place in
the larger scheme of creation. More than that, Doggett realizes that
his violence has consequences, and not always pretty ones. Similarly,
Fletcher comments to Harris after they have attended the wounded
Loker, "I've been a great hunter, in my day, and I tell thee I've seen
a buck that was shot down, and a dying, look that way on a feller
with his eye, that it reely most made a feller feel wicked for killing
him; and human creatures is a more serious consideration yet, bein',
as thy wife says, that the judgment comes to 'em after death" (239).
It is not surprising, then, that when *Uncle Tom's Cabin* appeared on
the popular stage Phineas Fletcher was converted into "a low-comedy
Kentucky roarer,"[56] for he conforms to one version of that comic archetype, the Jim Doggett type.

IV. REINVENTING THE AMERICAN ADVENTURE

In his study of "the great American adventure," Martin Green has commented that "adventure experience was the sacramental ceremony of the cult of manhood."[57] If the Southwestern humor tradition encoded an ethos of self-interest, cockiness, and victimization, the antebellum adventure narrative symbolized a male rite of passage that was closely tied to the imperial designs of the United States. As Green has further asserted, "adventure is the energizing myth of empire, taking empire to mean any expanding society dominant over others."[58] Cooper's seminal *The Last of the Mohicans* (1826) provides a paradigmatic instance of the American adventure narrative. Set during the French/Indian War, the novel negotiates the claims to ownership of America among the British, French, Native Americans, and colonial Americans. Through a process of elimination, the narrative ultimately affirms the colonials' domination over the New World. However, the colonies must *earn* this authority symbolically through the ritual maturation of Duncan Heyward. The initially awkward, dim-sighted Southern aristocrat undergoes an education in woodcraft by Natty Bumppo, Chingachgook, and Uncas. Symbolically, Heyward's acquisition of this knowledge makes him a suitable ruler for the American continent, once the native tribes have been extinguished. In a crucial moment of initiation, Heyward dons the disguise of a French juggler and enters the Huron camp, thus adopting the trickster behavior familiar to Bumppo and his Mohican allies. The young American now appears a more flexible, observant, daring individual than the rigid gentleman we meet at the beginning of the text.

But of course the American's success depends upon the failure of other factions, including the Delaware tribe. In one of Cooper's most moving evocations of an Indian perspective on the white incursion, Tamenund recalls in mythic terms the powerful past of the Delawares: "It was but yesterday . . . that the children of the Lenape were masters of the world! The fishes of the salt-lake, the birds, the beasts, and the Mengwe of the woods, owned them for Sagamores." This voice of racial memory rises in hope when Uncas reveals the blue tortoise upon his chest, symbol of Delaware royalty: "Is Tamenund a boy! . . . Have I dreamt of so many snows—that my people were scattered like floating sands—of Yengeese, more plenty than the leaves on the trees! . . . Tell me, ye Delawares, has Tamenund been a sleeper for a hundred winters?"[59] The answer to these questions will necessarily be "no," for Uncas will die in a futile attempt to save Cora, leaving the childless Chingachgook behind to mourn the death of his tribe. Indeed, this is a central irony of *The Last of the Mohicans,* an irony to which Cooper seems sensitive: the heroic Native American characters effect their own destruction by helping Duncan rescue Alice. They seem unwitting accomplices in their own undoing. The same can be said for Hawk-eye, who throughout the Leatherstocking series provides the chorus of doom, the voice for the wilderness, set against the drum-beat of American imperialism. And yet, time and again Bumppo aids the cause of empire by protecting the very forces of white hegemony, especially the future mothers of America such as Elizabeth Temple and Alice Munro. This is the ideological import of the famous chase sequences in the second of the Leatherstocking novels: the young American male, undergoing an initiation by wilderness testing, recap-tures his blond white bride with the help of wilderness advocates. In the process, the dark-skinned Cora, carrying the "tainted" blood of Munro's Caribbean lover, must die, assuring racial purity in the American elite. For all of Cooper's sensitivity to racial failures in the United States, when the plot is reduced to these radical elements, *The Last of the Mohicans* appears an uncompromising justification of white male authority over the New World.[60]

If we are tempted to see this famous Cooper novel as an isolated instance of the adventure narrative in antebellum America, we need only refer back to the New York epics discussed in chapter 2, for both Paulding's *The Dutchman's Fireside* and Cooper's *Satanstoe* advance the same argument by narrating the triumph of inexperienced white males over a recalcitrant wilderness and its defenders with the help of wilderness sages. Coming closer to home in terms of Stowe's political interests, Robert Montgomery Bird's *Nick of the Woods* (1837) trans-plants Cooper's archetypal adventure narrative to colonial Ken-tucky.[61] This overtly racist text provides a mirror image of Stowe's novel, for not only does it include the symbolic adventure, but it features a comic ring-tailed roarer in Ralph Stackpole, a sometimes cowardly boaster who ultimately manages to help the protagonists. If anything, Bird's novel is more blatant in its imperial and racial atti-tudes than Cooper's, for as the male protagonist Roland Forrester remarks, "And hence you see . . . that I come to Kentucky, an adven-turer and fortune-hunter, like other emigrants, to locate lands under proclamation-warrants and bounty-grants, to fell trees, raise corn, shoot bisons and Indians, and, in general, to do any thing else that can be required of a good Virginian or good Kentuckian."[62] Like *The Last of the Mohicans,* Bird's novel focuses on the chase and rescue of an American ingenue, Edith Forrester. Roland's arch enemy, the law-yer Dick Braxley, has dispossessed Forrester of his rightful inheritance and now plots to murder Roland and take Edith captive with the assistance of renegade Indians. But Braxley's plot is foiled through the ferocious heroism of Nathan Slaughter, the self-proclaimed Quaker who turns out to be "Nick of the Woods," the scourge of the Shawnees who had murdered his family and brutally scalped him. It is as though Bird anticipated Stowe's idealization of the Quaker settlement. Finally, then, we witness Dick Braxley's gruesome scalping by a Downeast character who mistakes him for an Indian (by now it must be apparent that *Nick of the Woods* shares many of the carnivalizing qualities of Stowe's novel). This catastrophe makes way for Edith and Roland's matrimonial triumph: "The deliverance of the cousins, the one from captivity and death, the other from a fate to her more dreadful than death; the restoration of the will of their uncle; and the fall of the daring and unprincipled villain, to whose machinations they owed all their calamities, had changed the current of their fortunes, which was now to flow in a channel where the eye could no longer trace obstructions. . . ."[63] Thus, both Cooper's and Bird's adventure narratives conform to the same archetypal romance structure discussed in chapter 2 as we examined Cooper's *Satanstoe*. We can reduce the narrative to three primary components: first, the plot follows a chase and rescue sequence, with a powerful erotic element; second, the narrative advances an ideology of empire; third, American adventure depends upon racial (often racist) assumptions, presupposing fundamental differences in kind rather than degree among black, Indian, and white races.

In what is generally called a "domestic" novel, Stowe includes a surprising number of adventure elements, but mainly toward the goal of subverting those conventions. Once again we see an antebellum writer imitating with a parodic difference the qualities of a sibling literary mode. In fact Stowe's novel partially demonstrates William Spengemann's claim that American writers waged a competition between "the poetics of adventure" and "the poetics of domesticity." The latter, dedicated to ahistorical eternal values centered on the home, devotes its energies to recuperating the adventurous male character. As we have already seen, *Uncle Tom's Cabin* does narrate the rehabilitation of active but misguided male characters. However, Spengemann loads the dice in favor of adventure narrative by describing it in terms such as "open-ended," "creative," and "daring," repeating the familiar notion that whereas domestic fiction preserves a status quo, a preexisting tradition, American literary adventures advance an experimental, experiential writing that liberates rather than constricts. At least in the case of *Uncle Tom's Cabin*, however, "domestic fiction" can be every bit as daring and surprising as the adventures discussed by Spengemann. Furthermore, American adventure narratives evince disturbing political implications overlooked in *The Adventurous Muse*.[64]

Stowe's novel inverts male adventure narrative by frustrating its forward movement, depicting blacks and women as adventure heroes, and subordinating adventure elements to Uncle Tom's picaresque narrative. In the earlier analyses of humor in *Uncle Tom's Cabin*, we observed how women and blacks thwarted the chase and capture designs of Dan Haley, Tom Loker, and Simon Legree. In each instance the male character represents a violent recasting of the archetypal stories coming out of the American adventure narrative tradition. If Duncan Heyward and Roland Forrester are maturing young men seeking white lovers, Haley and Legree are middle-aged cynics seeking black women for their own or others' prurient interest. The erotic element of American adventure thus takes a frightening direction away from procreation toward sexual exploitation. The male slave-holders become the heathen captors intent on "ruining" young women, much as Native Americans had appeared in the adventure novels founded on the captivity narrative tradition.[65] Stowe is not at all naive about these political implications, for she provides in Cassy a world-weary victim of the slave system who acts to protect Emmeline from Legree's lust. More than that, Cassy consciously plots to use Legree's desire for chase against him, for she remarks to Emmeline, "Don't you know that they must have their chase after us, at any rate?" (470). In this simple device of leading her tormenter on a wild goose chase Cassy exploits a male predilection for pursuit and capture that ultimately frustrates and maddens Legree, preparing the stage for his brutal treatment of Tom and his own descent into madness. By contrast, Cassy and Emmeline enter an enclosed space, a magical domestic sphere of their own design, created by taking from Legree what he would not give them. More than destroying Legree's psychic and domestic architecture, Cassy projects her own alternative home: "We see her transformed from a madwoman capable of murdering her children into a woman who can transform a *hus*, her temporary shelter from the wrath of Legree, into a matriarchal *domus*—complete with make-shift kitchen, sitting room, and bed—by which she gains power over her utterly masculine, materialistic 'master.'"[66] Stowe also plays Cassy's scheming off against Emmeline's still intact morality, showing that slavery reduces women to a condition of violating ethical norms in order to find safe haven within the slave regime.

Eliza and George go beyond frustrating male adventure, for each can be said to fulfill the requirements of adventure, but with an ideological twist. Eliza's flight with Harry has the teleological drive of male adventure, but with this crucial difference: whereas Cooper's protagonist is compelled by erotic as well as imperial designs, Eliza acts out of the "pure" motive of maternal love. In this inverted adventure story, then, the pursuer and the pursued are combined in a single character who rejects her dependent position and asserts her freedom through action. Throughout her novel Stowe toys with the possibilities of androgynous behavior by females and males alike, as in Cassy's insistence that Emmeline not faint. Eliza's heroic flight marks such a combined personality, one that fuses the values of public and private spheres. Male characters such as Simeon Halliday make the same point by their *refusal* to pursue adventure, for here is a male who has rejected "the cult of manhood."

As I suggested earlier, George's interpolated narrative conforms to the logic of Douglass's slave narrative. In the previous chapter we discovered that Douglass's story has the narrative force of *kairos*, a sense of time past and present leading to one crucial future: freedom. This most famous of slave narratives follows a carefully defined plot guiding the protagonist from subservience to manly independence. The plot has a providential tone, one injected by the narrator of course, for Douglass would insist that his flight was a miracle of sorts directed by a higher agency. However, like Franklin's *Autobiography*, Douglass's balances this superficial piety with a sense of autonomy, of personal authority. Ultimately the reader believes that Douglass is an exceptional individual who has triumphed through will and intelligence over an immoral system. George also takes the part of the adventure hero, both questing for freedom and being pursued by bounty hunters. If anything, Stowe amplifies the heroic qualities of the slave narrative by exploiting romantic conventions.

To further appreciate Stowe's revision of the adventure narrative, it is useful to reconsider the climactic incident of Harris's escape by comparing it with a similar scene in *The Last of the Mohicans*. Probably the most famous episode in the 1826 novel occurs at Glens Falls, where Hawk-eye, Uncas, Chingachgook, and the Heyward party are pinned down by Magua and his minions. Taking advantage of an American obsession with the sublime in landscape art, Cooper created a dramatic set piece complete with "gorgeous" scenery and a complex hiding place. Similarly Stowe locates her hero and heroine in a spectacular setting:

> The pursuers gained on them fast; the carriage made a sudden turn, and brought them near a ledge of a steep overhanging rock, that rose in an isolated ridge or clump in a large lot, which was, all around, quite clear and smooth. This isolated pile, or range of rocks, rose up black and heavy against the brightening sky, and seemed to promise shelter and conceal-

ment. It was a place well known to Phineas, who had been familiar with the spot in his hunting days; and it was to gain this point he had been racing his horses. (229)

Momentarily secure in this sublime setting, his head framed by the early morning light, George declares himself a freeman prepared to defend himself, a speech which prompts the narrator to remark ironically, "If it had been only a Hungarian youth, now bravely defending in some mountain fastness the retreat of fugitives escaping from Austria into America, this would have been sublime heroism; but as it was a youth of African descent . . . we are too well instructed and patriotic to see any heroism in it . . ." (232). After this self-conscious critique of American ideals of heroism, the narrator completes this story-within-a-story by describing the fugitive slaves' victory over the Satanic captors. Indeed, Stowe's characters double Cooper's, as the following chart demonstrates:

Duncan Heyward Uncas	George Harris
Alice Munro Cora Munro	Eliza
Hawk-eye Magua	Phineas Fletcher Tom Loker

This repetition-with-a-difference carries profound political significance. Stowe's male and female protagonists literally combine the qualities of white- and dark-skinned characters, so that Harris fuses Heyward's aristocratic bearing with Uncas's necessary guile. So also Eliza merges Alice's gentility with Cora's passion and maturity (Cooper frequently suggests that the older sister has a genetic predisposition toward knowledge-of-the-world because of her racial heritage). Similar to Hawk-eye, Phineas has the skills of a frontiersman and the values of a liberal democrat. And finally, in the most telling revision of all, Tom Loker, the ring-tailed roarer who would happily consort with the Devil, takes on the role of the violent pursuer. Stowe adds one element to Cooper's vignette, the child Harry, a reminder that George and Eliza are mature adults striving to preserve a family rather than create one. Overall, then, Stowe depicts how the imperial designs (the manifest destiny) of America has been perverted by the slave regime, for the bounty hunter becomes the pagan, pre-civilized victimizer intent on capture and sale of the noble mulattoes. In the twisted logic of antebellum politics, the heroic characters are outcasts, aliens, in need of help from a reformed roarer who is himself a member of a marginalized religious sect. In one sense, though, Stowe does replicate the imperial design of American adventure, for at the conclusion of her novel she casts George as a political hero in Liberia, suggesting that after all the escaped slave *is* an empire builder on the African continent.

If Stowe frustrates male adventure and describes successful risk-taking by black characters, she counters this narrative tradition in a more profound and subtle manner as well. Thus far my analysis of *Uncle Tom's Cabin* has said little about the title character. Largely this is a result of my focus on the humorous and parodic qualities of the novel, for Tom defies treatment as a comic character, except in the broad sense suggested by Dante's *Divine Comedy*. Similar to Little Eva, he is not susceptible to humor, for he is thoroughly earnest, thoroughly pious, thoroughly *sincere*. He will not employ trickster behavior, nor will he flee for his life when Eliza urges him to do so early in the text. His famous passivity emerges from the Christian values of patience and resignation. In an obvious sense Tom does foil Legree, for he will not relent and accept the master's code of violence as a substitute for his code of compassion. Even more fundamentally, Tom's story runs counter to the adventure tradition, for his tale conforms to the picaresque tradition. That is, this pious picaro subverts the salient features of adventure outlined above: the chase and rescue sequence, the ideology of empire, and the assumption of the black character's necessary inferiority.

At first this claim for Tom as picaro may seem preposterous, for after all the term means "rogue," and Tom is anything but a con man. But if we think of specific instances of American picaresque, we begin to perceive an affinity between Tom and picaros.[67] The single most famous example from nineteenth-century American writing is Huckleberry Finn, a rogue with a difference. Here is a poor white boy, raised by a violent, alcoholic father, enslaved by Tom Sawyer's middle-class romantic notions, on the whole powerless against social injustice. Despite the troubles he has seen, Huck retains his sound heart, striving to help Jim achieve freedom in a heartless world. This marginal character provides an episodic overview of antebellum American culture, for as he journeys down the Mississippi he encounters high and low culture, all classes, cons and saints-on-earth, etc. And perhaps most importantly, despite what he has seen, despite what he has learned, nothing really changes either about Huck or his world by the novel's conclusion. Only a deus ex machina saves Jim from reenslavement; the system itself remains very much in place.

Though Tom cannot tell a lie at the drop of a hat (one of Huck's least appreciated talents), his personality and his story bear striking resemblance to that of the fourteen-year-old white character. Like Huck, he is politically and socially marginal, the victim of an unjust regime who has no practical means for freeing himself or changing the system. Despite his encounters with the best and worst of antebellum Southern society, Tom also retains his sound heart. Moving from the Shelbys' genteel Kentucky farm, to St. Clare's overly refined plantation, to Legree's ramshackle prison plantation, Tom provides what Barbara Foley calls "encyclopedic portraiture" of a system.[68] But more than supplying the reader access to the system, Tom provides a point of reference, a measuring stick, for the moral condition of that system, much as Huck's pragmatic compassion contrasts sharply with the decadence of Mississippi River society. It is significant, then, that we see Tom on board riverboats twice in the course of the novel, for that vessel was an ideal setting for the picaro in antebellum literature, as demonstrated by Thorpe's "The Big Bear of Arkansas" and Melville's *The Confidence Man*. What better place to encounter a microcosm of American culture than the steamboat? Furthermore, what better image of Tom's passive movement through the American South could Stowe provide than one of his floating on this powerful machine of "progress" without any say concerning its destination: "Those turbid waters, hurrying, foaming, tearing along, an apt resemblance of that headlong tide of business which is poured along its wave by a race more vehement and energetic than any the old world ever saw. Ah! would that they did not also bear along a more fearful freight,—the tears of the oppressed, the sighs of the helpless, the bitter prayers of poor, ignorant hearts to an unknown God . . ." (172).

Tom's role as telling observer comes clearest following St. Clare's unexpected death. Thrown back onto the market dominated by calculation, the pious slave must watch helplessly as he and other, more vulnerable slaves (Emmeline) become subject to the whims of a Legree. Stowe cleverly exploits Tom as picaresque narrative eye in her description of the hideous slave warehouse, especially in the male slave's longing search for "a good master": "Tom saw abundance of men,—great, burly, gruff men; little, chirping, dried men; long-favored, lank, hard men; and every variety of stubbed-looking, commonplace men, who pick up their fellow-men as one picks up chips, putting them into the fire or a basket with equal unconcern, according to their convenience; but he saw no St. Clare" (387). The narrator repeats "men" for added effect, stressing once more the conflict between head and heart, between capitalist accounting and compassion. She also plays with the term "men" to emphasize Tom's status as a human being reduced to "chips." As if to underscore the connection between

the slave system and the calculating mentality, the narrator (still gaz-
ing through Tom's eyes) dwells upon Legree's hideous head: "From
the moment that Tom saw him approaching, he felt an immediate and
revolting horror at him, that increased as he came near. . . . His round,
bullet head, large, light-gray eyes, with their shaggy, sandy eye-brows,
and stiff, wiry, sun-burned hair, were rather unprepossessing items, it
is to be confessed . . ." (387). This encounter between profane and
devout manhood leads toward Legree's horrifying (literally hellish)
"estate," and so fittingly we catch another glimpse of Tom on board
a boat, this time Charon's raft taking him over the river Styx to the
hell of slavery:

> On the lower part of a small, mean boat, on the Red river, Tom sat,—
> chains on his wrists, chains on his feet, and a weight heavier than chains
> lay on his heart. All had faded from his sky,—moon and star; all had
> passed by him, as the trees and banks were now passing, to return no
> more. Kentucky home, with wife and children, and indulgent owners; St.
> Clare home, with all its refinements and splendors; the golden head of
> Eva, with its saint-like eyes; the proud, gay, handsome, seemingly careless,
> yet ever-kind St. Clare; hours of ease and indulgent leisure,—all gone! and
> in place thereof, *what* remains? (391)

In sharp contrast to George and Eliza, then, Uncle Tom is the passive
picaresque character who drifts according to the dictates of his white
handlers. He is locked into chronicity, the time scheme of sheer succession without beginning or end, the enemy of the self-reliant slave.
Except, of course, that Tom *does* have an alternative time frame, one
inaccessible to Haley, St. Clare, or Legree, the frame of sacred time
which exists in an eternal present, available to humanity through
recurring rituals of prayer and contemplation. Thus Tom is both inside
and outside the slave regime, for his eyes focus on an alternative home,
the home to which Eva has journeyed, the home called heaven.[69] Tom
leaves his cabin, never to return to it, because he must arrive at an
alternative cabin. Such is the condition of the slave South that this
saint-on-earth must perish rather than fulfill his duty as evangelist to
his fellow blacks. So it is that the slave South not only prevents the
millennium so vivid in the Beechers' eyes, but courts the apocalyptic
destruction of America.

V. There's No Place Like Home?

In my earlier analysis of female humor I stressed the complementary
relationship between satire and sentiment: while wit disarms destruc-

tive ideologies, sentiment affirms constructive ideologies. The textual
manuevers discussed so far primarily fulfill the first function, for
Stowe's humor and narrative inversions "tame" threatening male values. To fill the void created by this sibling rivalry toward male expressive forms, Uncle Tom's Cabin offers local color and domestic scenes
as alternatives. We have already discussed Cassy's successful creation
of a home within the wasteland of Legree's ruined plantation house.
Similarly George and Eliza drive toward a new home, first in Canada,
then in Africa. As we have just seen, Tom journeys toward that
ultimate home, heaven. So it is that Stowe's narrator promotes the
domestic ideology explicated by her sister: "Catharine began [her Treatise on Domestic Economy] with the premise that the home was a
perfect vehicle for national unity because it was a universally experienced institution recognizing no economic, political, or regional
boundaries."[70] Stowe was a "colonizationist" in more senses than one.
As she believed American blacks should colonize their native continent, so she sought to colonize American culture with an ethos of
domesticity. This aggressive rhetorical act was both her strength and
weakness as a political writer.

As her humor originated in her childhood experiences, so too did
her strong pull toward the pastoralized local color scene: "In retrospect, Stowe mused that her mother's childhood home in Nutplains,
Connecticut, Stowe's own childhood home away from home, had been
'a vision of Eden.' An original source, a place of her beginnings,
Stowe's Eden was like a dreamland, a setting yearned for and nostalgi-
cally recalled."[71] That nostalgia emerges full-blown in Stowe's representation of the Quaker settlement, a setting generally viewed as the
utopian center of Uncle Tom's Cabin. Fusing an ethic of nonviolence
with male/female equality, the Quaker settlement provides the model
for a reborn America. This fantasy of domestic/pastoral harmony
seems to support Habegger's observation that the idealization of literary homes points back to troubled conditions in actual homes.[72] After
all, we know that Uncle Tom's Cabin emerged from Stowe's stressful
domestic life, for the Stowes constantly lived on the edge of financial
failure, a fact painfully brought home by Harriet's being mistaken for a
poor immigrant mother on her journey from Cincinnati to Brunswick,
Maine, in 1850.

But lest we fall into the trap of pitying this persistently canny
writer, we should recognize that Stowe was to a large extent aware
of the fantasy function of the Quaker settlement, for she repeatedly
characterizes marriages as mixed affairs. After all, even Mrs. Shelby's
strongest rhetorical appeals cannot dissuade Mr. Shelby from selling
Tom and Harry (hence her use of trickster behavior to foil Haley).

While Mrs. Bird convinces her husband to help Eliza, theirs also has been a marriage fraught with sadness, both because of their political differences and because of the death of their child. Most dramatically of all, the St. Clares represent marriages gone awry for lack of conviction or deep concern. In a passage with implicit autobiographical force, Stowe describes the disillusionment of St. Clare following his marriage to Marie: "And thus ended the whole romance and ideal of life for Augustine St. Clare. But the *real* remained,—the *real*, like the flat, bare, oozy tide-mud, when the blue sparkling wave, with all its company of gliding boats and white-winged ships, its music of oars and chiming waters, has gone down, and there it lies, flat, slimy, bare,— exceedingly real" (185). Three times the narrator repeats the word "real," making it impossible for the reader to miss the importance of the actual in the face of the ideal. This passage conforms to the anti-romance impulse of Stowe's early local color fiction. Admittedly there is something disingenuous about this narrative interlude, for Stowe indulges romance at several turns in her fiction, especially in George and Eliza's melodramatic escape. My point here is that as the novel alternates between sentiment and satire, it also creates a dialectic between fantasy and realism, between idealized and realized experience, between the visionary and the mimetic. In short, Stowe is far more self-conscious about her nostalgia and longing than critics have admitted, for she contrasts the idealized Quaker marriage with more authentic portraits based on her own experience.

Still, in the millennial spirit of the novel, Stowe hopefully advances the cause of feminized religion in the teeth of capitalist America. Little Eva, that pre-sexual icon of piety, summarizes the narrative drive toward this value system. But for Stowe's political purposes, Ophelia, the comic New England spinster, is every bit as important a character as the Southern evangel. Though Eva remains the character every reader remembers, Ophelia's subplot models the reader's necessary conversion from abhorrence to love toward blacks. In a clever generic cross-breeding, Stowe transplants the quintessential local color character in the plantation romance. Here especially the writer seems sensitive to the ideological import of antebellum subgenres, for she uses this generic interplay to create a dialogue of values between the squeamish female and her lazy but insightful cousin. In a curious sense Stowe reaffirms the plantation tradition that her novel should presumably discredit. As Frank Meriwether of Kennedy's *Swallow Barn* combined qualities of *noblesse oblige* with whimsical folly, Augustine St. Clare blends a languorous temperament with an astute critical eye. After all, it is St. Clare who mouths the most devastating critiques of the slave system in the novel, stressing its demoralizing effects on slaves and masters alike. Furthermore, Augustine's astuteness drives his Northern cousin toward an important conclusion: the Northern abolitionist is often as much or more a racist than the Southern slaveholder. In literal dialogues of regional types, Augustine and Ophelia work out the categorical imperative for antebellum America: to embrace blacks as Christian brothers and sisters.

Similar to "Uncle Lot," Stowe's original local color story, the St. Clare section of Uncle Tom's Cabin follows a movement from playful levity to religious righteousness. Indeed, Ophelia is Uncle Lot revisited, for as that signature character of New England culture had to suffer in order to achieve wisdom, so Ophelia must endure Topsy's antics and Eva's death toward the larger goal of politicospiritual regeneration. The narrator falls into a comfortable trot when she shifts into her New England local color mode: "Whoever has travelled in the New England States will remember, in some cool village, the large farm-house, with its clean-swept grassy yard, shaded by the dense and massive foliage of the sugar maple . . ." (187). "Miss Ophelia" emerges full-blown from this northern home, perhaps a self-portrait of the writer, or more likely, a portrait of her older sister Catharine: "Miss Ophelia, as you now behold her, stands before you, in a very shining brown linen travelling-dress, tall, square-formed, and angular. Her face was thin, and rather sharp in its outlines; the lips compressed, like those of a person who is in the habit of making up her mind definitely on all subjects; while the keen, dark eyes had a peculiarly searching, advised movement, and travelled over everything, as if they were looking for something to take care of" (189). This conscientous-to-a-fault female becomes a walking parody of Beecher's Treatise on Domestic Economy, for she insists on creating order out of the chaos of the St. Clare house. Cut in the mold of Dickinson's horror-filled matrons, Ophelia reads the domestic sphere symbolically: disorder in the kitchen emblemizes spiritual failure. And yet, as Ophelia admits at several junctures, despite her moral convictions and her domestic tidiness, she cannot love the black slaves who swirl around Augustine, Marie, and Eva. In a climactic emotional scene, reformed by Eva's beatific life and death, Ophelia asserts, "Topsy, you poor child . . . don't give up! I can love you, though I am not like that dear little child. I hope I've learnt something of the love of Christ from her. I can love you; I do, and I'll try to help you to grow up a good Christian girl" (349). Just as Uncle Lot had to overcome his New England cragginess and reticence, so Ophelia had to journey to the "gorgeous" South to melt her heart and experience Christian love for an afflicted race. The New England spinster can now reverse the course of the St. Clare subplot by returning to New England with the emblematic black, fully embraced by her northern soul. The local color sketch has itself been transformed by the little evangel.

In many senses, then, Ophelia's story-within-a-story marks an impressive effort by the writer to come to terms with her own and her region's racism. Stowe asserts that the solution to this moral failure lies in evangelical religion and domestic nurture. And yet Stowe's attempt to colonize American society with these values left her blind to a more profound racism, one that goes hand in hand with her claims for female power. Because Stowe assumed that her domestic ideology cut across class and racial boundaries, she was unable to critique the assumptions about race which permeated her culture. Put differently, Stowe did not attempt to alter beliefs about blacks because she did not see her racial assumptions as an *issue*. So it is that her text affirms what Carolyn L. Karcher calls "romantic racialism": "A product of the historical theories about 'inbred national character and genius' that the romantic movement had diffused, romantic racialism . . . dwelled on the contrast between the Anglo-Saxon and the Negro, but credited the Negro with moral virtues compensating for his alleged intellectual inferiority to the Anglo-Saxon."[73] Stowe unequivocally affirms this racial distinction in her "Preface" to the novel, indeed, in the novel's very first paragraph: "The scenes of this story . . . lie among a race hitherto ignored by the associations of polite and refined society; an exotic race, whose ancestors, born beneath a tropic sun, brought with them, and perpetuated to their descendants, a character so essentially unlike the hard and dominant Anglo-Saxon race . . ." (9).

Ironically, then, in the most important white treatment of slavery in antebellum America, the very ideology of white/black difference never becomes a central issue. That difference is simply taken for granted. In combination with her assumptions about gender difference and her middle-class respectability, this romantic racialism comprises the undialogized residue of Stowe's sophisticated novelizing tactics. In the current rehabilitation of *Uncle Tom's Cabin,* it is this explicit racism which has been most difficult to acknowledge. And yet, as critics such as Hortense Spillers remind us, it is all well and good to affirm the woman-centered power of the novel, but black women readers garner little comfort from the text.[74] We must supplement Stowe's daring novel with Jacobs's *Incidents in the Life of a Slave Girl,* a narrative that not only discredits stereotypical views of black women but that disavows a naive view of blacks as innately pious and "exotic." Indeed, as Dana D. Nelson has cogently asserted, ". . . in order for there to be a truly constructive confrontation of the issue of 'race,' there must be a direct dialogue with the heretofore objectified Other. . . . 'Whites' must learn to occupy a more humble position,

and seek out the voices and experiences of the victim/object of American racial history and representation."[75] We must seek out, in other
words, a sympathetic conversation between literary siblings. Only by
reading side by side, in a kind of diptych, Stowe's novel and Jacobs's
autobiography can we approach a rounded vision of the antebellum
American home. We must recall Linda Brent's complex interaction
with white women, her resentment toward Northern racism, and her
resistance to male authority, qualities that bespeak a complex personality interacting with an often ambiguous social world. We must in
effect establish a dialogue between Linda and Ophelia, a conversation
that would go beyond the morphology of religious conversion and
allow individuals to confront prejudice and fear. Only through such
a dialogue could Ophelia complete her sentimental education concerning racial prejudice. Only by attending to these voices, the discourse
of the black and the white woman, could the twentieth-century reader
return to the riven home of antebellum America, with all that it has
to teach us about our contemporary dilemmas.

5

Twin Parodists: Rapport and Rivalry between Southworth and Melville

IN HIS FAMOUSLY PARODIC NOVEL *PIERRE*, HERMAN MELVILLE savaged the "common novels" of the antebellum period. Attacking "their false, inverted attempts at systematizing eternally unsystemizable elements," Melville critiqued popular fiction on ontological and psychological grounds.[1] He notes not only their insistence on happy endings, but the tendency of "the countless tribes of common novels [to] laboriously spin vails of mystery, only to complacently clear them up at last" (141). In a novel subtitled "The Ambiguities," a text dedicated to metaphysical uncertainty and the epistemological crises produced by that uncertainty, such ontological clarity, such confidence about the nature of the world, could only cause abhorrence. Melville extends his analysis of popular writing throughout the outlandish plot of *Pierre*, sardonically implicating the readership in the creation of such falsehood, further attacking the style of genteel writing through a hilarious satire of the young Pierre's ephemeral writings, and finally, most controversially, characterizing the aspiring genius as an alienated figure in an overly commercialized culture. Though ". . . *Pierre* has been a book that there were none to praise and very few to love,"[2] Melville's argument has carried the day in literary scholarship of the American Renaissance, for on the whole we have accepted his reading of popular fiction and his covert attack on sentimentalism and its proponents, a scholarly blindness best described by Jane P. Tompkins in *Sensational Designs*. If we cannot accept the novel itself as a literary success, we can at least appreciate it as a tormented writer's *cri de coeur*, the purging of just frustration in the face of an indifferent, even hostile readership.

However, there are at least two problems with this treatment of *Pierre*. First, we must resist the temptation to read this novel as Melville's raw, unvarnished autobiography. Modern readers seem too easily seduced by the biographical reading of what is, after all, a satiricotragic portrait of a failed naif.[3] To put my point bluntly, Pierre

Glendinning is *not* Herman Melville, but rather a mannequin representing a false idealism powered by sexual drives unacknowledgeable
in the culture. More importantly, a close reading of the writings of a
major popular writer of the period, those of E. D. E. N. Southworth,
reveals that Melville's critique, while astute in some aspects, gives an
altogether misleading impression of at least this mode of "common"
writing. I have not selected Southworth randomly, but instead have
isolated a writer nominated by scholars as Melville's prime target for
satire. Ann Douglas, for instance, suggests that "*Pierre* may actually
be a parody of the legendary and tempestuous best-sellers cranked out
by women like E. D. E. N. Southworth in this period."[4] While it is
accurate to write that Southworth clears up mysteries, ends her novels
happily (on the whole), and never seriously challenges the ideology
of sentimentalism, it is also fair to assert that her novels are not
particularly interested in the metaphysical and psychological issues
Melville raises. Instead, Southworth directs her considerable fictional
flair (to utilize her alliterative style) to raise over and over again the
ethical and *political* questions surrounding women's lives in antebellum culture. Not surprisingly, then, Southworth's novels are by turns
subversive and orthodox, subversive in their questioning of false ideals
of female behavior, orthodox in the ultimate answers provided for
those questions.

No doubt Southworth espouses a "comic" worldview at odds with
Melville's avowedly tragic view, and yet her fictions share surprising
similarities with Melville's sardonic text. Indeed, both *Pierre* and
many of Southworth's novels of the 1850s[5] are ideal instances of
"perverse fictions." These texts share an impish disregard for propriety, veering instead toward carnivalized and gothicized representations of so-called "mainstream" values. In the process, Melville's and
Southworth's fictions utilize similar conventions: the failure of patriarchal figures, the degeneration of the pastoral estate, the immersion of
main characters in gothicized scenes, and the general satire on "sentimental" behavior. In effect these seemingly unrelated writers compose
in the same subgenre toward different ends. Both Southworth and
Melville work the vein of "highly wrought fiction," "which was the
domestic novel's antithesis: a feverish, florid, improbable, melodramatic, exciting genre."[6] Indebted to the Gothic school of fiction popular in both England and the United States, highly wrought novels of
the 1850s seem more specifically influenced by the novels of Emily
and Charlotte Brontë, and especially the former.[7] Furthermore, both
writers exploited the Shakespearian lineage of Gothic fiction, injecting
unmistakably Shakespearian rhetoric into their characters' pronounce-
ments. Finally, both writers display impatience with domestic fiction

which celebrates "the cult of true womanhood" and the middle-class home. *Pierre* and several of Southworth's fictions flout those domestic values, linking an overdone domesticity to repressed creativity by males and females alike. Though as I argued in the last chapter one cannot easily classify *Uncle Tom's Cabin* generically, an important strand of that novel is the domestic mode, the celebration of mother love and the nurturing home. Fictions by Southworth and Melville often read like perverse inversions of Stowe's novel. In sum, we must read Melville and Southworth as "twin parodists," for they parodize similar literary conventions, doubling each other's subversive tactics. However, their genders influenced the direction they took those subversive strategies, producing sibling rivalry along gender lines.

We must inevitably attend to another source of friction between Melville and popular writers, the tremendous sales that eluded him. Why did *The Curse of Clifton* and *The Hidden Hand* become bestsellers while *Moby-Dick* experienced at best moderate success? And furthermore, what claims can a Southworth novel make on us as readers in the late-twentieth century? Until this chapter's conclusion I will bracket these important questions in order to highlight the literary kinship between "competing" writers. To begin that process of rapprochement I focus on their professional struggles, arguing that it was not Melville alone who could cry, "Dollars damn me."[8]

I. VICISSITUDES OF THE MARKETPLACE: THE PROFESSIONAL MANEUVERINGS OF SOUTHWORTH AND MELVILLE

We are familiar with the account of Melville's development as a writer from 1845 to 1857, a narrative Melville himself largely wrote through his personal letters, "Hawthorne and His Mosses," and *Pierre*. It is the morphology of a Romantic writer progressing from naive to fully conscious genius, a genius inevitably at war with philistine culture. After the popular success of *Typee* and *Omoo*, Melville cast a satirical eye on his early writings, resenting his identity as "Typee Melville." He opted for an experimental novel with *Mardi*, but that performance met with an indifferent response, sparking the writer's anger that American readers had not found a place for his daring novel in their "Republic of Letters."[9] Following a professional retrenchment with *White Jacket* and *Redburn*, Melville once again broke free from commercial limitations in *Moby-Dick*, unquestionably his best book and one of the great fictions of the nineteenth century. This progress of the artist culminated in *Pierre*, yet another experimental text, a preposterous combination of melodrama and Shakespearian tragedy that is nonetheless a fascinating study of failed American idealism. But the savage response to *Pierre* by the reviewing establishment redirected Melville's energies toward a doubly duplicitous style of magazine writing exemplified by "Bartleby the Scrivener" and "Benito Cereno." The dense, difficult, thoroughly ironic *The Confidence Man* really marks a point beyond which Melville's fiction could not go, for that byzantine text essentially renounces the novel as a genre.

If Melville's dramatic account of the vicissitudes of the literary marketplace is well known, Southworth's is all but unknown.[10] In surprising ways this "American George Sand" followed the same professional path as Melville, and, like her sibling writer, told her story in melodramatic terms. (It would seem that the highly wrought style of their fiction carried over into their personal narratives.) In an autobiographical sketch, Southworth described herself as a loner by nature, given over to imaginative flights at odds with her family's orthodox values. Curiously Southworth casts this self-characterization in the schematic terms of "regular romance," converting her sister into the blond Angel of popular art and herself into the dark-haired troubled female: "[My sister] was a very beautiful child, with fair and rounded form, rosy complexion, soft blue eyes, and golden hair, that in after years became of a bright chestnut. She was of a lively, social, loving nature, and, as she grew, won all the hearts around her—parents, cousins, nurses, servants, and all who had been wearied to death with two years' attendance on such a weird little elf as myself—yes—and *who made me feel it too.*"[11] Southworth created a series of fictional surrogates for this "weird little elf" with Hagar (*The Deserted Wife*), Nettie (*The Discarded Daughter*), and Capitola (*The Hidden Hand*). Rather than writing against passion and the fantastic, Southworth claimed those very qualities for herself and her most compelling heroines. This little elf developed into a mature woman who suffered through a disastrous marriage: "Let me pass over in silence the stormy and disastrous days of my wretched girlhood and womanhood—days that stamped upon my brow of youth the furrows of fifty years—let me come at once to the time when I found myself broken in spirit, health, and purse—a widow in fate but not in fact—with my babes looking up to me for a support I could not give them."[12] Southworth turned to prose fiction as a means of support and so began her long career as one of America's most read writers. Her fiction registers her anger both at patriarchal demands on women and misleading descriptions of the middle-class marriage. As the narrator of her first novel declares, "Marriage is a sort of crucible, into which the ore of love is thrown, to be tried, whether it be good or whether it be evil. Happy is the marriage, when the pure gold of affection is found in the ashes, when the fire has burned out."[13] Southworth was especially sensitive to urban poverty suffered by abandoned women, as indicated by this passage from her relatively cautious novel, *The Lost Heiress*:

> Ellen's only friend in the city was Father Goodrich, and it was through his kind offices that she obtained as much needle-work as she could possibly do. And she worked steadily, from the earliest dawn of day, till twelve or one o'clock at night, while old Abishag took care of the house, the children and the lunatic grandmother. But alas! alas! what could one frail pair of woman's hands do towards supporting a family of six, when house-rent, and fuel, and lights, and food, and clothing were to be purchased for them all? Ellen worked very hard, but without making her family comfortable, without doing more than just keeping their souls and bodies together.[14]

Like Melville, then, Southworth had been "disillusioned" by life experience, a disenchantment registered in a number of her characters. She transcribes her life experiences into fiction, projecting both her suffering and her fantasies of power onto her characters. Rather than composing in the genteel, "smooth" style attributed to the young Pierre, she asserts her sometimes dark vision of female experience in high-flown language indebted to Shakespeare and the Brontë sisters.

However, Southworth's passionate self-representations and advocacy of women's self-reliance did not meet with universal acceptance. Indeed, reviewers felt uncomfortable with her fantastic plots and biting accounts of male/female relationships. Sarah Josepha Hale, the powerful editor of *Godey's Lady's Book*, sternly remarked that Southworth's first four novels were "written in a wild and extravagant manner, and occasionally with a freedom of expression that almost borders on impiety.... She seems carried, by a fervid imagination, in an enthusiasm for depicting character as it is actually found (in which she excels,) beyond the limits prescribed by correct taste or good judgment."[15] Similarly, a reviewer for *Harper's* discovered "an intolerable glare of gas-light; truth is sacrificed to melodramatic effect" in *The Discarded Daughter*.[16] Her editor at the *Saturday Evening Post* objected to her lack of decorum and threatened her "literary perdition."[17] If her sensational novels were indeed the obverse of the respectable domestic novels such as *The Wide, Wide World*, Southworth faced a potential professional problem: how to maintain her position as a credible writer for her female readership?

Analogous to Melville's retrenchment following *Mardi*, Southworth "tamed" her fiction following the publication of *The Discarded*

Daughter (ca. 1852).[18] Reading six of her early novels in sequence one is struck by a marked change in tone and characterization of women. While never completely sacrificing her theme of female self-reliance, Southworth toned down the melodramatic rant of her female protagonists, displacing that violent language to out-and-out villainesses or madwomen. She further highlighted accepted "feminine" values such as piety and domesticity. *The Curse of Clifton* (ca. 1852) is a faithful reproduction of the romantic conflict between the light-haired heroine and the dark-haired temptress. Kate Kavanaugh embodies the accepted values of mainstream periodical literature, while Georgia Clifton becomes the apotheosis of heretical rant. True to the formula made popular by Scott and Cooper, Kate survives to marry the humbled male protagonist, while Georgia dies a repentant woman. This summary oversimplifies the text to the extent that it downplays Southworth's interest in female "power." Not only is Kate the active protagonist in the fiction, but the male lead's mother, Mrs. Clifton of Hardbargain, exemplifies the self-made woman who has developed her own thriving farm without her husband's assistance. Still, one notices a telling contrast between *Godey's* review of *The Curse of Clifton* and Hale's displeased characterization of Southworth's first four novels:

> We should not do justice to our own feelings did we hesitate to confess how thoroughly, how deeply they were interested during the perusal of these volumes. The characters are all drawn with the greatest skill, and with all the truthfulness of nature. But that of the humble, the bashful, and uncomplaining Catharine [Kate Kavanaugh], strange as it may appear, is the most exalted, the most commanding, and, we might say, the most enchanting that we have seen drawn in a book of fiction for many a day. We do not think our readers will find fault with us for commending this work to their attention. We have the profoundest respect for truth in all things. But, although we have had many days of experience in this world, we do not see how such a fiction as this, if indeed it be all fiction, can do injury to pure womanhood, or to the honest manhood of any heart.[19]

Despite the reviewer's obvious discomfort with fiction itself, she unequivocally recommends *The Curse of Clifton* for inculcating suitably orthodox values. No wonder this text became Southworth's first "best-seller."

Two novels written on the heels of *The Curse of Clifton* also tame the more exotic qualities of the earlier fiction. In *India: The Pearl of Pearl River* (ca. 1853) and *The Lost Heiress* (ca. 1853) the influence of *Uncle Tom's Cabin* is unmistakable. This is no chance connection, for not only were Stowe and Southworth friends, but the *National Era* specifically mentioned Southworth's *Retribution* when advertising Stowe's novel.[20] In *India* Southworth openly advocates abolition and colonization, though she does not soft-sell the financial and psychological difficulties of this radical economic change. The title character is the voluptuous, dark-haired Southern aristocrat, India Sutherland, affianced to the idealistic plantation master Mark Sutherland. Converted by northern abolitionists to the cause of emancipation, Sutherland frees his slaves and leaves his plantation home to journey West as a lawyer and settler. While the haughty, spoiled India spurns him, the fair-haired, Eva-like Rosalie marries and supports him in this dramatic move. Though the consumptive Rosalie lives to the age of twenty-one, her beatific death bears all the hallmarks of Eva's saintly expulsion to Heaven. Ultimately proud India, reduced to poverty by a bad marriage and her father's financial misdeeds, earns Sutherland's love by working as a teacher in New York City. Thus Southworth narrates the familiar revivalist story of the proud sinner's conversion, a conversion directly linked to the cause of abolition. On the whole, Southworth eschews the passionate declamations of *The Deserted Wife* and *The Discarded Daughter,* granting India occasional bursts of fury along the lines of Georgia Clifton.[21]

In *The Lost Heiress* Southworth nearly depletes her fiction of her highly wrought style, producing what is surely one of her dullest novels. It is as though the novelist had determined to compose exclusively in the domestic voice with melodramatic plot twists for leavening. Once again her female protagonist signals her commercial designs: Augusta Hunter, an English aristocrat by birth married to Maryland's earnest governor Daniel Hunter, is all that one could hope for in conventional femininity: loving, pious, beautiful, patient, etc. Southworth modifies the iconography of popular art to the extent that she allows this dark-haired beauty to perform the function of pious heroine. The only moments of female passion are attributed to Norah O'Leary, a lower-class "genre" character who goes mad upon the unjust execution of her son William (an execution Daniel Hunter refuses to stay). Pursuing vengeance against the governor, Norah kidnaps the Hunters' daughter Maud, who is, then, "the lost heiress." However, Norah's deathbed confession to Augusta effects a reunion between mother and daughter, providing Southworth all the license she needs for a tearful celebration of mother-love. If Southworth's debt to Stowe is implicit in these familial scenes, her borrowing becomes explicit in a chapter entitled "The Last of Earth," an obvious echo of Stowe's chapter dedicated to Eva's death. Here Southworth describes the deaths of Daniel and Augusta, deaths that inspire the pious conduct of Maud and her fiancé, Falconer O'Leary. In contrast to fictions discussed below, *The Lost Heiress* raises few questions about patriarchal values, instead celebrating a continuity of ethical norms from the Hunters to their children.

And yet, despite this professional retrenchment during what I might call "the second phase" of Southworth's career, we know that she went on to compose the outlandish *The Hidden Hand* in 1859. Clearly this writer was no simpleminded follower of popular taste. While carefully adjusting her "product" to demands enunciated by the reviewing establishment, Southworth never completely abandoned her first impulses as a writer. Careful reading of select fictions from the 1850s reveals that Southworth possessed critical intelligence, savvy, and a commitment to her own artistic voice. In a sense *The Hidden Hand* is reminiscent of Melville's various experiments with two-tiered writing. Most famously in "Hawthorne and His Mosses," Melville theorized that a great tragic artist such as Hawthorne could fool his readership with "sunny" surfaces. The narrator of *Pierre* develops a similar argument in a sneering tone when describing Pierre's reading of Dante's *Inferno:* "Fortunately for the felicity of the Dilletante in Literature, the horrible allegorical meanings of the Inferno, lie not on the surface . . ." (169). Melville's increasing fascination with duplicitous writing seems to have coincided with his overwhelming experience of reading Shakespeare, a popular playwright who mouthed "the sane madness of vital truth."[22] Indeed, Melville's attitude toward Shakespeare and his art is strikingly similar to Emerson's in *Representative Men* (1850). Emerson develops the concept of the concealed genius when analyzing Shakespeare's relationship with his contemporaries, both "the groundlings" and the sophisticated literati: "A popular player;—nobody suspected he was the poet of the human race; and the secret was kept as faithfully from poets and intellectual men as from courtiers and frivolous people." But Emerson does more than speculate about the genius's relationship with his own time, for he theorizes about Shakespeare's use of popular conventions in creating his masterful art:

Shakspeare [sic], in common with his comrades, esteemed the mass of old plays waste stock, in which any experiment could be freely tried. Had the *prestige* which hedges about a modern tragedy existed, nothing could have been done. The rude warm blood of the living England circulated in the play, as in street-ballads, and gave body which he wanted to his airy and majestic fancy. The poet needs a ground in popular tradition on which he may work, and which, again, may restrain his art within the due temperance. It holds him to the people, supplies a foundation for his edifice, and in furnishing so much work done to his hand, leaves him at leisure and in full strength for the audacities of his imagination.[23]

It is quite possible that Melville knew this passage when he composed *Pierre*.[24] Though Emerson places far more emphasis on the genius's rapport with his audience, an emphasis that after all comports with the theme of "representative men," he may have provided Melville with an operative theory for combining popular appeal with intuitive insights into the metaphysical and psychological realities of nineteenth-century humanity. That is, Emerson argues for a "hollowing out" of the popular conventions to allow for universal, profound material. It is apparent that in his experimental *Pierre* Melville aspired to this cohabitation of the accessible and the arcane. Unfortunately for his pocketbook, he did not find a subtle narrative voice (in the Hawthorne vein) which could nimbly handle both these demands. As mentioned above, it would be in the magazine pieces of the 1850s that Melville found a means for effecting his two-tiered scheme.

The Hidden Hand relies upon a somewhat similar approach to the merging of popular with less conventional materials. Southworth was also deeply influenced by Shakespeare, for as one of her more conventional heroines, Hester Grey, asserts, "Shakspeare's [sic] divination of woman's nature, and delineation of woman's heart, is as wonderful as any thing else in his god-like genius"(*Retribution*, 62). As Hester's comment would suggest, Southworth responded to a different aspect of the master dramatist than did Melville. As we know from Charles Olsen's analysis, Melville was fired by the tragedies of Timon, Macbeth, Lear, and Hamlet.[25] Generally speaking he responded to the *textualized* writer rather than the performed text; that is, Melville found inspiration from the printed language of the master rather than the spectacle of the dramaturge. By contrast, Southworth imitated the staged dramas, with particular attention to Shakespeare's double plotting, alternation of serious and comic materials, and his mature comic heroines. Many of Capitola's speeches read like set pieces for antebellum popular theater, and indeed, *The Hidden Hand* "was dramatized in forty versions."[26] A glance at the epigrams for *The Hidden Hand* shows a predominance of quotations from the familiar tragedies (*Hamlet, Lear,* and *Romeo and Juliet*), mature comedies such as *Measure for Measure* and *Much Ado about Nothing,* and the mature romance *A Winter's Tale.* In tone and structure the 1859 novel has more in common with the comedies and romance than the tragedies, which supply familiar (and respectable) signals for the mood or action of specific chapters. For instance, similar to *Much Ado about Nothing, The Hidden Hand* follows two distinct but related plotlines: the "high" or serious plot focused on Clara Day, and the "low" or comic plot focused on the inimitable Capitola Black. Like Shakespeare's Hero, Clara is victimized by male oppressors, mainly in the form of the

villainous Colonel Le Noir, an able stand-in for Don John. So also
does Capitola fulfill Beatrice's role, for she is witty, self-directed, and
to a degree duped by love (after all Cap frees the outlaw Black Donald
because of a crush on this tall, dark, handsome male!). Cap is also
strongly reminiscent of Viola, the cross-dressing female protagonist of
Twelfth Night. Viola mixes "female" sentiment with "male" wit to
survive and even triumph in an often gloomy, demoralizing setting.
But of all the Shakespearian connections the most important would
seem to be that of *The Winter's Tale,* which transcribes the victimization of women and the ultimate repentance of Leontes for his sins
against Hermione. Not only in *The Hidden Hand* but in Southworth's
first phase of novel writing, male mistreatment of females is a recurring theme. These novels, then, are not as simple as Melville's dis-
missive comments in *Pierre* would suggest, for even as they provide
a fantasy resolution of female traumas, they openly describe those
distresses and bring them before the readership for censure. Hence
the overwhelmingly ethical bias of Southworth's woman-centered
writing.[27]

So far, then, I have claimed that Southworth was as equally indebted to Shakespeare as Melville, though she responded to the theat-
rical and comic possibilities of the playwright rather than the
textualized tragic possibilities. But in a fundamental sense Southworth's *The Hidden Hand* conforms to Melville's argument for a two-
tiered method, for it is apparent that Southworth plays Cap's and
Clara's plots against each other, with a decided preference for the
former. In other words, Southworth's novel is not an even-handed,
balanced treatment of the two storylines, but instead gives preference
to the daring, often subversive Cap. This comment leads us back to
my claim in the introduction to this chapter that Southworth's highly
wrought materials are perverse doubles for domestic fiction. Clara
Day is a quintessential "good girl" who gets into deep trouble because
of her passivity.[28] Cap, on the other hand, a veritable "imp of the
perverse" (she is described as "impish" and "perverse" at several points
in the novel), repeatedly courts physical danger, only to triumph time
and again. Indeed, it is Capitola who rescues Clara, and even teaches
her the ways of female independence, for Clara rides to freedom while
Cap stands in at her forced wedding! I suggest, then, that Southworth
is herself duplicitous in her popular novel, for she proffers the conventional models of female behavior (including Marah Rocke) only to
idealize their very opposite. It would seem that the sophisticated novelist had found a method for balancing her subversive and orthodox
materials in such a way that she could escape the censure that greeted

her earliest, most autobiographical texts. In effect she merged the writing of her first and second phases, with a decided bias toward the former. However, by putting the villainous Le Noir to death, clearing up the mysteries surrounding Traverse Rocke's and Capitola Black's births, and marrying off the main characters at the end, Southworth could get away with her subversive innuendoes.

If nothing else, this survey of Southworth's fictions calls into question the monolithic characterization of "common novels" presented in *Pierre*. Put in Bakhtinian terms, Southworth's texts are not monologic but full of heteroglossia, the multiple languages and ideologies of a culture. Dobson characterizes that multiplicity of voices when she describes the novelist's style in these terms: "Conventional pieties, personal passions, and radical departures from gentility intermingle in Southworth's work with an almost confounding sincerity, reflecting not only the author's intimate involvement with the values of her society, but also the complexity and self-contradictions inherent in that culture."[29] Thus, Southworth's fictions perform the function Bakhtin ascribed to the novel, that of encoding competing representations of social reality, creating a dialogic texture that resists simple closure. In the process Southworth held out the possibility of limited female independence, especially by carnivalizing narrow definitions of female conduct. Furthermore, as a professional writer who supported herself and her family (including the husband who deserted her) through her craft, she faced many of the dilemmas of "sincerity" Melville described so eloquently. Her solution seems to have been a "two-track" (rather than two-tiered) structure that allowed the reader to shift desire between poles of independence and conformity.[30] Quoting Melville's description of his attitude toward *Moby-Dick,* through the management of reader desire Southworth permitted her middle-class reader to relish "a wicked book, and feel spotless as the lamb."[31] The narrator of *The Hidden Hand* all but admits to this ploy in one of her many asides: "Reader! I do not defend, far less approve, poor Cap! I only tell her story and describe her as I have seen her, leaving her to your charitable interpretation."[32] The narrator puts on the mask of propriety only to peek out from behind and wink at the reader. This remark conforms to Southworth's many protestations that her wildly fanciful texts conformed to the actual. In reality her novels, most notably *The Deserted Wife* and *The Hidden Hand,* project vivid fantasies of female power. Part of that wickedness a reader experiences is attributable to a thorough critique of patriarchy in the novels of both Southworth and Melville, a subversive design to which we now turn.

II. VISITING THE SINS OF THE FATHERS UPON THE CHILDREN

To this point we have observed how both Melville and Southworth challenged genteel taboos through their duplicitous art. In a sense these writers are thumbing their noses at the critical "fathers" who would censure them, "fathers" such as Henry Petersen of the *Saturday Evening Post* and Evert Duyckinck of the *Literary World*. Their anti-patriarchal methods match a pervasive anti-patriarchal theme in their texts, for Melville and Southworth stubbornly assault the deforming values of cultural and political fathers. In surprisingly open ways, texts by these two writers interrogate the legitimacy (ethical and otherwise) of paternalistic figures, ultimately calling into question the Revolutionary heritage of antebellum America. These subversive themes emerge from the carnivalization of two classic American patri-archal genres, the New York epic and the plantation novel.

Melville attempts a comprehensive critique of patriarchy on onto-logical, political, psychological, and even generic grounds. The text openly speaks its subversive designs in the mincing Reverend Fals-grave's quotation of the Biblical injunction, "The sins of the father shall be visited upon the children to the third generation" (100). In its representation of this Biblical prophecy, *Pierre* can be read as Mel-ville's reprise of Cooper's Littlepage Trilogy in condensed form. In chapter 2, I showed the devolution of the Littlepage clan in the course of the three "manuscripts," a degeneration culminating in the decadent values of Hugh and Ro Littlepage in *The Redskins*. Set on the Dutch patroonships of upstate New York, Cooper's Trilogy, though projected as a defense of the landed gentry in the Anti-Rent War, concluded by deconstructing the aristocratic claims of that gentry, for the reader comes to see that the Littlepages are not Horatian pastoralists immune to the economic pressures of Jacksonian society but are themselves embodiments of the capitalist ethos of their culture.[33]

Melville perversely chose the same setting for his only "regular romance." Writing out of his own family heritage, he locates the young Pierre, "just emerging from his teens," on the Saddle Meadows estate of upstate New York. The pastoral setting allows the narrator to attack one of Melville's favorite targets, "pantheism," defined most clearly in a rousing letter to Hawthorne shortly before he took up the composition of *Pierre*:

> N. B. This "all" feeling, though, there is some truth in. You must often have felt it, lying on the grass on a warm summer's day. Your legs seem to send out shoots into the earth. Your hair feels like leaves upon your head. This is the *all* feeling. But what plays the mischief with the truth is

that men will insist upon the universal application of a temporary feeling or opinion.[34]

The "'all' feeling" and "pantheism" are Melville's terms for what Rus-kin called "the pathetic fallacy," the pervasive notion that Nature sympathizes with the self. The "Mast-head" chapter in *Moby-Dick*, which describes Ishmael's close brush with death through an optical and psychological illusion of Nature's benevolence, most clearly repre-sents this Romantic folly. At the beginning of his narrative, Pierre lives in a mirror world, a narcissistic never-never land, in which he cannot but help believe he is embowered in a sympathetic Nature and society. Mirror imagery abounds in the text (even Pierre's horses seem his twins!). Melville's narrator takes delight in washing the lacquer off this pastoralized mirror world to reveal the rather hideous inner workings of the patriarchal machine which supports it. Unlike *Moby-Dick*, which critiques pantheism almost exclusively on metaphysical grounds, *Pierre* explicitly challenges the political and economic foun-dation for an American form of pantheism. Poor Pierre is the hapless strawman in Melville's sardonic assault on the ideology embodied in the Dutch patroonships. In his analysis of the correspondences be-tween Glendinning's and Melville's genealogies, Michael Paul Rogin has established the relationship between pastoral estate and patriar-chal order: "Melville harmonized nature and patriarchy in the pastoral beginning of his tale, the better to destroy the family. . . ."[35]

We begin to see, then, that while *Pierre* occupies the same social terrain as Cooper's Littlepage Trilogy, Melville drives toward an even harsher indictment of that patriarchal heritage. After all, *Satanstoe*, the quintessential New York epic, celebrated Corny's personal and social maturation in the charmed, magical style of undialogized ro-mance. By contrast Melville's depiction of Pierre's ancestry demeans the patriarchal heritage, foregrounding the violence of the Glendin-ning clan.[36] Here the narrator "celebrates" Pierre's revolutionary gen-eration grandfather in mock heroic terms: "The grandfather of Pierre measured six feet four inches in height; during a fire in the old mano-rial mansion, with one dash of his foot, he had smitten down an oaken door, to admit the buckets of his negro slaves; Pierre had often tried on his military vest, which still remained an heirloom at Saddle Mead-ows, and found the pockets below his knees, and plenty additional room for a fair-sized quarter-cask within its buttoned girth; in a night-scuffle in the wilderness before the Revolutionary War, he had annihi-lated two Indian savages by making reciprocal bludgeons of their heads. And all this was done by the mildest hearted, and most blue-eyed gentleman in the world . . ." (29–30). In a novel devoted to parodic misprision of diverse representational strategies, this passage surely marks Melville's satire on the epicizing mode of Cooper's historical fiction. More generally Melville critiques the inflated presentation of military leaders in popular accounts of various American wars, including the Mexican-American War of the mid-1840s. The text recasts such popular iconography in a sneering tone by highlighting the presence of slaves and native tribes in the grandfather's world, suggesting that this is no mere "blue-eyed gentleman," but a powerful patriarch who ruthlessly wields his authority when necessary. The narrator explicitly correlates the old Pierre's political power to ontological concerns when he concludes this character sketch with the offhand remark that in his "meek, majestic soul, the lion and the lamb embraced—fit image of his God" (30). Pierre's disillusionment with his pantheistic youth will combine genealogical and religious doubts.

Thus, the Glendinning family has flourished through suppression of native tribes and through economic ruthlessness (class issues are foregrounded by Isabel's dependent status on the patroonship). Of course Melville's novel goes beyond a critique of the male ancestors, for *Pierre* satirizes "feminized" domestic values as well. Mary Glendinning represents the stultifying power of the domestic ideal. She colludes with the patriarchal past to suppress Pierre's latent anarchic drives, for it is Mary who enforces the idealized images of Pierre's grandfather and father. She further conspires with the insipid Falsgrave to inculcate a thoroughly sentimentalized religion in the impressionable Pierre.[37] The narrative presents her worldview in the double-voiced declaration, "Love is this world's great redeemer and reformer" (34). More blatantly the narrator undermines this affectional theory of the world by dismissing "the dreary heart vacancies of the conventional life" (90), a transparent hint that the intellectual, fervid Pierre would have no choice but to abandon Saddle Meadows. Ann Douglas has clear grounds for asserting that "in *Pierre* . . . Melville presents a savage study of the conspirational interaction between genteel religion, feminine morality, and polite literature against the interests of genuine masculinity."[38]

If *Pierre* is indeed the novelist's defense of masculine genius, then it achieves that apology through the tortured psychomachia of the main character, for this "hothouse" text examines the *psychological* effects of Glendinning patriarchal norms on a young American. On the one hand, Pierre is dominated by family legend, for he fetishizes such family relics as his grandfather's campbed and sword. On the other hand, Pierre desires liberation from the weight of that history. He finds justification for his break in his father's presumed infidelity (though Pierre can only infer that philandering from weak circumstantial evidence such as his father's deathbed rantings and "the chair portrait"). The Hamlet-like protagonist enacts both adulation and re- volt by claiming Isabel as his sister. That is, Pierre sublimates his rebellious rage into an apparently noble gesture, one which compen- sates for his father's neglect of his "daughter" while preserving his mother's illusions about his father's nobility. We discover, then, that his sentimental education allows him neither clear insight into his sexual drives nor an alternative to self-immolation. Pierre's "enthusi- astic" "crossing of the Rubicon" only compounds his psychological difficulties, then, for as Michael Davitt Bell has pointed out, "Pierre, having fully internalized the taboos of his culture and being thus incapable of rebelling consciously against ancestral authority, turns from the assertion of his buried self to benevolent rhetoric and, ulti- mately, by his guilty self-destruction, to fulfillment of the biblical prophecy."[39] Pierre's sublimation does not work; desire, both sexual and political, must out. Only the apocalyptic destruction of self, kin, and betrothed will fulfill that desire. Ultimately only extermination of the Glendinning family will end Pierre's patriarchal madness.

While less subtle and comprehensive than Melville in her critique of American patriarchy, Southworth is no less daring. From her first novel until the serialization of *The Hidden Hand,* Southworth persist- ently represented the sins of the fathers and the disastrous conse- quences of those acts for women and children. Her narrator openly espouses this view in this passionate declamation from *The Discarded Daughter:* "And what words are these to write! and what a position was hers when that divinely appointed parental authority—that pro- tective and beneficent power—was perverted by pride, ambition, and selfishness into an engine of mighty torture, inflicting a fatal and life- long calamity!"[40] Southworth's assault on patriarchy is patently clear in her first published novel, *Retribution; or, The Vale of Shadows* (ca. 1849). The novel's title refers to a curse placed on "the Vale of Shad- ows" because of atrocities committed by settlers against native tribes. For this reason the narrator quotes the same Biblical threat as Fals- grave, but with an ominous conviction lacking in the genteel minister's voice (23). This ancestral curse is fulfilled in the career of Colonel Earnest Dent, the novel's tragic protagonist. A Revolutionary War hero, Dent first marries, then abandons, a sentimental heroine, Hester Grey. As the narrator writes of this failed marriage upon the female character's death, "So Hester Dent, the loving, but unloved; the gentle, yet oppressed; the confiding, though deceived, was dead at last" (67). Dent's infidelities mar the heroic image of the founding fathers as devoted parents. Indeed, one cannot help thinking of Wash- ington's personal foibles when reading Dent's fictive history.[41] But

Dent's failures are not merely personal, for they represent larger political lapses, especially in the treatment of Indians and blacks. Most dramatically, Dent tears up a manumission order written by Hester upon her deathbed. (We have to remember that Southworth serialized her early fiction in the abolitionist *National Era*.) The male character's marital and political sins are figured in the decline of his Virginia estate. In a final prospect the once-pastoral Vale appears a pale imitation of itself: "What had wrought this change? When the soul departs, the body falls into dissolution. The soul of liberty and hope had departed from the model farm, and it was sharing the same fate" (106).

Retribution not only introduces the theme of masculine betrayal that recurs throughout Southworth's novels, but it also links that betrayal to the Southern plantation novel and its pastoralization of the "patriarchal institution." In chapter 3 I showed how Caroline Lee Hentz's *The Planter's Northern Bride* in particular converted the plantation into a macrocosmic version of the ideal American family, with the slave master as benevolent patriarch, his wife as affectionate helpmate, and the slaves as docile children. Earnest Dent's failed plantation is the moral retribution against the unkind master and father. In *India*, Southworth's most overt defense of abolition, the moral degradation of the Sutherland and Ashley families is imaged in the shocking decline of the Southern plantation. Here Mark Sutherland approaches his homeland after several years' absence in the middle West:

> It might have been the waning season, for it was now late in a dry and burning September; but the beauty and glory had departed from the vale. The luxuriant green freshness of summer had departed, and the brilliant and gorgeous magnificence of autumn had not come. All the vegetation— forests, and shrubberies, and grasses—was dry and parched in the sun, and the very earth beneath seemed *calcined* by the dry and burning heat. The springs, ponds, and water-courses were low, muddy, and nearly exhausted; and over all the sun-burned, feverish earth, hung a still, coppery, parching sky.[42]

Similarly, in *The Discarded Daughter* Southworth "signifies" upon the theme of aristocratic intermarriage common in plantation novels of the antebellum period. In *Swallow Barn*, for instance, John Pendleton Kennedy developed a lengthy (even tedious) subplot of Bel Tracy and Ned Hazard's courtship, a ritual that culminates in the linking of two estates through marriage. John Esten Cooke's *The Virginia Comedians* climaxes with the marriage between two plantation aristocrats, Champ Effingham and Clare Lee. By contrast, in Southworth's 1852 novel the villainous plantation master General Garnet, husband of and father to "discarded daughters," plots to marry his beloved Elsie to the neighboring plantation heir. When the noble Magnus Hardcastle is dispossessed by Lionel Hardcastle (originally thought to be dead), Garnet demands that his daughter shift allegiance from the former to the latter male. But the spirited Elsie refuses to go along with her father's social and economic ambitions: "[Garnet's] very neighbors and associates had fallen into the habit of yielding to his inflexible will; and here was a little girl of seventeen years of age, with positively her own notions of right and wrong, of faith and infidelity, of honour and dishonour—and telling him, with a high, unblenching cheek, and a clear, unfaltering voice, that she meant to abide by right, and eschew wrong!" (I, 161).

Elsie's self-reliant stand against her father's ambitions represents another important strand in Southworth's fictional weave: the novelist often links the subversion of male dominance to a critique of genteel female conduct. Various versions of Mary Glendinning appear in Southworth's novels, generally toward critique of that value system for its disempowerment of women. We can see, then, that it was not "genuine masculinity" alone which suffered under "the conspirational interaction" described by Douglas, but "genuine femininity" as well. Judging from Southworth's second novel, *The Deserted Wife* (ca. 1850), "genuine femininity" could only be realized outside the middle-class marriage. That message is driven home by the story of Hagar, one of Southworth's evident fictional surrogates. Raised on the Maryland heaths, herself a "weird little elf," Hagar develops an obsession with spirited horses and passionate rant. This nature's child (a predecessor to Isabel) comes under the control of Raymond Withers, a Hawthornian egotist who marries Hagar under the false pretense of matrimonial equality. The narrator describes the subsequent hierarchical power relations within the marriage: "It was curious; her very name and title were gone, and the girl, two minutes since a wild, free maiden, was now little better than a bondwoman; and the gentle youth who two minutes since might have sued humbly to raise the tips of her dark little fingers to his lips, was now invested with life-long authority over her" (78). This legal transformation brings about a psychological transformation in Withers, who insists that his wife keep her passions "latent" (89). Despite this injunction upon his wife's desires, Withers expresses his own passion for Rosalia Aguilar and thus betrays his marriage vows. So it is that Hagar becomes the deserted wife, abandoned with a child and no means of support. In a heroic recasting of her own rags-to-respectability story, Southworth narrates Hagar's rise to fame through her singing talent. Furthermore, Hagar returns to the Maryland heaths that nurtured her romantic soul, there to revive a country estate in a pastoralized reversal of Earnest Dent's masculine failure. In a characterization which antici-pates Maxine Hong Kingston's *The Woman Warrior,* Hagar combines her art of singing, pleasure in hunting, and delight in raising her child. As one shocked character remarks, "She has cut off her hair, and dresses like *a man!*" (148). In the end Withers does return to Hagar, a chastened man who must depend upon his wife's wealth. But this "happy ending" does not diminish the power of Hagar's suffering, for like Shakespeare's Viola, Hagar has passed through the transforming fire of loss and alienation.

These various anti-patriarchal maneuvers culminate in *The Hidden Hand.* This novel features several abusive male figures, most promi-nently Major Ira Warfield and Colonel Gabriel Le Noir. Warfield or "Old Hurricane," a veteran of an unspecified military campaign, rages and storms through the novel, yet another blustering male who must undergo an education in pity. Similar to Raymond Withers, he has deserted his wife Marah Rocke, in this case because he believes she has been unfaithful to him with Le Noir. Not only has he cast off this patient, suffering female, but he has spurned his only son, Traverse Rocke. Capitola educates him by returning rage for rage, abusive word for abusive word. In a truly funny parody of the demeaning patriarch, Cap takes Old Hurricane to task for returning to the plantation late at night: "DIDN'T you know, you headstrong, reckless, desperate, frantic veteran! *didn't* you know the jeopardy in which you placed yourself by riding out alone at this hour? Suppose three or four great runaway negresses had sprung out of the bushes—and—and" (128). This perverse imp, operating with the savvy of the streetwise urchin she once was, redirects abusive language at the general and openly names his character flaws. She uses humor much as Stowe utilized female wit in *Uncle Tom's Cabin,* toward the goal of discrediting destructive (mainly male-centered) ideologies. Much as the clever nar-rator of Stowe's novel double-voices the language of Senator Bird and Dan Haley, so Cap revises Old Hurricane's insulting language. However, one is not surprised to read that "Cap isn't *sentimental*" (175), for her behavior could not be farther from the norm of Stowe's mothers. She has far more in common with Hagar than with Mrs. Shelby. By contrast, the victimized Marah Rocke, Clara Day, and Mrs. Le Noir (Cap's mother) are painful reprises of the Griselda archetype, pure victims who implicitly argue for Cap's self-reliance. Ultimately, Melville questions the revolutionary heritage on the grounds that American forms of oppression make a mockery of the rhetoric of inde-pendence. Southworth prefers the less radical position of extending the rights enunciated in "The Declaration of Independence" to women

and blacks. If hers is a less extreme position, arguably it is more efficacious than Melville's. It is not surprising, then, that one of her favorite
words was "power," and that she applied it with conviction to such
diverse heroines as Kate Kavanaugh and Capitola Black.

III. Angels and Monsters in the Houses of Melville and Southworth

If Southworth and Melville enunciate similarly anti-patriarchal
themes, they also approach those arguments through a common
method: the gothicization of normalized, pastoralized settings and
characters. These writers share a strong regard for "the fortunate fall,"
the necessary plunge from innocence to experience, from a "sopho-
moric" overconfidence to a mature understanding of individual liabili-
ties and strengths. The Gothic mode of antebellum writing provided
an ideal vehicle for narrating this psychological process, as Frederick
Douglass's *Narrative of the Life of an American Slave* has demonstrated. However, we see a striking gender difference in Melville and
Southworth's handling of Gothic conventions. In *The Madwoman in
the Attic,* Sandra Gilbert and Susan Gubar have exposed the competing images of woman as Angel and Monster in the "patriarchal" tradition of Western writing. "Woman" thus combines qualities of the
ethereal and heavenly with attributes of the earthly and hellish. Furthermore, female writers of the nineteenth century were not immune
to this demeaning stereotyping, for fictions such as *Frankenstein* and
Jane Eyre replicate the typecasting. Indeed, *Uncle Tom's Cabin* utilizes
this dichotomy in the split between Little Eva and Cassy, the tragic
mulatto. As we shall see, *Pierre* largely conforms to this dichotomous
tradition, while Southworth's fictions on the whole subvert it. It
would seem that Southworth sought to bring her angels to earth and
her monsters to respectability, processes that would deconstruct rather
than affirm the Angel/Monster hierarchy.

I have described above the tortured progress of Pierre's psychomachia, his unfortunate fortunate fall into knowledge of ancestral
guilt, sexual desire, and the limitations of "the conventional life." This
bildungsroman requires a virtual gothicization of Mary Glendinning's
worldview. Melville narrates that Gothic degeneration through
Pierre's encounter with two female types, Lucy, the Angel of the
House, and Isabel, the mysterious "monster" who represents all that
is inscrutable in the cosmos.[43] While on the whole Melville utilizes
these types in an uncritical manner, he is sensitive to a dimension of
male/female relations that was taboo in his culture: sex. After all, it

is largely Pierre himself, nurtured in the sentimentalized worldview of his mother, who needlessly converts Lucy into an unapproachable Laura. Several of Lucy's gestures, most dramatically her flight to New York City to join Pierre, suggest a strong physical attraction to the male character. Furthermore, in the "climactic" vision of Enceladus, Pierre finally confronts the sexual pull toward Isabel, the repressed or latent drive that made him treat her as a victim of fate in need of his care. In other words, by filtering the stereotypical images of "woman" through Pierre's diseased mind, Melville intimates the dubious grounds for those icons.

Lucy is indeed the Angel of patriarchal tradition, for Pierre feels only remorse at the prospect of marrying her:

> This is to be my wife? I that but the other day weighed an hundred and fifty pounds of solid avoirdupois;—I to wed this heavenly fleece? Methinks one husbandly embrace would break her airy zone, and she exhale upward to that heaven whence she hath hither come, condensed to mortal sight. It can not be; I am of heavy earth, and she of airy light. By heaven, but marriage is an impious thing! (58)

From a Freudian perspective (and isn't *Pierre* the ultimate pre-Freudian novel?[44]), Pierre's treatment of Lucy can be linked to his vexed relationship with his mother. Ernest Jones's well-known analysis of Hamlet is useful here. The analogy between Pierre and Hamlet is of course not merely gratuitous, for the text calls attention to the literary kinship (135–36). Pierre seems most similar to Shakespeare's protagonist in his averred disgust with the carnal aspect of human nature. Thus, in Pierre's declaration that "marriage is but an impious thing" one hears an echo of Hamlet's soliloquy on "this too too sallied flesh." Given this correspondence between the characters, Jones's remarks are at least suggestive: "The underlying theme relates ultimately to the splitting of the mother image which the infantile unconscious effects into two opposite pictures: one of a virginal Madonna, an inaccessible saint towards whom all sensual approaches are unthinkable, and the other a sensual creature accessible to everyone."[45] This description suggests the curious mixture of "sibling" and "sexual" interaction between Pierre and "Sister Mary." Furthermore, the "rarefied" Lucy is Pierre's idealized self-image, a projection of the asexual "enthusiasm" for social justice he consciously adopts. As Douglas points out, "it is one of the greatest ironies of the novel that Pierre, while revolting officially against Mrs. Glendinning's code, is himself the Virgin Absolute of the story."[46] If, however, the male character cannot resolve the dichotomous image of "woman" into a single complex whole, and if he has learned to identify with the idealized, angelic image, and if further Lucy becomes the vivid icon of that purity, then Pierre's continued abstinence, especially with his betrothed, makes sense.

Isabel, then, the other half of this ambivalent female image generated by Pierre's mother, embodies the "earthly part" that is excluded from Saddle Meadows. She is, in other words, the quintessential Gothic "monster," for she is

> . . . a magical creature of the lower world who is a kind of antithetical mirror image of an angel. As such, she still stands, in Sherry Ortner's words, "both under and over (but really simply outside of) the sphere of culture's hegemony." But now, as a representative of otherness, she incarnates the damning otherness of the flesh rather than the inspiring otherness of the spirit, expressing what—to use Anne Finch's words—men consider her own "presumptuous" desires rather than the angelic humility and "dullness" for which she was designed.[47]

Isabel is truly other, truly uncanny, precisely because she *is* "outside of culture," a point made through her often incoherent, untrained, even idiot-like personal narrative. Imagery of primal landscapes, landscapes *prior* to cultivation, dominate her narrative, along with the mysterious music that is preverbal and strongly erotic. Most importantly for Melville's purposes, Isabel is "under . . . culture's hegemony" in the sense that her naive narrative reveals the primordial (that is, ontological) *ground* beneath the hothouse culture of Saddle Meadows: ". . . but somehow I felt that all good, harmless men and women were human things, placed at cross-purposes, in a world of snakes and lightnings, in a world of horrible and inscrutable inhumanities" (122). Associatively linked to such "ambiguous" natural phenomena as the Memnon Stone, Isabel expresses the metaphysical "Truth" that invalidates Pierre's moral earnestness. Furthermore, that metaphysical ambiguity, that psychological inscrutableness, is joined to an openly sexual appeal, for the narrator acerbically comments upon Pierre's physical attraction to his "bewitching" "sister": "How, if accosted in some squalid lane, a humped, and crippled, hideous girl should have snatched his garment's hem, with—'Save me, Pierre—love me, own me, brother; I am thy sister!'—Ah, if man were wholly made in heaven, why catch we hell-glimpses?" (107). Thus, the narrative ironically confirms Pierre's earlier self-distrust, for the narrator explicitly describes the protagonist's "hellish" part. Finally, like the "monsters" of tradition discussed in *The Madwoman in the Attic*, Isabel is "presumptuous" in her behavior, for she openly seduces Pierre and later, when Lucy arrives in their crowded apartments, reveals her possessiveness. She insists that they act like husband and wife in front of Lucy, ultimately forcing Pierre to recognize the charged physical relationship they share but which has apparently not been consummated.[48]

Just as Isabel conforms to the monster archetype in behavior and symbolic import, she literally replicates two grotesque characters from British literary tradition: Lady Macbeth and Mary Shelley's eloquent creature. In her heroic, seductive pledge of allegiance to Pierre, Isabel echoes the scheming Lady to her Macbeth: "Thy catching nobleness unsexes me, my brother; and now I know that in her most exalted moment, then woman no more feels the twin-born softness of her breasts, but feels chain-armor palpitating there!" (160). Rarely one to understate his irony, Melville underlines the hypocritical public relationship between male and female by placing the word "brother" in Isabel's mouth, an obvious substitution for the more appropriate "lover" or "husband." Isabel's duplicity consists in her avowal of an "unsexed" relationship, a relationship that is in reality anything *but* unsexed. True to his perverse strategies throughout the novel, Melville calls into question the idealized sibling relationships of antebellum culture.[49] Given Shakespeare's misogynistic characterization of women not only in *Macbeth* but in *King Lear* and *Hamlet,* perhaps it is less surprising that Southworth would turn away from the tragedies toward the comedies for inspiration.

Isabel also doubles Shelley's monster in the telling of her tale, for like the tormented product of Frankenstein's frenzy, Isabel tells a mysterious tale of growing up parentless, the ultimate orphan in search of a home and a genealogy.[50] Like his Gothic predecessor, Melville attempts to trace "the growth of a character's mind" (to roughly paraphrase Wordsworth's famous subtitle for *The Prelude*), but with this critical difference: Isabel's ambiguous story is wholly lacking in the sophisticated literary education described by the male monster, suggesting once again the "pre-cultural" import of the female character. Of course Melville gains certain thematic advantages by casting Isabel's narrative in these "uncouth" terms, such as foregrounding Pierre's willful assertion of brotherhood in the face of inconclusive evidence. That is, Isabel's inscrutable narrative squarely places responsibility for interpreting their relationship on Pierre, who then accedes to their sibling relationship out of the confused motives of idealism and revolt. Thus, the difference in sophistication between Melville's and Shelley's monsters is partly attributable to competing metaphysics and divergent ethical implications. However, we cannot miss the gender implications as well, for while the maturing male character recapitulates the history of Western civilization, the female character

remains wholly natural, wholly witchlike. Put differently, Isabel
makes no claim on the reader's sympathy through her pathetic story,
for she remains altogether "other," chaotic and undefined. And at no
point in the novel is that "ambiguity" firmly resolved; she appears a
cypher to the end. Though the analogy may strike one as ludicrous,
Isabel is *Pierre*'s version of the great white whale, the hieroglyphic
natural phenomenon that triggers the tragic protagonist's torment and
death. As Rogin has described her, "this savage child is the return of
the dispossessed child of nature."[51] Appropriately enough, then, upon
their death this natural force embowers the male character, now transformed into an exact image of the Memnon Stone: ". . . her long hair
ran over him, and arbored him in ebon vines" (362).

Melville's "dark lady" is never granted a fully defined, articulate
subjectivity. By contrast, Southworth's fictions create "monster" females who are fully expressive, complex personalities who progress
toward respectable marriage. It is as though the female writer, indebted to Stowe's overtly sentimental tactics in her second phase, had
chosen to place Cassy's marginalized narrative at the center of her
more subversive texts. After all, Cassy exploits Gothic conventions
to drive the oppressive master to madness, a tactic that culminates in
her reunion with her lost children. If, as Leslie Fiedler claims, Cassy
is the forgotten character in our memories of *Uncle Tom's Cabin*,[52]
Southworth's Hagars and Capitolas make "female Gothic" unforgettable. Ultimately, Southworth's Gothic tactics both reaffirm a female
tradition of Gothic writing and generally revise the male tradition.

It would be misleading, however, to assert that Southworth entirely
escaped the angel/monster stereotyping that ensnared other women
writers of the nineteenth century. In *Retribution*, for instance, she
creates the ultimate *femme fatale* in Juliette Summers, the beautiful
antagonist to Hester Grey. Cast in the molds of Lady Macbeth and
Catherine Earnshaw, Juliette repeatedly affirms her identity as
"temptress." Following the pattern of Georgia Clifton in *The Curse
of Clifton*, Juliette asserts rather than denies her "hellish" character:

". . . between [Earnest Dent's] wicked passion for my wicked self, and his
compunctious affection for his fading wife, his soul is made the scene of a
civil war. He can't abandon his passion, and won't abandon his integrity.
Verily, a most unhappy condition. Truly, one should be a faithful servant
of God, or a thorough-going ally of the Devil, to get along tolerably well
in this world." (60)

Juliette's "wicked self" infects more than Earnest Dent's susceptible
mind, for the narrator confesses to an uncontrollable attraction to the

character: ". . . I am fevered and excited with this dark Juliette, with whom one can not even deal without danger of receiving and communicating evil. She comes upon me like a fiend, or a fit of insanity; so I wish to hurry on to the end of her story, and be done with her" (97). We have returned to the narrator's winking denial of responsibility for Capitola in *The Hidden Hand,* for this passage manifests Southworth's duplicity as she suggests the powerful fantasy appeal of the self-directed, fully independent villainess. More than that, the narrator's confession of attraction intimates that even when male and female writers utilize similar female types, they do so toward different ends. Whereas Isabel remains a "flat" symbol in Pierre's struggle between the Good and Bad Angel, Juliette becomes the embodiment of the narrator's desire for power. Southworth features other "monstrous" females in *The Deserted Wife* and *The Lost Heiress,* but once again toward different ends than those exemplified by Melville. In the former novel, Nancy Withers, abandoned by her husband because she has been raped, "haunts" John Withers' life. She becomes the repressed victim who uncannily returns to claim justice, a futile gesture which culminates in her drowning. As discussed earlier, Norah O'Leary, a powerless Irish immigrant, takes the only action that makes sense to her when she kidnaps the charismatic governor's infant daughter. In such scenes Southworth's Gothic females have a great deal in common with the Bertha Mason developed by Jean Rhys in *Wide Sargasso Sea,* a female character uprooted from her Caribbean home because of the financial maneuverings of a petty, selfish Rochester. Her vengeful act of burning down the house strikes the reader as a sane alternative to maddening imprisonment.

If Southworth reorients the madwoman archetype toward woman-centered concerns, she also precisely challenges a male Gothic tradition that represents women as pure victims. In Matthew Lewis's *The Monk,* the hapless Antonia suffers violation and death at the hands of the damned Ambrosio, an action that inspires some of Lewis's most sensational and lurid prose. In Poe's "The Fall of the House of Usher," the maddened brother buries his twin sister prematurely, an apparent attempt to end a nightmare of doubling for the product of an inbred family. Southworth often challenges male Gothic by subverting conventions of male oppression of females in horrific settings. *The Discarded Daughter* exemplifies her counter-Gothic strategies, for repeatedly female characters elude entrapment and even death at the hands of males. Elsie, forced into the attic by her enraged father, asserts the bride's right to consent to marriage, extending Southworth's theme of female self-reliance, especially in the matter of marriage. Rather than developing into the maddened, imprisoned Bertha archetype, Elsie gains her freedom through her eloquence, a freedom that allows her to marry her betrothed despite her despotic father. Later in the novel Southworth virtually rewrites "The Fall of the House of Usher" from a female perspective. In a melodramatic sequence, Elsie and her husband Magnus journey to the burial chamber of her "dead" mother Alice, only to discover that the unconscious woman is still alive! We later learn that General Garnet, in a fit of rage, had knocked Alice unconscious, and believing her dead, had buried her prematurely. Southworth continues her revision of Poe by having Alice return by night to her husband's home, where the guilt-ridden male suffers remorse over his "homicidal" act. When Garnet confronts his shrouded wife on the stairs, he believes her ghost has returned to haunt him, collapses, and dies.[53] Unlike Poe's tragic denouement, however, *The Discarded Daughter* grants Alice a happy ending when she marries her first love, a pious minister. Once again we are led to speculate that Southworth rejected the tragic in favor of the comic precisely because the former tradition granted female characters so little status, so little power. In a final dramatic revision of the male Gothic tradition, the spirited Nettie is trapped on a deserted island during a storm and there threatened with rape by Lionel Hardcastle. Similar to Southworth's other patriarchal characters, he represents his sexual violence as an opportunity to demean the "haughty" female: "'Ha! trapped, palsied, helpless!' he exclaimed, exultingly, 'where is now your vaunted independence? your pride? your scorn? gone! quite gone! why, so much the better. You will make the better wife for the loss of that'" (II, 115). However, Hardcastle's triumph is cut short when yet another maddened woman returns to wreak vengeance upon the male. Agnes Seabright (her name links her with another of Lewis's victimized females), having escaped from years-long captivity by pirates, looms up out of the darkness and kills the would-be rapist. So it is that the reputed female monster liberates her younger sister from male violence.

At the same time she revises the male tradition of Gothic, Southworth extends a distinctive female practice of writing exemplified by the fictions of Radcliffe and Emily Brontë, writers who grant their female characters the freedom to travel (literally or metaphorically). As Ellen Moers has written of "female Gothic," specifically with reference to novels such as *The Mysteries of Udolpho* and *The Italian*:

For Mrs. Radcliffe, the Gothic novel was a device to send maidens on distant and exciting journeys without offending the proprieties. In the power of villains, her heroines are forced to do what they could never do alone, whatever their ambitions: scurry up the top of pasteboard Alps, spy

out exotic vistas, penetrate bandit–infested forests. And indoors, inside
Mrs. Radcliffe's castles, her heroines can scuttle miles along corridors,
descend into dungeons, and explore secret chambers without a chaperone,
because the Gothic castle, however much in ruins, is still an indoor and
therefore freely female space. In Mrs. Radcliffe's hands, the Gothic novel
became a feminine substitute for the picaresque, where heroines could
enjoy all the adventures and alarms that masculine heroes had long experienced, far from home, in fiction.[54]

Southworth must have "conned [her] novel-lessons" (to borrow Melville's phrasing in *Pierre*), for several of her heroines demonstrate
Moers's generalization. In *The Deserted Wife*, for instance, Hagar becomes the living and breathing embodiment of "the traveling heroine":
"More than ever she took to the desolate scenes around her native
hall. She made wider excursions upon the bay, and deeper inroads
into the forest—in the wild wantonness of her nature she would scale
the most difficult rocks, and skim along the edge of the most fearful
precipices, or climb the tallest trees . . ." (45). Capitola Black conforms
to the Gothic heroine even more dramatically, though there is a parodic quality to Gothic effects in *The Hidden Hand*: "Southworth's
basic and brilliant maneuver . . . is to begin the novel with the old
gothic machinery . . . and then to subvert the genre by introducing
this streetwise and self-reliant female prankster."[55] Indeed, both out-
doors and in, Cap is anything but helpless in the face of Gothic terrors.
Two paradigmatic scenes demonstrate her intense pleasure in the supposedly disabling encounter between the male aggressor and the female victim. In a chapter entitled "Cap's Fearful Adventure," the
heroine encounters Craven Le Noir (son of the villainous Colonel) in
a desolate stretch of countryside as night falls on the sublime Virginia
landscape. Alone and seemingly vulnerable, Cap is approached by "a
gentlemanly ruffian about forty years of age, well dressed in a black
riding suit; black beaver hat drawn down close over his eyes; black
hair and whiskers; heavy black eyebrows that met across his nose;
drooping eyelashes, and eyes that looked out under the corners of the
lids; altogether a sly, sinister, cruel face, a cross between fox and tiger!"
(115). Aware of her danger, Cap cleverly procrastinates, feigning interest in the ruffian's advances but delaying their fulfillment. In a ballad-
like style replete with incremental repetition, Southworth rewrites
"La Belle Dame Sans Merci," for the playful "faery child" here evades
the aroused male. Finally Cap pretends to stop and prepare for a
sexual liaison, convincing the "craven" male to place his saddle blanket
on the ground so that she can sit comfortably. Once Le Noir has

removed his saddle, Cap rides off unpursued. The narrator describes Cap's victory with a familiar mixture of delight and put-on shock:

> Hearing the shout, the lash, and the starting of the horses, the baffled villain turned and saw that his game was lost! He had been outwitted by a child! He gnashed his teeth and shook his fist in rage.
>
> Turning, as she wheeled out of sight, Capitola—I'm sorry to say—put her thumb to the side of her nose, and whirled her fingers into a semi-circle, in a gesture more expressive than elegant. (118)

The narrative virtually duplicates this episode in the encounter between Cap and the imposing Black Donald inside her bedroom at Hurricane Hall. The legendary ringleader of a band of thieves, Black Donald has pursued Cap throughout the novel, first under a contract to murder her, later out of a powerful erotic attraction. In the late-night encounter he would seem to have it all his own way, for he has trapped Cap in an isolated part of the house while most of the servants are away. Cap's motives in this action are less clear than in the earlier encounter with Craven Le Noir, for she has demonstrated her own physical attraction to the dashing outlaw, an attraction she explains by commenting to him, "I always *did* like people that made other people's hair stand on end!" (386). Rather than dreading the Gothic moment this protagonist all but embraces it. Nonetheless, she once again uses her guile to escape rape. As Black Donald slowly removes his clothing, Cap tries to talk him out of his lust, urging him to turn from his hellish desires toward heavenly repentance. (Even the impish Cap is an evangel in the Stowe school.) Little does Donald realize that Cap has seated him on a trapdoor which leads to a Poe-like bottomless pit, one that she believes would plunge the male character toward hell. Despite these qualms of conscience, Cap will not relent on her self-reliance, even for the alluring Donald. When he refuses to repent of his desires, Cap sends him to perdition: "The outlaw shot downwards! There was an instant's vision of a white and panic-stricken face, and wild uplifted hands as he disappeared, and then a square, black opening was all that remained where the terrible intruder had sat" (393). This is a prototypical instance of female vengeance against the Gothic villain, but the protagonist does not relish her victory, for "Capitola turned and threw herself, face downwards, upon the bed, not daring to rejoice in the safety that had been purchased by such a dreadful deed, feeling that it was an awful, though a complete victory!" (393). In contrast to Lewis's Ambrosio, she cannot luxuriate in the abuse of others. Eventually Cap learns that Black Donald has not been killed, and she even helps him to escape hanging.

Thus, our Gothic heroine need never stand accused of murdering a fellow mortal. She has experienced the heights and depths of terror without ever harming a single soul.

I earlier claimed that Melville and Southworth shared a fascination with the necessary (if not always fortunate) fall, and further, that gothicized incidents aid and abet that process. In Pierre's case it is apparent that Isabel's mysterious story thoroughly estranges the maturing patriarch's pastoral world, for she speaks out of a psychological and economic background of which he is thoroughly unaware. Isabel manifests psychic pressures repressed in Mary Glendinning's official narrative, and so projects Pierre on his futile search for an alternative philosophy to replace his sentimental faith. If Pierre is a representative American male, his fall exemplifies a necessary fall for Young America into a knowledge of political and theological terror. In this sense Pierre's Gothic education continues in the surreal episodes in "The First Night of Their Arrival in the City," a Poesque chapter that describes not only Glen Stanley's cruel rejection of his cousin but the abusive and abused inhabitants of the city's street culture.

Southworth puts her heroines through a similar process of gothicization, though finally they arrive at a mature self-possession. It would seem that for Southworth the Gothic allowed her female characters the scope to explore their self-reliance and the opportunity to confront male oppression head-on. Through their trials and triumphs in Gothic settings, her female protagonists discover the terrors that await women in a patriarchal culture and the very means for survival despite those terrors. Hagar, for example, begins life as a self-reliant elf on the Maryland heaths, only to come under the Gothic tyranny of her husband Raymond. Ultimately she incorporates that youthful freedom and knowledge of evil into her mature adult character. Similarly, Nettie in *The Discarded Daughter* progresses from a literal elf in a tree to a fully controlled, disciplined adult woman who is willing to sacrifice her fortune for moral duty. Her grim encounter with Lionel Hardcastle contributes to that maturation by revealing both her courage and her vulnerability. In a striking sense, then, Southworth's mature heroines are reminiscient of Hawthorne's Hester, the most famous "dark woman" from pre-Civil War American writing. Like Hester, these characters are not static symbols, neither "angels" nor "monsters," but are fully conscious, complex, sometimes ranting characters who develop in the course of their narratives. But where do they come to a rest? What value system finally governs their adult roles? To these questions we must now turn, for it is on these grounds that the differences between these twin parodists become unavoidable.

IV. SIBLING RIVALRY BETWEEN SOUTHWORTH AND MELVILLE

Despite their shared aggressions and perverse tactics, Southworth and Melville also shared an intense literary rivalry. I do not claim that they consciously assaulted each other but that these two writers, male and female, represented *classes* of antebellum writers that waged discursive warfare, a conflict we observed in depth in *Uncle Tom's Cabin*. That discord is apparent in the texts themselves, painfully so in the case of *Pierre* and implicitly so in Southworth's more daring fictions. It is suggestive that her male characters' paternalistic diatribes often focus on women's intellect, as in General Garnet's snide aside on his wife Alice's pretensions to knowledge: "'A little learning is a dangerous thing.' It makes any one conceited—especially, I think, a woman who has few opportunities of comparing her ignorance with other people's knowledge . . ." (109). Furthermore, these two writers could not escape gender issues in their professional lives, for as Southworth had to contend with her male editors, so Melville felt the need to woo a female readership typified by his Berkshire neighbor Sarah Morewood.[56] In a culture with clearly defined spheres of male and female conduct, a phenomenon described by astute foreign observers such as Frances Trollope and Alexis de Tocqueville, writers would no doubt experience anxiety attempting to cross over from one sphere to the other. That anxiety could turn into outright resentment, as most famously demonstrated by Hawthorne's letter to William Ticknor concerning "the d—d mob of scribbling women." However, as I have attempted to demonstrate in this chapter, we must not be too quick to assume an undiluted scorn between male and female writers. It is at least suggestive that Melville allowed Lucy to attempt her art of portraiture in New York City, thereby granting her a degree of artistic license. It is equally telling that Southworth balances against her villains sensitive, philanthropic male characters who make suitable husbands for her maturing heroines. Apparently the two sexes really could not live without each other in antebellum literature and life.

But granting a complex of emotions swirling around competition between male and female writers, what precisely were the grounds for dispute between Melville and Southworth's texts? We immediately recall Melville's financial struggles, his painful recognition in the early 1850s that he was not making a living at his writing. But of course that comment begs the deeper question, which is simply: why didn't Melville sell more books when Southworth was able to establish financial independence through her writing? That question in turn leads us to the readership for these novels. In her reader-response approach to pre-Civil War fiction, Jane P. Tompkins has theorized that these consumers demanded a strong dose of reform and religious sentiment.[57] Time and again Southworth provides that elixir, for amidst her sensational narratives she sprinkles prescriptions for reform. Indeed, she is careful to frame her narratives in easily conceptualized issues such as the evils of premature marriage and the psychological pitfalls of jealous passion. She thus grants her readers a didactic rationalization for reading what are often downright fun books.[58] The savvy Melville was by no means unaware of his readers' predilection for the didactic and the reformist, for he gave them large portions of both in *Redburn* and *White Jacket*. In *Pierre,* a novel dedicated to satirizing enthusiastic philanthropic gestures on the grounds that they often emerge from "hellish" rather than "heavenly" parts, Melville does not even attempt to supply that didactic fix.

In another important study of readers and romance literature, Janice Radway has argued that contemporary American female readers of Harlequin romances discover a blend of the subversive and the conformist in those fictions that comports with their own aspirations *within* patriarchy:

> Romances purport to be open-ended stories about different heroines who undergo different experiences. They manage such a suggestion by using the conventions of the realistic novel, which always pretends to be telling the as-yet-uncompleted story of a singular individual. Despite this realistic illusion, however, each romance is, in fact, a mythic account of how women *must* achieve fulfillment in patriarchal society. . . . By reading the romance as if it were a realistic novel about an individual's unique life . . . the reader can ignore the fact that each story prescribes the same fate for its heroine and can therefore unconsciously reassure herself that her adoption of the conventional role, like the heroine's, was the product of chance and choice, not of social coercion.[59]

Of course this reading model cannot be applied directly to Southworth's fictions because of differences in historical milieu between contemporary and antebellum readers. Nonetheless, Radway's argument seems relevant to Southworth's novels, first, because she rightly emphasizes the "realistic" quality of women's romance writing, a realism embodied in graphic urban scenes (such as the depiction of urban poverty quoted earlier), historical fact, and careful description of even exotic foreign scenes. As Radway suggests, such mimetic qualities construct a bridge between the fantasy elements of women's romance and the reader's life. The critic's assertion that modern romances grant female readers a comforting illusion of choice also seems pertinent when reexamining Southworth's heroines, for curiously, despite their

radical gestures of revolt against overweening patriarchs such as Garnet, "Old Hurricane," and Le Noir, time and again her female protagonists opt for respectable marriage. Hagar, the woman warrior of
Southworth's fictions and in my view the most complex image of
antebellum woman projected by the fictions discussed here, finds fulfillment as a mother and a wife. Kate Kavanaugh, the noble heroine
of *The Curse of Clifton,* demonstrates all the qualities of the self-
reliant female, even rescuing the often hapless romantic lead, Archer
Clifton. And yet, in the end, she recoups her gentility and marries
the man she has earned through her pious labors. Perhaps most shockingly of all, Cap marries Herbert Greyson at the conclusion of *The
Hidden Hand,* though the reader is relieved to learn from the narrator
that she "know[s] for a positive fact, that our Cap sometimes gives
her 'dear, darling, sweet Herbert,' the benefit of the sharp edge of her
tongue, which of course he deserves" (485). Can Southworth imagine
no other option for her vivid heroines than marriage? After all, the
writer herself, despite an extended relationship with a man following
her husband's desertion, never remarried and so modeled a kind of
professional independence. In part the modern reader can justify
Southworth's happy endings by attending to genre, for if she is indeed
writing in the Shakespearian comic tradition, then surely such endings
are a prerequisite. But that seems too simple an answer, for as Dobson
writes, "While Southworth obviously adores her nonconforming
heroine, her true real-life ideal would seem to be a conventional
woman who adds to the domestic virtues the integrity and self-
reliance of Capitola."[60] In the sensational, fervid, *earnest* prose of her
novels, Southworth does indeed reaffirm the "conventional woman"
of middle-class respectability, while allowing that woman to hollow
out a space of *relative* independence in patriarchy. There is no question
that her female protagonists should marry, but Southworth would
add that they should marry the men of their choice at an appropriate
juncture in their lives. Despite the melodramatic pyrotechnics of her
plotting, then, Southworth reinscribes the domestic power espoused
by Catharine Beecher.[61]

Perhaps late-twentieth-century readers would prefer a more radical
writer (I speak autobiographically here), and yet there is something
compelling about Southworth's mixture of the radical and conventional, a combination that does not seem cynical though at times disingenuous. Ultimately, Southworth believed both in the Revolutionary
legacy of freedom and the sentimental ideology that undergirded the
reformist culture of antebellum America. In this sense the writer demonstrates my claim in chapter 1 that writers created their perverse
fictions out of a desire to extend the rhetoric of equality to their own

social subgroups. Southworth's savaging of cruel fathers and gothiciz-ing of women's experience function much as Stowe's carnivalizing humor, which disarmed the hierarchical politics of male social leaders toward the larger goal of affirming female sentimental power.

The Herman Melville of *Pierre* believed in none of this, for finally he could not believe in any foundational ethics other than the kind dramatized in *King Lear,* in which the blind supply comfort to the blind in a savage world. Put simply, Melville deconstructed the senti-mental ideology of his epoch. He did so by revealing the violence concealed behind the blue eyes of Pierre's powerful grandfather, by exposing the hypocrisy of Mary Glendinning's family narrative, and by describing an alternative, pre-Freudian psychology powered as much by sex as by "affection." Furthermore, he did not succeed in veiling these critiques behind the fantastic plot elements taken over from highly wrought fiction, for he *foregrounds* the literary quality of those conventions. In the overripe pastoral opening, in the over-wrought narrative of Isabel, in the "spasmodic" description of Pierre's psychomachia, Melville adds a heavy ironic overlay which is nearly unavoidable on first reading. Curiously, it was a reviewer for *Godey's* who most appreciated Melville's tactics, for despite the requisite moral objection she observes, "It may be, however, that the heretofore intel-ligible and popular author has merely assumed his present transcen-dental metamorphosis, in order that he may have range and scope enough to satirize the ridiculous pretensions of some of our modern literati."[62] Here the reader has responded to Melville's tactics of *de-familiarization* of literary convention, his overbearing repetition of those motifs toward the goal of estranging not only the conventions themselves but the *conventional life* that lies behind those literary qualities. Melville never grants his reader the room to daydream or fantasize as he had in *Typee* or *Moby-Dick*. His double-voiced novel makes a mockery of fiction, all but destroying itself in the process of its making. No wonder modernist critics have been drawn to a text for which "there were none to praise and very few to love," as Brod-head has put it. *Pierre* is a textbook study in the modernist strategies made famous by the Russian Formalists. However, I reiterate my argu-ment that the novel's commercial failure need not convert us into Melville's apologists. This creative writer took a wild risk with *Pierre;* on the whole he seems to have succeeded at his original design, despite the irruptions of satire toward editors and readers in the chapters dedicated to Pierre's juvenilia.[63] After all, if Pierre died his senseless death in the Tombs, Melville went on to write some of his best fiction over the next five years. The writer did not die with his character, nor did he necessarily sympathize with the premature attempt to write a great book. Melville had served his own apprenticeship in five full-length narratives before attempting *Moby-Dick*. Pierre was the artist Melville might have become but did not.

Indeed, Brown has argued that Melville saw masculinity and the marketplace as incompatible terms: ". . . the relation between author and market that *Ruth Hall* [or *The Hidden Hand*] forges exemplifies the literary commerce from which Melville would extricate the (male) author."[64] To understand that seemingly self-destructive logic, we must attend to David Leverenz's thoughtful account of images of manhood in the antebellum United States. He contrasts three versions of masculinity, the patrician, artisan, and middle-class (entrepreneurial), emphasizing that the Jacksonian era witnessed the rise of the last and its conflict with the two earlier definitions. Thus, during the pre-Civil War years "manhood becomes a more intense anxiety."[65] Melville seems to have experienced this "anxiety" fully, perhaps because he was torn between the patrician and capitalist definitions of his masculinity. Though bereft of social status in his adolescence, he seems to have clung to its trappings, especially in his theory of "Genius," the potent "Truth Teller." From the perspective of the patrician artist, the marketplace would appear petty, vulgar, obscene. In light of this self-image, Melville's frequent complaints about dollars damning him take on added significance. And yet, like Cooper and the plantation apologists, Melville could not deny his necessary transaction with the capitalist economy. Furthermore, in a kind of rage toward his failed father, he assaulted genteel patriarchy through his savage parody of the Glendinning family. We can speculate, then, that the boundless ambiguity, duplicity, and downright confusion of *Pierre* arose from Melville's confounded sense of himself as a man in antebellum culture.

To highlight the competing values of these sibling writers, I want to conclude by attending to a remarkable coincidence of naming and plotting between *Pierre* and *The Hidden Hand*. In this intertextual encounter we see full-blown the blindness and insight of Southworth and of Melville. To this point in my discussion of Southworth's most famous novel I have all but ignored Cap's mother, the unfortunate Mrs. Capitola Le Noir, sister-in-law of the infamous Colonel. And yet she is another of those madwomen in the attic who populate nineteenth-century fiction, yet another Bertha Mason incarcerated for her crimes of womanhood. Indeed, Mrs. Le Noir's offense was giving birth to Capitola, the heiress who would strip Le Noir of his fortune. For her "crime" this woman in white has been imprisoned in the attic of the Hidden House, there presumably to remain until her death. But the appearance of Cap on a mission of mercy (and curiosity) toward Clara Day inspires the mother's desire for freedom, culminating in her second abduction by Le Noir and her incarceration in an insane asylum outside New Orleans. Remarkably (for our purposes), Mrs. Le Noir has been given the pseudonym Mademoiselle Mont de St. Pierre. She is, in a sense, Pierre's identical twin, the female wounded by life and trapped in an asylum that may be seen as a microcosm of the world itself. Similar to Pierre, she has been disillusioned, having lost her romantic love to her brother-in-law's violence. Her world has been profoundly gothicized by experience.

But the doubling of texts becomes even more uncanny, for it is Traverse Rocke, the discarded son of Old Hurricane, now a young physician who has lately returned from the Mexican-American War, who takes up the cause of this unfortunate "maniac." If Melville's Pierre is a parody of the New Testament Peter and is himself destined to return to the inanimate condition of the Memnon Stone, Southworth's Rocke appears the Rock of Ages, an antebellum Christ who heals suffering in both a physical and a mental sense. Indeed, unlike Pierre, who is trapped by the Memnon Stone, this male character *traverses* the rock of Mrs. Le Noir's mystery to effect justice. He does so by granting the suppressed woman the opportunity to tell her story for herself; it is Rocke who listens to the narrative of this slave and takes that account seriously. In short, this idealized male character allows Mrs. Le Noir a personhood, an autonomy, a subjectivity that all other males had denied her. Mrs. Le Noir must in some sense be a facet of E. D. E. N. Southworth, the Southworth who was psychologically wounded by her husband's desertion and her poverty. She is also an alternative version of the preverbal, dream-like Isabel who remains more a natural force than a fully-defined character. Mrs. Le Noir has a *history,* and she tells that story with the understated bitterness of a mature, assured, Christian mind. Clearly she knows whereof she speaks. As if to underscore the correspondence between the Pierre/Isabel and Traverse/Mrs. Le Noir plots, Traverse proposes that the injured but beautiful Madam (the male character himself repeatedly calls attention to her beauty and its effect upon him) live with himself, his wife, and his own suffering mother. The more experienced Mrs. Le Noir replies, "Boy, . . . do you know what you are promising—to assume the whole burden of the support of a useless woman for her whole life! What would your mother or promised wife say to such a proposition?" (447). In that last sentence she hints at the sexual implications of an arrangement in which she might well appear Rocke's mistress. But safely ensconced within a sentimental ideology, Rocke dismisses these innuendoes, assuring the wronged woman that he acts philanthropically. While Pierre's encounter with Isabel inspires a tortured reexamination of all his beliefs, Traverse's engagement with a female "Pierre" becomes the occasion to reaffirm his ethical norms. As Mrs. Le Noir remarks, invoking the term that is so crucial to Pierre's tragedy, "I see that life has not deprived you of a generous, youthful enthusiasm" (448). Ultimately, this ethical test becomes a moot point, for Traverse discovers the real identity of his patient, who turns out to be the victim of his hated enemy and mother to his friend Capitola. In a sense the narrative rewards the kind male for his ethical enthusiasm by bringing all complications to a resolution.

As Stowe's domestic ideology remained the undialogized residue of *Uncle Tom's Cabin,* so Southworth's faith in the powers of sympathy remains fully pastoralized. Capitola Le Noir's Gothic nightmare is replaced by the beatific image of her reunion with her daughter at a refurbished Hidden House. The ghosts have indeed been exorcised, making way for "a fair amount of human felicity" (485). Moreover, that happy issue is made possible by efficacious benevolence motivated by asexual drives. For Melville the Gothic terrors afflicting his protagonist are everywhere and nowhere.

If Traverse Rocke's Christ-like conduct rewrites Pierre's Gothic tragedy, so Melville in a sense parodically anticipated Rocke's story in "Benito Cereno," the ironic narrative of mindless benevolence insisting upon universal justice. In the concluding scene between Amasa Delano and Benito Cereno, the American captain argues for a pantheistic vision of the world as kind at the core and cruel only in its aberrant moments. Cereno's mordant, simple reply is "The negro," referring not only to violent race relations but to the reality of duplicitous evil at work in the world, an evil to which Delano is wholly blind. For Melville it was this blindness to the ambiguous moral and metaphysical worlds that infuriated him about "common novels." For Southworth "the regular romance" was more than a means to earn a living; it was the vehicle for narrating the partial liberation of her heroines from patriarchal domination. In a sense these sibling writers wrote past each other, utilizing similar conventions toward different ends. By listening to their voices in chorus we hear the urgent longing for a cultural space that would grant expressive power to both men and women.

Conclusion: The Fall of the House of America

I

As EDGAR ALLAN POE SUPPLIED THIS STUDY A POINT OF DEPARTURE, so he provides the sense of an ending. One could imagine no more appropriate writer for this task, for what other fictionist in the literary history of the United States has so eagerly anticipated the apocalypse?[1] What other writer has so luxuriated in the prospect of doom, of that final judgment followed by release into an exotic if factitious Neoplatonic afterlife? Of course, we are used to reading Poe's tales as symbolic testaments to psychological crises rather than as sociological exposés; yet as "The Imp of the Perverse" implicitly assaulted a sentimentalist consensus on the psyche, so "The Fall of the House of Usher" covertly challenges American confidence in the enduring edifice of the United States constructed by founding fathers working with the Constitution as blueprint. Lewis Simpson for one has suggested that Poe's most famous short story is in part the anxious Southern writer's vision of the destroyed plantation.[2] More recently, Joan Dayan has asserted that "we need to reread Poe's romantic fictions as bound to the realities of race. . . . There is a logic to his excessive attention to blood, things dirtied, and bodies mutilated. Lurking in every effusion of ennobling love is the terror of literal dehumanization . . . the reduction of human into thing for the ends of capital."[3] Poe himself was immersed in the intertextual conflicts over the Republic, revealing in explicit and implicit ways his complex fate of being a Southerner. We should not forget, then, that Madeline Usher can be compared to slaves in her bondage, humiliation, and suffering.[4] We can extend these political readings of that peculiar narrative to encompass the class, gender, and racial issues discussed throughout this study.

But what precisely is wrong with Roderick Usher? And why does he refuse to release his sister once he becomes aware that she is alive? The narrator, the reader's surrogate who duplicates Usher's madness in the course of the story, makes the source of Roderick's insanity apparent from the start: the nightmare of all-encompassing doubling.

As the narrator approaches the House of Usher, he observes its similarity to a human face, complete with its "vacant eye-like windows."[5] The correspondence between the master and his dwelling is immediately apparent. But the image of this personified house is again replicated in the tarn, now with an uncanny effect: ". . . I reined my horse to the precipitous brink of a black and lurid tarn that lay in unruffled lustre by the dwelling, and gazed down—but with a shudder even more thrilling than before—upon the remodelled and inverted images of the gray sedge, and the ghastly tree-stems, and the vacant and eye-like windows" (318). As if to underscore the double significance of the gloom-inspiring Gothic mansion, the narrator further informs the reader that the house's "appellation . . . seemed to include, in the minds of the peasantry who used it, both the family and the family mansion" (319). And so it goes throughout the story. We next learn that Madeline is Roderick's *twin* in an inbred aristocratic family, a doubling that assures a psychic bond between the siblings. Furthermore, Roderick doubles himself in his poem, "The Haunted Palace," a virtual reduplication of the House of Usher and its twin master. Finally, the narrator enters this web of mirroring completely in the climactic episode, for he unwittingly takes up a narrative (Poe's hilarious version of medieval romance) that literally re-presents the action going forward in the homicidal relationship between brother and sister.

Thus Roderick Usher is trapped at the center of an unstoppable process of doubling. He knows that the inevitable outcome of his relationship with Madeline will be procreation of yet another generation of Ushers, who will themselves be images of the male character. Locked in a solipsistic, narcissistic, incestuous mirror world, Roderick takes the only action short of suicide that makes sense: he puts his catatonic sister in the vault, more hoping than believing she is dead. Usher's action virtually assures the end of his family line; at least at a metaphoric level, once Roderick banishes his sister to the vault, the House of Usher must fall because it has no issue to extend it. As readers tend to remember long after perusing the tale, Roderick realizes his sister is alive in the vault: "Long—long—long—many minutes, many hours, many days, have I heard it—yet I dared not—oh, pity me, miserable wretch that I am!—I dared not—I *dared* not speak!" (334). In part, no doubt, this sham aristocrat (another of Poe's images of the gentleman he himself could not be) could not humble himself before his boyhood friend to admit so catastrophic a mistake. After all, this ultimate narcissist would serve his vanity in a crisis. More importantly, having secured his sister in the distant part of the house, he will not free her to threaten his mental stability again. Once she has been imprisoned, why release her and risk sexual intercourse? Poe does not downplay the male violence of Roderick's decision, for the narrator informs us that the "temporary" tomb "had been used, apparently, in remote feudal times, for the worst purposes of a donjon-keep" (329).

Madeline's return from the grave is Poe's perverse revision of the central Christian story, Jesus's return from his burial cave. The sister's "resurrection" symbolizes female vengeance against the oppressive male, a vengeance that culminates not in redemption but in the collapse of master and house: "For a moment she remained trembling and reeling to and fro upon the threshold—then, with a low moaning cry, fell heavily inward upon the person of her brother, and in her violent and now final death-agonies, bore him to the floor a corpse, and a victim to the terrors he had anticipated" (335). Ironically Roderick's dread of coupling with his sister is all but fulfilled, but only in an embrace of death. That homicidal union assures the literal death of the Usher line, a significance driven home by one of the most famous images in American writing: "While I gazed, this fissure rapidly widened—there came a fierce breath of the whirlwind—the entire orb of the satellite burst at once upon my sight—my brain reeled as I saw the mighty walls rushing asunder—there was a long tumultuous shouting sound like the voice of a thousand waters—and the deep and dank tarn at my feet closed sullenly and silently over the fragments of the 'House of Usher'" (335–336). So it is that Roderick's mirror world is irrevocably destroyed; primal nature has claimed even the fragments of the Usher line, calling back to primordial being the hyper-refined, inbred Usher progeny. The ending symbolizes the victory of the pre-cultural over the cultural; it returns us to *Pierre* and the other perverse fictions studied here, fictions that time and again threaten or provide the apocalypse for which Roderick longs.

Poe's unforgettable story presents in an extreme way (as only Poe can) the issues and motifs that have structured this study. "The Fall of the House of Usher" figures the perversity and incestuous obsession of antebellum prose. After all, Roderick is himself afflicted by the imp, for why else would he insist on burying his sister in a temporary tomb rather than assuring her destruction through permanent burial? Perhaps a modicum of decency, of moral compunction, restrains him from effecting his murderous intention. Or, more likely, he cannot put an end to his desire for his sister, despite the longing to end his madness of doubling. He finds a halfway measure between enacting her destruction and withholding her from dissolution. That halfway measure is a perverse countermove to his dominant desire for freedom from the Usher funhouse.

The texts studied here have quite literally doubled the action of Poe's story. Cooper's Littlepage Trilogy narrates the devolution of the Littlepage "house" upon its approach to the historical present. The concluding narrative overturns the Littlepage claim to social leader-ship by characterizing the latter-day Littlepages as materialistic ego-tists. Hugh and Ro mirror the all-consuming male vanity of Roderick Usher. The internecine struggle between plantation novels and slave narratives anticipates the apocalyptic destruction of the master's "Big House," for Douglass and Jacobs become surrogates for the repressed Madeline, returning from the hell of slavery to articulate their auton-omy and indict the slave regime. Though their death struggle with dehumanizing racism provides only a partial victory—the abolition of chattel slavery—it is nonetheless a victory. Stowe's pangeneric, panregional novel foreshadows a more encompassing destruction, the destruction of the house of America itself, the just retribution for an American family that has failed its responsibility. In Stowe's eschata-logical vision, Legree's inverted plantation house can be seen as the microcosm of the larger Gothic mansion of "America," haunted by the multiple Cassys who will seek vengeance for inhumane suppres-sion. And finally, both Southworth and Melville proffer visions of the fallen house, in the former case, the house of an overweening, unquestioned patriarchy, in the latter case, the house of Glendinning, brought down by the incestuous struggle between Isabel and Pierre. Time and again these writers image in less overt ways Poe's apocalyp-tic falling house.

In part these fallen houses symbolize the collapse of the dominant antebellum subgenre during the 1820s and 1830s, the complex histori-cal novel. In effect prose of the 1840s and 1850s brought down the house of Marmaduke Temple. Divided between claims to epic idealiza-tion and historical "realism," these novels generally supplied an ideo-logical foundation for the anxious young nation, virtually providing a *history* or *pretext* for the culture. These were by no means simple-minded affirmations of the past, for novels such as *The Pioneers* and Lydia Maria Child's *Hobomok* (1824) raised ethical issues surrounding settlement of the wilderness and suppression of native tribes. On the whole, however, these narratives allowed American readers to inhabit comfortably the houses of their fathers. In the reformist culture of the last two decades preceding the Civil War, writers turned from the past to the present as the primary field of analysis. Emerson's call in *Nature* for attention to the present rather than the past signaled this shift of perspective, a shift powered by the Jacksonian emphasis upon the people and a "leveling down" democracy. A text such as Orestes Brownson's *The Laboring Classes* (1840), written in the aftermath of the disastrous Depression of 1837, provides another benchmark of this altered focus, for Brownson demands attention to the immediate problem of class inequities within a supposedly egalitarian society. Brownson's diatribe not only suggests the broader turn toward social issues, but it indicates the new interest in specific class issues within the culture, an interest that is reflected in the diverse subgenres examined in the preceding chapters.

This reformist culture replaced the house of Temple with Uncle Tom's Cabin. Stowe's novel inevitably typifies the new emphasis on immediate social issues, but one could also point to the slave narratives, Southwestern humor tales, novels by Fanny Fern and Susan Warner, and even Melville's *Pierre,* which though superficially located in the past speaks to immediate cultural and social issues. Cooper's Littlepage Trilogy exemplified this fall into time, this plunge into history, in his successive narratives of the Littlepage clan. Hawthorne also mirrors this progression in his three novels of the early 1850s, which move from Puritanical Boston to contemporary Salem to nearly contemporaneous Brook Farm. E. D. E. N. Southworth's novels provide a somewhat more complicated case, for the writer persistently locates her highly wrought, sensational narratives in past epochs, generally preferring to include scenes from conflicts such as the War of 1812 (*The Curse of Clifton*) and the Mexican-American War (*The Hidden Hand*). However, despite this gesture toward the romantic "neutral territory" defined so famously by Hawthorne, Southworth does not develop the historical settings for the action, focusing instead on her female characters' struggles for independence, especially in heterosexual relationships. Southworth's settings are atemporal while her narratives are very much centered on the gender issues of the writer's own time. Finally, writers such as William Gilmore Simms continued to churn out historical novels in the Cooper tradition, but that generic choice seemed increasingly retrograde in the 1850s, the gesture of a pro-slavery advocate who wished to rewrite the American past to incorporate the peculiar institution.

It becomes clear, then, that the rivalrous fictions of the antebellum United States replaced the gentrified mansion with a humbler version of "the American home." But Poe's symbolic narrative suggests that even this more fraternal America suffered apocalypse during the Civil War. To begin to understand the impetus for this second fall, we can turn to another canonical text from pre-Civil War culture.

II

Just as Poe's "The Fall of the House of Usher" is arguably the most famous short story from the antebellum epoch, Lincoln's Speech to

the Republican State Convention in 1858 provided the most memorable *figure* for the political crisis moving the United States inexorably
toward civil war:

> "A house divided against itself cannot stand."
> I believe this government cannot endure, permanently half *slave* and
> half *free*.
> I do not expect the Union to be *dissolved*—I do not expect the house
> to *fall*—but I *do* expect it will cease to be divided.
> It will become *all* one thing, or *all* the other.[6]

In an era officially dedicated to the home as the site of nurture and
reformation, Lincoln's evocation of the house must have held special
power for his contemporaries. Indeed, Lincoln was repeatedly asked
to explicate this speech, a task he deferred by referring his questioners
back to the original text. Either Lincoln considered his metaphor transparent, or else he cannily avoided literalizing his argument by paraphrase. In one such letter of response Lincoln contrasted the house of
the United States to a conventional marriage, which after all can be
dissolved by divorce in a nondestructive way. Thus the future president suggests that the national home is even more sacred than the
idealized private sphere.

But did Lincoln thereby prophesy the doom of the American house,
much as Stowe does in her "Concluding Remarks" to her novel? At
least in the texts of his speech and letters, the prospective President
claimed quite the contrary. Lincoln believed the house would be pre-
served, the issue would be settled, but that it would take a crisis to
heal the division within the American family. No doubt Lincoln hoped
for a political rather than a military climax, and yet even in his relatively areligious rhetoric the argument for a providential purging of
national sin can be detected. Following this line of analysis, the Civil
War was not a "fall" at all but a necessary stage in the spiritual and
political regeneration of the United States. We should substitute the
term "millennial" for "apocalyptic" in describing such an interpretation of that oxymoronic "civil" war, for the painful catharsis of conflict
should produce a better America, not a sadly reduced nation.

From the point of view of the younger Henry James, however, the
Southern War for Independence was indeed a fall, but a fall into
knowledge of good and evil, and thus the dispersion of that most
endurable American dream, the vision of innocence. As James wrote
of Hawthorne and his cavalier treatment of slavery:

> Like most of his fellow-countrymen, Hawthorne had no idea that the
> respectable institution which he contemplated in impressive contrast to

humanitarian "mistiness", was presently to cost the nation four long years
of bloodshed and misery, and a social revolution as complete as any the
world has seen. When this event occurred, he was therefore proportion-
ately horrified and depressed by it; it cut from beneath his feet the familiar
ground which had long felt so firm, substituting a heaving and quaking
medium in which his spirit found no rest. Such was the bewildered sensa-
tion of that earlier and simpler generation of which I have spoken; their
illusions were rudely dispelled, and they saw the best of all possible repub-
lics given over to fratricidal carnage.[7]

An almost ideal witness to the transformation of the United States
by the war, a scion of antebellum idealism and advocate for postbellum
critical acumen, James suggests another way of reading Lincoln's metaphor of the house, a way that returns us to Poe's uncanny narrative.
James's reference to "fratricidal carnage" reminds us that the Civil
War was universally viewed as a *sibling* struggle, a kind of incestuous
death wish within the American family romance. As we have seen
throughout this study, pre-Civil War culture elevated sibling relations
above heterosexual marriage. To return to Larzer Ziff's analysis of
The Blithedale Romance:

> As a response to increasing depersonalization in their daily lives, Ameri-
> cans would appear to have fantasized fulfillment of the qualities they felt
> to be missing, and to have done so in terms of family bonds that were, at
> the time, dissolving. To be married figuratively to one's sibling was to be
> safe from outside forces. When those forces caused a person to stray, then
> the counterforce was visualized as familial, most commonly an avenging
> sibling.[8]

Taking Ziff's cultural analysis to its logical limit, the Civil War can
be seen as the ultimate instance of "avenging siblings" punishing their
ideological rivals. But as I have already suggested, that fraternal violence did not emerge from a vacuum but was anticipated in antebellum
culture, in particular by the narratives discussed in this study. We
have witnessed imaginative anticipations of the dire sibling conflict
described by James.[9] With the exceptions of Cooper and Kennedy,
the writers analyzed in the preceding chapters were virtual contemporaries, struggling to claim discursive precedence within the house of
American narrativity. Interestingly, brother/sister relationships were
extraordinarily important to these writers. As she revealed in her
Incidents, Jacobs felt a strong bond to her brother John (given the
pseudonym "William" in the narrative), a male who must follow a
different route to freedom than the concerned mother. In *Ruth Hall*,
Fanny Fern attacked the male vanity of Hyacinth Ellet, a parody of her

brother Nathaniel Willis.[10] By contrast, Stowe was deeply attached to her brother Henry Ward, who perhaps served as a model for her idealized male figures. As a final example, Melville's sisters apparently figured large in his conception of his first book, for "passages in *Typee* were obviously written as a way of teasing his household of sisters."[11] These biographical glimpses suggest that fraternal relations influenced the narratives, for siblings appear in fictional guise as either fools or role models.

Not surprisingly, then, at times these writers served as loyal adher-ents to their narrative siblings, such as in Stowe's overdetermined repetition of slave narratives in *Uncle Tom's Cabin*. More often, how-ever, these brothers and sisters assaulted each other's texts through parody and even derision, explicitly claiming equality in the ideal American home but implicitly demanding ascendancy. Jacobs must in some way challenge the claims of Douglass and Stowe, for both writers reduce the female slave to a melodramatic victim; similarly, South-worth must defame male Gothic and the tragic mode, for both trans-form woman into the dichotomous angel/monster. Clearly there was a great deal at stake, rhetorically and politically, in these narratives, for one is struck by the discursive violence of so many of these texts. It is not sufficient to point to a crude taste for the melodramatic and horrific in antebellum prose; as David S. Reynolds asserts, that overt violence marks a turbulent, troubled culture, indeed "divided" along class, racial and gender lines,[12] a culture pursuing but not achieving the Emersonian, pantheistic "'all' feeling" affirmed by Lincoln and satirized by Melville.

From this perspective, as Poe had projected in his haunting narra-tive of 1839, the American house did in fact fall. It fell precisely because of repetition compulsions within the culture that were analo-gous to Roderick's nightmare of doubling. One has a sense upon x-raying the dialogic narratives of writers such as Cooper, Jacobs, and Stowe that recurring contradictions had surfaced for which the cul-ture had no practical solution. The contradiction between Cooper's claim for the American gentleman and an emerging capitalist economy was so palpable that the apologist himself could not complete his defense of his social class. And yet, that character type reappears in various fictions discussed here, in both parodized and affirmative forms, as though American writers could not surrender the idealized patriarchal figure. Perhaps the brothers and sisters felt abandoned by the fathers of America and glanced back longingly at iconic images such as Pierre's grandfather. Similarly, the contradiction between the legal definition of the slave as subhuman and the cultural recognition of intelligent, resourceful black persons tore at the fabric of antebellum narratives, producing strained defenses of the status quo and frenzied counterassaults. As a final instance, we can note the contrapuntal themes of woman as cultural mother and woman as self-reliant individual. Even Stowe, supposedly the most conscious advocate of sentimental power, contrasts the dangerous passivity of Emmeline with the aggressive self-help tactics of Cassy.

The Civil War did not resolve these issues but only exacerbated them. While the war forever sealed the fate of a landed gentry in the United States, it empowered a class of financiers who asserted a similar kind of cultural ascendancy. So also in the disastrous racial politics of Reconstruction and after do we see the repetition of these prior compulsions, these antecendant dilemmas. Finally, as dramatic narratives by women writers suggest, "the woman question" was far from resolved by the war. And yet, James asserts that the war precipitated "a social revolution as complete as any the world has seen." To discover that new social order in postbellum culture, we must attend to the redefinition of the American home by late-nineteenth-century writers. If indeed the American home fell during the war, later writers rebuilt it, but with a stunning difference from its predecessor dwellings. A brief tour of that late-nineteenth-century version of "America" will provide a final perspective on the narrative rivalry of the antebellum epoch.

III

Recollecting the protagonists of postbellum literature, especially those populating narratives of the 1890s, one is struck by the number of orphans and unhappily married characters: Huckleberry Finn, Bartley Hubbard, Sister Carrie, Edna Pontellier, McTeague, the narrator of "The Yellow Wallpaper," Isabel Archer, Undine Spragg, etc. These names suggest a cultural epoch in which the sentimental home has been abandoned as a lost cause. Kate Chopin's *The Awakening* demonstrates that leaving that "home" was not a simple psychic process, for the narrative focuses on two contrasting structures: the home of the husband/patriarch Leonce, and "the pigeon house," Edna's private sanctuary. The "awakening" woman must abandon her husband's house, a repository of idealized images of her roles as wife and mother, in order to affirm her desires for sex and power. Her quest for the latter collapses when Robert refuses her offer of a sexual relationship, resulting in Edna's controversial death. Despite Edna's "defeat" by bourgeois respectability, her tale of two houses symbolizes a larger redefinition of "power" and psychology within the culture, a redefinition that provides a new idiom for describing the troubling conflicts that divided the pre-Civil War house of America.

Eric J. Sundquist both exemplifies and hints at the foundation for this new idiom when he writes, "Not Captain Ahab but the Captains of Industry were the new cultural embodiments of heroism. If we only see this clearly in retrospect ... it is because we live in the society that they—as forefathers do—made possible and necessary, and therefore feel more fully the psychological implications of the transfiguration of 'father' and 'family' into 'boss' and 'corporation.'"[13] Sundquist points to "the incorporation of America" that Alan Trachtenberg describes as "the emergence of a changed, more tightly structured society with new hierarchies of control, and also changed conceptions of that society, of America itself."[14] This post-Darwinian culture substituted "force" for "sentiment," "desire" for "affection," and "corporation" for "family." Whereas writers of the pre-Civil War epoch *repressed* "power and appetite" within marriage,[15] these later writers openly embraced them. Within this amoral frame of reference, the conflicts between classes, races, and genders could be understood as functions of biological, even cosmic *drives*. McTeague's gruesome murder of Trina, while horrifying in its violence, does not provoke a reader's moral condemnation but a kind of numb acceptance of primal drives within this archetypal male. Carrie's "success story" mirrors McTeague's brutal treatment of his wife, for the aspiring actress abandons Hurstwood to his fate once it becomes convenient for her to establish her independence. Once again the text works hard to dissuade a "sentimental" reading of the action, for Hurstwood's descent to death is presented in the cold-blooded documentary fashion of a trained journalist.

Indeed, as Philip Fisher shows, naturalist documentary narrative contrasts with earlier representational styles in the United States by its insistence on *the actual* as opposed to *the possible*. Unlike Stowe's Quaker settlement, which was "a sanctuary from, not a faithful account of, a larger social world[,] the Dreiserian city was a perfect fit, both representing the psychological dynamics of the individual and the politics of America itself."[16] At least by 1900 narratives had abandoned idealized "homes" in favor of the terrifying public spaces of industrialized, commercialized American culture. Rather than the House of the Seven Gables, or the House of Usher, or even Uncle Tom's Cabin, we have "the House of Mirth," that Veblenarian nightmare of a home, complete with flashy sights, sensual gratification, and spiritual emptiness. Wharton's is the garish (or gilded) substitution for all those antebellum homes to which we have attended. As representative structure for its age, it helps us understand the nature of

perverse fictions of the prior historical epoch. That perversity, a turning away from the accepted and the "normal," depended upon secure
assumptions about the self and society. Even the iconoclastic Melville
needed a foundational ethos to assault. A sentimentalized Romanticism, fusing "feminized" religion with the dominant practices of European Romanticism, supplied that ethos. It was exemplified in those
idealized homes and parodied by the inverted houses of Poe, Cooper,
Douglass, and Southworth. Furthermore, the idealization of sibling
relationships within that sentimentalized culture permitted a confidence, even smugness in dealing with the political crises of the epoch,
for the writers assumed the possibility of effecting change through
their prose. Uncowed by hierarchical assumptions, the brothers and
sisters believed they could convert their equals.

Put differently, the narrative subgenres of antebellum culture combined political controversy with reformist designs. Postbellum "realist"
and "naturalist" prose rarely pretends to such an audacious union of
analysis and amelioration. Twain seems content to skewer American
hypocrisy with few designs upon *altering* the culture; Dreiser articulates the raw, unembarrassed *desire* of his fellow Americans without
ever propounding a transformation of those yearnings. Thus, the contrast between these narrative epochs could be framed in these terms:
whereas antebellum narratives confronted *modern* political crises
within the framework of eighteenth- and nineteenth-century ideologies, Dreiser and his contemporaries presented those same crises
through the medium of a modern discourse. This is not to suggest that
the Bakhtinian processes of novelization and carnivalization ceased
with the Civil War. Parody, inversion, pastoralizing, and gothicizing
are all evident in the later prose, especially in the narratives of Twain,
Crane, and Wharton. However, these novelizing tactics go forward
within a horizon of narrative possibility defined by irony. Whether
we discuss the social irony of Twain or the cosmic, naturalist irony
of Crane, we see over and over again the subversion of the assumed
or the apparent by "the real." We might say that "defamiliarization"
had become *the* "normalizing" strategy of postbellum prose. That is,
the estrangement of the taken-for-granted in a novel such as *The Red
Badge of Courage* is a common gesture in a literary culture dedicated
to irony in all its forms. Henry Fleming's disillusionment, marked by
his fall from the pastoralized hometown ardor for war, typifies the
disillusionment of many of the characters listed at the start of this
section. In postbellum culture, then, you can't go home again, for the
falls are irrevocable and complete. I would argue that this is largely
so because the sentimental alternative to irony was represented by
"the genteel tradition" savaged so famously by Santayana. In contrast

to what we might call the "tough sentimentalism" represented by Stowe, postbellum culture proferred a "soft," idealizing sentimentalism summarized by writers such as Maurice Thompson.

Henry Adams's *Education* provides us a synopsis of the sea-changes in American narrativity during the nineteenth century. He of course exemplifies the ironic mode of late-nineteenth-century prose, for one can imagine no more sardonic analysis of American subjectivity than his *Education*. That irony emerges from his carnivalizing of the auto-biographical tradition in American writing, stretching from the Puritans through Franklin to Thoreau. Indeed, this mock autobiography provides a cornucopia of dialogized narrative modes, ranging from the pastoralizing nostalgia of "Quincy" to the astute political analysis of British-American politics during the war to the pseudoscientific discourse of the closing chapters. Through these diverse voices Adams narrates his forced march through a series of "American homes." Simplifying the text for the purposes of this discussion, we can follow Adams's movement from the home of the early Republic to the antebellum home to the terrifying world of force in Chicago.

John Quincy Adams's home immersed the young Henry in an "atmosphere of education" that "was colonial, revolutionary, almost Cromwellian, as though he were steeped, from his greatest grandmother's birth, in the odor of political crime."[17] The world of the founding fathers is *palpable* for the young scion of this political tradition, a point made clear by the description of the grandfather's home: "The old house at Quincy was eighteenth century. What style it had was in its Queen Anne mahogany panels and its Louis Seize chairs and sofas. The panels belonged to an old colonial Vassall who built the house; the furniture had been brought back from Paris in 1789 or 1801 or 1817 . . ." (11). We have returned to the epic time of the fathers described by Bakhtin and recreated in *Satanstoe;* we have once again entered the mansion of grandfather Glendinning. However, this eighteenth-century edifice is superseded by the nineteenth-century Boston home in the narrative's next chapter. That home typifies the antebellum compulsion for improvement: "Politics offered no difficulties, for there the moral law was a sure guide. Social perfection was also sure, because human nature worked for Good, and three instruments were all she asked—Suffrage, Common Schools, and Press" (33). Similar to Cooper, Adams seems impatient with sentimental politics, as of course any self-respecting ironist would be. Interestingly, he ties that political climate to a new family organization that contrasts strongly with the patriarchal order of Quincy. While the chapter on "Boston" explicitly praises the writer's father for his sanity and decency, it also suggests the predominance of fraternal over filial relation-

ships in the quintessential American family: ". . . the family was rather
an atmosphere than an influence. The boy had a large and overpowering set of brothers and sisters, who were modes or replicas of the same
type, getting the same education, struggling with the same problems. . . . They knew no more than he what they wanted or what to
do for it, but all were conscious that they would like to control power
in some form . . ." (36). In yet another uncanny instance Adams's
personal narrative provides a microcosm of the American polity, refut-
ing Adams's own repeated claim of insignificance. At the very least
he and his family were "representative."

Thus, as the larger culture abandoned the eighteenth- and
nineteenth-century structures for modernity, Adams's education culminates in his encounter with "force" in the White City of the 1893
Chicago Columbian Exposition. As Trachtenberg observes, "It was,
of course, a city without residences, though it offered advice in great
detail about how families might live in cities of the near future. . . ."[18]
This comment is doubly ironic from our present perspective, for the
universe of force was indeed a world without homes. In effect the
White City was another House of Mirth, or, in Frederick Douglass's
phrase, "a whited sepulcher."[19] This architectural wonder embodied
the split between genteel culture and power within the society, for
the neoclassical facades masked the implicit authority of capital in the
creation of the Fair. Looking into the tomb of the City, Adams discovered the dynamos, which prompted "the question whether the American people knew where they were driving" (343). Quite certain that
the people did *not* know, Adams next learned who did, the capitalists
who had displaced his own social class. Reacting to the repeal of the
silver standard, Adams expressed a grudging admiration for "the
whole mechanical consolidation of force, which ruthlessly stamped
out the life of the class into which Adams was born, but created
monopolies capable of controlling the new energies that America
adored" (345). Adrift in the chaos of this incorporated America, Adams contents himself with the cool intellectual task of calculating the
direction and intensity of force—cultural, political, and economic.
Breathing the thin oxygen of this homeless fin de siècle America, the
quintessential gentleman must content himself with clinical
assessment.

In this regard also Adams represents the postbellum generation, for
utilizing the new idiom of naturalism he sidestepped the reformist
confidence of his father's generation. Adams concedes that power
within his culture lies elsewhere, beyond the conscious designs of the
citizen, in sex, capital, and political machines. But if these later writers
gained in sophistication at depicting these *forces*, they lost that earlier

generation's "capacity for wonder," as Fitzgerald put it so famously, that expectation of the millennium. After all, the fictions of writers as different as Harriet Ann Jacobs and Herman Melville were efforts to remake reality in the image of a textualized value system. Ultimately the producers of perverse fictions believed they could make a difference for their class of antebellum citizens. If those gestures now seem naive they also seem compelling in their activism, in their assumption that writing and writers can make a difference.

Notes

CHAPTER 1: THE UNCANNY HOME

The Downing quote is from *The Architecture of Country Houses* (New York: D. Appleton, 1850), 269.

1. See Jay Fliegelman, *Prodigals and Pilgrims: The American Revolution against Patriarchal Authority, 1750–1800* (Cambridge, England: Cambridge University Press, 1982).

2. *Democracy in America* (New York: Mentor, 1956), 232.

3. David E. Shi, *The Simple Life: Plain Living and High Thinking in American Culture* (New York: Oxford University Press, 1985), 108.

4. For example, in *The American Family Home, 1800–1960* (Chapel Hill: University of North Carolina Press, 1986), Clifford Edward Clark Jr. has asserted, "Tocqueville was only one of the numerous nineteenth- and twentieth-century writers who proclaimed the virtues of the single-family dwelling. Insecure about the chaotic growth of American society, these writers have constantly held up the twin ideals of family and home as benchmarks against which the progress of the nation might be measured" (15–16).

5. In his charming (even seductive) *Home: A Short History of an Idea* (New York: Penguin, 1986), Witold Rybczynski establishes the necessary relationship between "house" and "family": "'Home' brought together the meanings of house and of household, of dwelling and of refuge, of ownership and of affection. 'Home' meant the house, but also everything that was in it and around it, as well as the people, and the sense of satisfaction and contentment that all these could convey" (62).

6. See Marilyn R. Chandler, *Dwelling in the Text: Houses in American Fiction* (Berkeley and Los Angeles: University of California Press, 1991) for an especially rich reading of the house as symbol in American writing. Chandler speculates that "this symbolic treatment of houses is not simply a literary fancy: houses in their various ways are obviously visible histories of personal and collective life. One of the problems that preoccupied writers and artists throughout the nineteenth century was that our collective identity had rather shallow roots; we had, as a nation, no significant past. For that reason, artists tended to mythologize the immediate and personal past ... and, borrowing a note from the Puritans who so profoundly formed our habits of imagination, regarding both American history and personal history as reiterations of the timeless cycle of salvation history" (11).

7. Representative studies of antebellum domesticity are Nancy F. Cott, *The Bonds of Womanhood: "Woman's Sphere" in New England, 1780–1835* (New Haven: Yale University Press, 1977); Mary P. Ryan, *Cradle of the Middle Class: The Family in Oneida County, New York, 1790–1865* (Cambridge, England: Cambridge University Press, 1981); and T. Walter Herbert Jr., *Dearest Beloved: The Hawthornes and the Making of the Middle-Class Family* (Berkeley: University of California Press, 1993). I should immediately add that historians such as Elizabeth Fox-Genovese have shown

how "partial" this domestic ideology could be. Specifically, in *Within the Plantation Household: Black and White Women of the Old South* (Chapel Hill: University of North Carolina Press, 1988), Fox-Genovese demonstrates that the plantation resisted the capitalist division of labor and, by necessity, thwarted reduction to the northern model of a bourgeois home. By way of making her argument, Fox-Genovese suggests that this middle-class norm did not speak to working-class women either. This historian's qualifications remind us that the domestic ideal was indeed a constructed belief, and one that emerged from a specific social system prevalent in the northern United States. However, as Fox-Genovese concedes, that "bourgeois" standard presented a powerful ideological force that tended to sweep all counter-ideologies before it. In other words, whether Southern women conformed to the middle-class ideal or not, they were certainly aware of and influenced by it. In short, that ideology could aptly be described as "dominant" in that it defined the controlling assumptions of the culture.

8. Michael Paul Rogin, *Subversive Genealogy: The Politics and Art of Herman Melville* (New York: Knopf, 1983), 164.

9. Kenneth Silverman, *Edgar A. Poe: Mournful and Never-Ending Remembrance* (New York: HarperCollins, 1991), 107.

10. *The Wide, Wide World* (New York: Feminist Press, 1987), 569.

11. Cott, *The Bonds of Womanhood,* 187.

12. Donald Yacovone, "Abolitionists and the 'Language of Fraternal Love,'" in *Meanings for Manhood: Constructions of Masculinity in Victorian America,* ed. Mark C. Carnes and Clyde Griffen (Chicago: University of Chicago Press, 1992), 86–87.

13. *The Letters of Herman Melville,* ed. Merrell R. Davis and William H. Gilman (New Haven: Yale University Press, 1960), 126, 128, and 132.

14. Letter dated 17? November 1851, in *The Letters of Herman Melville,* 142.

15. *The Blithedale Romance* (New York: Norton, 1978), 23 and 38–39.

16. Larzer Ziff, *Literary Democracy: The Declaration of Cultural Independence in America* (New York: Penguin, 1982), 170.

17. In *Manhood and the American Renaissance* (Ithaca: Cornell University Press, 1989), David Leverenz has traced this masculine rivalry in pre-Civil War writing: ". . . I've tried to show the presence of a common rhetorical pattern in the diverse masterpieces of Thoreau, Melville, and Whitman. A conventionally manly 'you' is accused and appealed to, as double, potential convert, and comrade for the self-refashioning 'I.' Male rivalry looms under the fraternity, I've argued, and the rivalry returns in the self-fashioning" (34).

18. *Domestic Individualism: Imagining Self in Nineteenth-Century America* (Berkeley and Los Angeles: University of California Press, 1990), 20.

19. In *Catharine Beecher: A Study in American Domesticity* (New York: Norton, 1976), Kathryn Kish Sklar observes, "The major ambiguity faced by American women in the 1830s and 1840s was . . . how, in an egalitarian society, the submission of one sex to the other could be justified. Women in America had always experienced such inequity, but they had never before needed to reconcile it with a growing ideology of popular democracy and equal rights" (155–56).

20. *A Treatise on Domestic Economy, for the Use of Young Ladies at Home and at School* (Boston: Marsh, Capen, Lyon, and Webb, 1841), 1–3. Commenting on this vexed section of the *Treatise,* G. M. Goshgarian has cleverly remarked, ". . . the 'presiding divinity' of domesticity was the divided subject par excellence. She was rendered whole, and holy, by virtue of her subjection to God and man. . . . Woman's condition was—exemplarily—(w)holeness." *To Kiss the Chastening Rod: Domestic Fiction and Sexual Ideology in the American Renaissance* (Ithaca: Cornell University

Press, 1992), 73. Goshgarian claims, then, that the American home was essentially incestuous, for the hidden sin of domesticity was "the true woman's" subjugation to male figures. In less scandalous terms, we might agree with one historian who observes that "when closely examined, it was evident that a tension existed within this image of the ideal family between the encouragement of freedom and the need for social control" (Clark, *The American Family Home*, 35).

21. *A Treatise on Domestic Economy*, 16.

22. Herbert, *Dearest Beloved*, xvi. "A madwoman, a criminal, and a saint" refers, respectively, to Una, Julian, and Rose Hawthorne.

23. Robert Doherty, *Society and Power: Five New England Towns, 1800–1860* (Amherst: University of Massachusetts Press, 1977), 71.

24. Alan Dawley, *Class and Community: The Industrial Revolution in Lynn* (Cambridge: Harvard University Press, 1976), 1.

25. *The Anxiety of Influence* (New York: Oxford University Press, 1973), 85–86.

26. See, for instance, Sandra M. Gilbert and Susan Gubar, *The Madwoman in the Attic: The Woman Writer and the Nineteenth-Century Literary Imagination* (New Haven: Yale University Press, 1979), for these two scholars deploy a revised Bloomian approach in order to read the relationship between literary "daughters" and male precursors.

27. *Edgar Allan Poe: Poetry and Tales* (New York: Library of America, 1984), 827. All further references will be cited in the text.

28. "Discourse in the Novel," in *The Dialogic Imagination: Four Essays*, ed. Michael Holquist, trans. Caryl Emerson and Michael Holquist (Austin: University of Texas Press, 1981), 368.

29. *Problems of Dostoevsky's Poetics*, ed. and trans. Caryl Emerson (Minneapolis: University of Minnesota Press, 1984), 124–25.

30. "Epic and Novel," in *The Dialogic Imagination*, 6.

31. Robert Young, "Back to Bakhtin," *Cultural Critique* 2 (1985–86): 76.

32. *The Political Unconscious: Narrative as a Socially Symbolic Act* (Ithaca: Cornell University Press, 1981), 144, 115.

33. Jameson's method has the added advantage of substituting the term "narrative" for "novel." Bakhtin himself questioned the distinction between the "literary" novel and other "non-literary" narrative forms ("Epic and Novel," 33). This strategy is appropriate for at least two reasons. First, "narrative" suggests how fundamental storytelling is to the process of making sense of experience: "Like the Kantian concepts of space and time . . . narrative may be taken not as a feature of our experience but as one of the abstract or 'empty' coordinates within which we come to know the world, a contentless form that our perception imposes on the raw flux of reality, giving it, even as we perceive, the comprehensible order we call experience." William C. Dowling, *Jameson, Althusser, Marx: An Introduction to The Political Unconscious* (Ithaca: Cornell University Press, 1984), 95. Beyond this general claim for narrative's epistemological function, we can observe that fictional and nonfictional narratives share so many representational conventions that neatly distinguishing between the two becomes difficult at a practical level. Once we realize that *Narrative of the Life of Frederick Douglass, an American Slave*, and *Swallow Barn* organize experience through shared conventions, we are positioned to read the dialogue between autobiography and novel.

34. *Sensational Designs: The Cultural Work of American Fiction, 1790–1860* (New York: Oxford University Press, 1985).

35. Cathy N. Davidson has discovered a similar impulse behind the early American novel: "By no means an isolated phenomenon, the emergence of the novel was part

of a movement in the late eighteenth century toward a reassessment of the role of the 'average' American and a concomitant questioning of political, ministerial, legal, and even medical authorities on the part of the citizens of the new nation who, having already accepted the egalitarian rhetoric of the Revolution, increasingly believed that the Republic belonged as much to them as to the gentry." *Revolution and the Word: The Rise of the Novel in America* (New York: Oxford University Press, 1986), 44.

36. Nina Baym, *Novels, Readers, and Reviewers: Responses to Fiction in Antebellum America* (Ithaca: Cornell University Press, 1984), 200.

37. *The Jacksonian Persuasion: Politics and Belief* (Stanford: Stanford University Press, 1957), 12.

38. In "Mysterious Laughter: Humor and Fear in Gothic Fiction," *Genre* 14 (1981), Paul Lewis has shown the close connection between Gothic and humor by pointing to their common origin in "the incongruous" (310).

39. I want to distinguish carefully between narrative *subgenres* and *modes*. The former refers to a cluster of narrative conventions that coalesced into a recognizable category of writing during the antebellum period. Typically a distinct subgenre, serving the ideological purposes of a subclass of antebellum society, combines distinguishing character types, settings, and plots. This study examines such subgenres as "the historical novel of New York," "the plantation novel," "the slave narrative," "the Southwestern humor tale," and "the local color sketch." "Mode" refers to a narrative radical that recurs in a wide array of subgenres. Thus the terms "gothicizing" and "pastoralizing" name modes of representation that move across generic boundaries. We may say the same for "adventure narrative," a mode that recurs in Cooper's novels, Douglass's slave narrative, and Stowe's *Uncle Tom's Cabin*.

40. *Beyond the Pleasure Principle*, trans. James Strachey (New York: Norton, 1961), 30.

41. "The Uncanny," trans. Alix Strachey, in *On Creativity and the Unconscious: Papers on the Psychology of Art, Literature, Love, and Religion* (New York: Harper and Row, 1958), 123–24, 131, 148.

Chapter 2: Home as Lost

The quote is from Marylin R. Chandler, *Dwelling in the Text: Houses in American Fiction* (Berkeley and Los Angeles: University of California Press, 1991), 1.

1. In *Versions of the Past: The Historical Imagination in American Fiction* (New York: Oxford University Press, 1974), Harry B. Henderson III makes a similar point about the significance of the Littlepage Trilogy when he comments: "The trilogy in large part is a subtle assessment of the special ways in which New World history has modified and subverted the *a priori* precepts, definitions, distinctions, and categories of the holist frame. This is Cooper's special quality: having accepted the holist categories from the first, he found them in conflict with the stresses and tensions of the historical process as he imagined it" (89). I take issue with Henderson on the degree of Cooper's authorial control over the Trilogy, especially on the grounds that the supposed representatives of the landed gentry devolve in the course of the Manuscripts. Furthermore, I establish crucial interrelationships among Cooper's historical vision, class sympathies, and narrative subgenres.

2. Emory Elliot, *Revolutionary Writers: Literature and Authority in the New Republic, 1775–1810* (New York: Oxford University Press, 1982), 22. For a full (and witty) analysis of this "strain" in American writing, see John P. McWilliams Jr., *The*

American Epic: Transforming a Genre, 1770–1860 (Cambridge, England: Cambridge University Press, 1989).

3. *Home as Found: Authority and Genealogy in Nineteenth-Century American Literature* (Baltimore: Johns Hopkins University Press, 1979), xi.

4. *Revolution and the Word: The Rise of the Novel in America* (New York: Oxford University Press, 1986), 153.

5. *The Pursuit of Happiness* (Ithaca: Cornell University Press, 1953), 105.

6. For a discussion of the relationship between the historical romance and epic, see George Dekker's definitive *The American Historical Romance* (Cambridge, England: Cambridge University Press, 1987), 54–61. For a more general discussion of Scott's influence on Cooper and American historical writers, see Dekker, chap. 2, "The *Waverley*-model and the rise of historical romance," 29–72.

7. *The Pioneers, or the Sources of the Susquehanna* (New York: Library of America, 1985), 39.

8. *The American Democrat* (New York: Penguin, 1969), 153 and 191.

9. Mark R. Patterson, *Authority, Autonomy, and Representation in American Literature, 1776–1865* (Princeton: Princeton University Press, 1988), 135.

10. Sundquist, *Home as Found*, 30.

11. John P. McWilliams Jr., *Political Justice in a Republic: James Fenimore Cooper's America* (Berkeley and Los Angeles: University of California Press, 1972), 307.

12. *The Letters and Journals of James Fenimore Cooper, Vol. 5, 1845–1849*, ed. James Franklin Beard (Cambridge: Belknap, 1968), 7.

13. *A World By Itself: The Pastoral Moment in Cooper's Fiction* (New Haven: Yale University Press, 1977), 167.

14. George Dekker has remarked in *The American Historical Romance*, ". . . *Satanstoe* has the extraordinarily rich and mixed current, the ample social and generic inclusiveness of epic, bringing together an astonishingly wide range of narrative kinds, dialects, races, nationalities, and social levels" (127).

15. "Epic and Novel: Toward a Methodology for the Study of the Novel," in *The Dialogic Imagination: Four Essays*, ed. Michael Holquist, trans. Caryl Emerson and Michael Holquist (Austin: University of Texas Press, 1981), 15.

16. *A History of New York* (New Haven: College and University Press, 1964), 346.

17. Similarities between the two novels have not been lost on literary historians, and indeed at least one scholar prefers Paulding's text: "The hero is not a hero at the beginning but must prove himself one by pluck and resourcefulness. This is one advantage *The Dutchman's Fireside* has over Cooper's yet-to-be-written *Satanstoe*, which it resembles in much of its narrative agenda and portions of its setting. It is also a livelier and more varied book than *Satanstoe*, and its re-creation of old Dutch life seems more authentic than that of Cooper's story." Alexander Cowie, *The Rise of the American Novel* (New York: American Book Company, 1946), 192.

18. *The Dutchman's Fireside* (New Haven: College and University Press, 1966), 83. All further references will be cited in the text.

19. *The Jacksonian Persuasion: Politics and Belief* (Stanford: Stanford University Press, 1957), 58–59. In *Writing in the New Nation: Prose, Print, and Politics in the Early United States* (New Haven: Yale University Press, 1991), Larzer Ziff has proposed a more direct solution to this riddle: ". . . Cooper's considerable fictional achievement . . . constitutes a powerful conservative political statement that overwhelms any nonfictional claims to the contrary" (147).

20. *Satanstoe or The Littlepage Manuscripts, A Tale of the Colony* (Boston: Houghton Mifflin, n. d.), 5–6. All further references will be cited in the text.

21. *Versions of the Past*, 89.

22. *The Secular Scripture: A Study of the Structure of Romance* (Cambridge: Harvard University Press, 1976).

23. "Epic and Novel," 15.

24. This analysis of Cooper's historical novel is deeply indebted to Dekker's seminal *James Fenimore Cooper: The American Scott* (New York: Barnes and Noble, 1967). More specifically, I am influenced by Dekker's analysis of how Cooper transplanted Scott's "wavering hero" to the American scene. However, Dekker's interpretation of the Littlepage Trilogy hastily dismisses the second and third volumes. For example, Dekker writes, "If *Chainbearer* is about half as good as *Satanstoe*, it is incomparably better than *The Redskins.* . . . This third member of the Littlepage trilogy is probably the only book Cooper ever wrote which can be justifiably termed contemptible" (232). I would counter that because he wrote quickly, Cooper unconsciously revealed aspects of his ideology often more carefully concealed in his polemical writings.

25. *The Chainbearer or The Littlepage Manuscripts* (Boston: Houghton Mifflin, n.d.), 90. All further references will be cited in the text.

26. *Waverley* (New York: Harper and Brothers, n.d.), 311 and 328.

27. *Versions of the Past,* 79.

28. David S. Reynolds, *Beneath the American Renaissance: The Subversive Imagination in the Age of Emerson and Melville* (New York: Knopf, 1988), 454.

29. *Dreaming Revolution: Transgression in the Development of American Romance* (Iowa City: University of Iowa Press, 1993), 55.

30. *Beneath the American Renaissance,* 444.

31. *The Letters and Journals of James Fenimore Cooper,* 166.

32. "Family Lineage and Narrative Pattern in Cooper's Littlepage Trilogy," *Forum* 12 (1974): 7.

33. *The Redskins or Indian and Injin, being the conclusion of the Littlepage Manuscripts* (Boston: Houghton Mifflin, n.d.), 5. All further references will be cited in the text.

34. 171.

35. *Confidence Men and Painted Women: A Study of Middle-Class Culture in America, 1830–1870* (New Haven: Yale University Press, 1982), 34, 40, and 33.

36. *Struggles and Triumphs Or, Forty Years' Recollection* (New York: Penguin, 1981), 103.

37. In *Comic Relations: Studies in the Comic, Satire, and Parody,* ed. Pavel Petr, David Roberts, and Philip Thomson (Frankfurt am Main: Verlag Peter Lang, 1985), 185.

38. For a useful commentary on the unifying elements of the Trilogy, see Donald A. Ringe, "Cooper's Littlepage Novels: Change and Stability in American Society," *American Literature* 32 (1960): 280–90.

39. Allan M. Axelrad, *History and Utopia: A Study of the World View of James Fenimore Cooper* (Norwood, Penn.: Norwood Editions, 1978), 53.

40. Bakhtin, "Epic and Novel," 31.

41. Heinz Ickstadt, "Instructing the American Democrat: Cooper and the Concept of Popular Fiction in Jacksonian America," in *James Fenimore Cooper: New Critical Essays,* ed. Robert Clark (London: Vision and Barnes and Noble, 1985), 33.

42. *Fenimore Cooper: A Study of his Life and Imagination* (Princeton: Princeton University Press, 1978), 246–47.

43. *The Letters and Journals of James Fenimore Cooper,* 131.

44. Ibid., 106.

45. Richard Godden, "Pioneer Properties, or 'What's in a Hut?'", in *James Fenimore Cooper: New Critical Essays,* 138–39.

46. David E. Shi, *The Simple Life: Plain Living and High Thinking in American Culture* (New York: Oxford University Press, 1985), 101–2.

CHAPTER 3: OF MASTERS AND MEN

1. I am indebted here to Elizabeth Fox-Genovese's rich analysis of Southern culture and images of the family in *Within the Plantation Household: Black and White Women of the Old South* (Chapel Hill: University of North Carolina Press, 1988), esp. chap. 2, "The View from the Big House," 100–45.

2. Gillian Brown, *Domestic Individualism: Imagining Self in Nineteenth-Century America* (Berkeley and Los Angeles: University of California Press, 1990), 23.

3. *The Signifying Monkey: A Theory of Afro-American Literary Criticism* (New York: Oxford University Press, 1988).

4. Raymond Hedin, "The American Slave Narrative: The Justification of the Picaro," *American Literature* 53 (1982): 634.

5. As William S. Osborne observes in "An Introduction," *Swallow Barn, or A Sojourn in the Old Dominion* (New York: Hafner, 1962), "[Kennedy] had followed closely the debates in the Virginia legislature in 1831–1832 over abolishing slavery in the state; and like the legislators themselves, he was unwilling to endorse emancipation at the cost of economic ruin to Virginia" (xviii).

6. Craig Werner, "The Old South, 1815–1840," in *The History of Southern Literature* (Baton Rouge: Louisiana State University Press, 1985), 91; J. V. Ridgely, *John Pendleton Kennedy* (New York: Twayne, 1966), 60–61.

7. *The Dispossessed Garden: Pastoral and History in Southern Literature* (Athens: University of Georgia Press, 1975), 51. Richie Devon Watson Jr. presents this reading even more bluntly, asserting that "counter tendencies toward romantic inflation and realistic introspection are never successfully resolved in the fiction of . . . Kennedy." *The Cavalier in Virginia Fiction* (Baton Rouge: Louisiana State University Press, 1985), 71. Lucinda MacKethan has been more frankly critical of Kennedy's multifarious text, suggesting that "Readers have continued to find whatever they look for in *Swallow Barn*, a phenomenon that is indicative of the book's strengths as well as its weaknesses." "Introduction," in *Swallow Barn, or, A Sojourn in the Old Dominion* (Baton Rouge: Louisiana State University Press, 1986), xii.

8. *The Intricate Knot: Black Figures in American Literature, 1776–1863* (New York: New York University Press, 1972), 29.

9. Ridgely, *John Pendleton Kennedy*, 36–37.

10. For a thorough discussion of Kennedy's handling of time in *Swallow Barn*, see Jan Bakker, "Time and Timelessness in Images of the Old South: Pastoral in John Pendleton Kennedy's *Swallow Barn* and *Horse-shoe Robinson*," *Tennessee Studies in Literature* 26 (1981): 75–88. Bakker argues that *Swallow Barn* not only aspires to timelessness, but the text critiques that posture in the moment of its creation.

11. *Swallow Barn, or A Sojourn in the Old Dominion* (Philadelphia: Carey and Lea, 1832), I, 9. All further references will be cited in the text.

12. John W. Blassingame, *The Slave Community: Plantation Life in the Antebellum South* (New York: Oxford University Press, 1972), 134.

13. *The Dispossessed Garden*, 45.

14. Charles H. Bohner, *John Pendleton Kennedy: Gentleman from Baltimore* (Baltimore: Johns Hopkins University Press, 1961), 9.

15. In *Roll, Jordan, Roll: The World the Slaves Made* (New York: Pantheon, 1974), Eugene D. Genovese argues that the white man's burden view of slavery was typical

in the antebellum South: "The twin themes of duty and burden, which grew stronger over time, appeared throughout the master class, not merely in the more propagandistic writings of public figures" (78).

16. *The Intricate Knot,* 57.

17. Blassingame, *The Slave Community,* 134.

18. "Introduction," xxvi.

19. *Narrative of the Life of Frederick Douglass, an American Slave, Written by Himself* (Boston: Anti-Slavery Office, 1845), 64. All further references will be cited in the text.

20. As H. Bruce Franklin has observed, ". . . we are forced to sense a tremendous disparity between the emotional level of the prose, running on that matter-of-fact norm, and the potential rage and violence implicit in the slave's situation." *The Victim as Criminal and Artist: Literature from the American Prison* (New York: Oxford University Press, 1978), 12.

21. Charles T. Davis and Henry Louis Gates Jr., "Introduction" to *The Slave's Narrative,* ed. Charles T. Davis and Henry Louis Gates Jr. (New York: Oxford University Press, 1985), xvii. Gates introduced this line of analysis in "Binary Oppositions in Chapter One of *Narrative of the Life of Frederick Douglass an American Slave Written by Himself,*" in *Afro-American Literature: The Reconstruction of Instruction,* ed. Dexter Fisher and Robert B. Stepto (New York: MLA, 1979), 212–32. In *The Signifying Monkey,* Gates reasserts the claim by remarking, "Frederick Douglass, a masterful Signifier himself, discusses this use of troping in his *Narrative* of 1845" (66).

22. Here I treat Douglass's *Narrative* as a "representative text" for slave narratives of the 1840s. In *Black Autobiography in America* (Amherst: University of Massachusetts Press, 1974), Stephen Butterfield has pointed out that the 1845 *Narrative* shared with other slave narratives values such as "hard work, forceful resistance, and education as tools to win freedom, both for the individual slave and the entire slave class" (66). In *To Tell a Free Story: The First Century of Afro-American Autobiography, 1760–1865* (Urbana: University of Illinois Press, 1986), William L. Andrews devotes a chapter to "The Performance of Slave Narrative in the 1840s" (97–166), arguing that cultural and social conditions enabled slave narratives to claim equality, even prestige in the literary marketplace. Andrews primarily discusses the narratives of Henry Bibb, William Wells Brown, James W. C. Pennington, and Douglass.

23. *The Sacred and the Profane: The Nature of Religion* (New York: Harper, 1959), 70.

24. Frank Kermode, *The Sense of an Ending: Studies in the Theory of Fiction* (New York: Oxford University Press, 1967), 46.

25. In *The Peculiar Institution: Slavery in the Ante-bellum South* (New York: Vintage, 1956), Kenneth M. Stampp observes, "Slavery was above all a labor system. Wherever in the South the master lived, however many slaves he owned, it was his bondsmen's productive capacity that he generally valued most. And to the problem of organizing and exploiting their labor with maximum efficiency he devoted much of his attention" (34).

26. "Identity and Art in Frederick Douglass's *Narrative,*" *CLA Journal* 17 (1973): 201.

27. For an especially subtle analysis of the correspondences between Franklin's *Autobiography* and Douglass's *Narrative,* see Annette Niemtzow, "The Problematic of Self in Autobiography: The Example of the Slave Narrative," in *The Art of the Slave Narrative,* ed. John Sekora and Darwin T. Turner (Carbondale: Western Illinois University Press, 1982), 96–109.

28. Butterfield has discussed Douglass's turn from the spiritual to the secular auto-biography in these terms:

> But unlike Thompson and Pennington, [Douglass's] identity is not formed primarily in Chris-tian terms. Where Pennington or Noah Davis, for example, will oppose alcoholism as a sin and condemn slavery for encouraging the sin of intemperance, Douglass, penetrating directly to the political motive of the master in giving his slaves alcohol, advocates temperance as a political defense. Where Pennington considers lying and violence to be sinful in themselves and condemns slavery because it forces these things on the slave, Douglass supports them as positive forms of struggle when they are directed toward the master class. (*Black Autobiogra-phy in America*, 66)

29. In *The Journey Back: Issues in Black Literature and Criticism* (Chicago: Univer-sity of Chicago Press, 1980), Houston A. Baker Jr. has stated this position most dramatically, claiming:

> Unable to transplant the institutions of his homeland in the soil of America—as the Puritans had done—the black slave had to seek means of survival and fulfillment on that middle ground where the European slave trade had deposited him. He had to seize whatever weapons came to hand in his struggle for self-definition. The range of instruments was limited. Evangeli-cal Christians and committed abolitionists were the only discernable groups standing in the path of America's hypocrisy and inhumanity. (36–37)

Laura E. Tanner is more sharply critical of Douglass's cooptation by mainstream American discourse, arguing that ". . . Douglass has succeeded so well in assimilating the authenticating documents and strategies into his tale that he has assimilated also the generalizations and prejudices of the white authenticator's narrow-minded consciousness" ("Self-Conscious Representation in the Slave Narrative," *Black Ameri-can Literature Forum* 21 [1987]: 423). See also Frances Smith Foster, *Witnessing Slavery: The Development of Ante-bellum Slave Narratives* (Westport, Conn.: Green-wood, 1979), for a discussion of how rhetorical necessity compelled slave narrators to adopt the discourse of white abolitionists and their "sentimental" audience. Finally, Andrews contrasts the restraint of Douglass's *Narrative* with the self-assertion of *My Bondage and My Freedom* (280–91).

30. Douglass expands upon the content of this first speech in *My Bondage and My Freedom* (New York: Dover, 1969), specifically mentioning the *narrative* elements of the speech:

> Mr. William C. Coffin, a prominent abolitionist in those days of trial, had heard me speaking to my colored friends, in the little schoolhouse on Second Street, New Bedford, where we worshiped. He sought me out in the crowd, and invited me to say a few words to the convention. Thus sought out, and thus invited, I was induced to speak out the feelings inspired by the occasion, and *the fresh recollection of the scenes through which I had passed as a slave.* (357–58; emphasis mine)

31. "We Wear the Mask: Deceit as Theme and Style in Slave Narratives," in *The Art of the Slave Narrative*, ed. John Sekora and Darwin T. Turner (Carbondale: Western Illinois University Press, 1982), 72. In "The American Slave Narrative: The Justification of the Picaro," Hedin has argued, ". . . in his cunning, strategic manipulation of already existing arguments and narrative modes, the slave narrator demonstrated that, far from being deprived of his old trickster skills, he had simply found new territory in which to use them" (632). Henry Louis Gates Jr. has discussed Douglass's trickster tactics in "Binary Oppositions in Chapter One of *Narrative of*

the Life of Frederick Douglass," with particular attention to Douglass's overturning of plantation codes.

32. Here Douglass exemplifies what Gates calls "motivated signifin'": "Signifyin(g) revision is a rhetorical transfer that can be motivated or unmotivated. Motivated Signifyin(g) is the sort in which the Monkey delights; it functions to redress an imbalance of power, to clear a space, rhetorically. To achieve occupancy in this desired space, the Monkey rewrites the received order by exploiting the Lion's hubris and his inability to read the figurative other than as the literal" (124).

33. *Black Autobiography in America,* 74.

34. *Swallow Barn, or A Sojourn in the Old Dominion,* Revised ed. (New York: George P. Putnam, 1851), 8. All further references will be cited in the text.

35. Jay B. Hubbel, *The South in American Literature, 1607–1900* (Durham, N.C.: Duke University Press, 1954), 514.

36. *The Cavalier in Virginia Fiction,* 132.

37. *The Virginia Comedians: or, Old Days in the Old Dominion. Edited from the MSS. of C. Effingham, Esq.* (New York: D. Appleton, 1854), II, 44.

38. Ibid., II, 190–91.

39. *The Dispossessed Garden,* 55.

40. *The Intricate Knot,* 73.

41. *Woodcraft or, Hawks about the Dovecoat: A Story of the South at the Close of the Revolution* (New York: Norton, 1961), 367.

42. Yellin, *The Intricate Knot,* 77.

43. *Woodcraft,* 456.

44. Ibid., 397.

45. *Hard Facts: Setting and Form in the American Novel* (New York: Oxford University Press, 1985), 19.

46. *The Act of Reading: A Theory of Aesthetic Response* (Baltimore: Johns Hopkins University Press, 1978), 77.

47. *The Planter's Northern Bride* (Chapel Hill: University of North Carolina Press, 1970), 32. All further references will be cited in the text.

48. *Roll, Jordan, Roll,* 74.

49. Andrews has analyzed the "novelization" of Afro-American autobiography during the 1850s in *To Tell a Free Story,* with particular attention to Douglass's *My Bondage and My Freedom* and Jacobs's *Incidents* (265–91).

50. *Incidents in the Life of a Slave Girl, Written by Herself,* ed. Jean Fagan Yellin (Cambridge: Harvard University Press, 1987). These claims are made, respectively, on the following pages: 31; 184; 36; 43; 74; 146. All further references will be cited in the text.

51. In *Manhood and the American Renaissance* (Ithaca: Cornell University Press, 1989), David Leverenz has made a similar observation: "Despite his ardent, lifelong public feminism, Douglass's preoccupation with manhood and power all but erases any self-representation linking him to women, family, and intimacy or to lower-class black people" (109).

52. Fox-Genovese, *Within the Plantation Household,* 378.

53. *Specifying: Black Women Writing the American Experience* (Madison: University of Wisconsin Press, 1987), 14.

54. *Gender, Fantasy, and Realism in American Literature* (New York: Columbia University Press, 1982).

55. *Specifying,* 6.

56. "An Interview conducted by Nellie McKay," *Contemporary Literature* 24 (1983): 416.

57. At a conference on African-American literature, Deborah E. McDowell challenged the canonical "priority" granted Douglass's *Narrative* precisely because black females are "objectified" and "fetishized" by the male narrator. In a dramatic formulation of her critique, McDowell claimed that the male narrator's freedom was achieved through female slavery ("In the First Place: Making Frederick Douglass and the Afro-American Narrative Tradition," paper presented at "'Looking Back with Pleasure': A Bicentennial Commemoration of Equiano's *Narrative*," University of Utah, 28 October 1989). In "Critiques from Within: Antebellum Projects of Resistance," *American Literature* 64 (1992), Maggie Sale has made a similar argument: "While maintaining a sense of racial solidarity . . . Jacobs also perceived limitations in the way the rhetoric of the Revolution was used to support only the claims of black men to natural rights, and [her] writings challenged these limitations by replacing representations of women as passive and voiceless, such as Douglass's, with ones of black women's articulate expression and agency" (712).

58. In its portrayal of active, intelligent black slaves, Jacobs's narrative is typical of other narratives by black women of the nineteenth century. See Frances Smith Foster, "'In Respect to Females . . .': Differences in the Portrayals of Women by Male and Female Narrators," *Black American Literature Forum* 15 (1981): 66–70.

59. *In a Different Voice: Psychological Theory and Women's Development* (Cambridge: Harvard University Press, 1982), 169.

60. "Introduction" to *Incidents in the Life of a Slave Girl, Written by Herself*, ed. Jean Fagan Yellin (Cambridge: Harvard University Press, 1987), xiv.

CHAPTER 4: AT HOME IN KITCHEN AND CABIN

1. "Changing the Letter: The Yokes, the Jokes of Discourse, or, Mrs. Stowe, Mr. Reed," in *Slavery and the Literary Imagination*, ed. Deborah E. McDowell and Arnold Rampersad (Baltimore: Johns Hopkins University Press, 1989), 30.

2. *Dwelling in the Text: Houses in American Fiction* (Berkeley and Los Angeles: University of California Press, 1991), 17.

3. *Novels, Readers, and Reviewers: Responses to Fiction in Antebellum America* (Ithaca: Cornell University Press, 1984), 220–23.

4. Philip Fisher, *Hard Facts: Setting and Form in the American Novel* (New York: Oxford University Press, 1985), esp. 17.

5. Jean W. Ashton, *Harriet Beecher Stowe: A Reference Guide* (Boston: G. K. Hall, 1977), xvi.

6. Alice C. Crozier, *The Novels of Harriet Beecher Stowe* (New York: Oxford University Press, 1969), 3–33, and Jane P. Tompkins, *Sensational Designs: The Cultural Work of American Fiction, 1790–1860* (New York: Oxford University Press, 1985), 135.

7. To further appreciate the dialogic texture of the novel, one need only contrast it with Stowe's *A Key to Uncle Tom's Cabin* (1853), which relentlessly, humorlessly argues for abolition and colonization. The "key" constitutes Stowe's later reading of her novel, one which monologizes the earlier text, cleaning it up, as it were, making it politically correct.

8. *The Victorian Multiplot Novel: Studies in Dialogical Form* (New Haven: Yale University Press, 1980).

9. Eric J. Sundquist describes the energy and creativity Stowe poured into serial publication in these terms: "When the serial version of the novel began to appear . . . her audience was given to expect a tale that would run about fourteen weekly

installments. In the end, it ran for ten months, gaining a steadily larger audience, as new characters and events came to life and as Stowe discovered the pleasures and suspense of serial publication." "Introduction," in *New Essays on Uncle Tom's Cabin*, ed. Eric J. Sundquist (Cambridge, England: Cambridge University Press, 1986), 9.

10. "Introduction" to *Uncle Tom's Cabin or Life among the Lowly* (Cambridge: Belknap, 1962), xi.

11. *The Act of Reading: A Theory of Aesthetic Response* (Baltimore: Johns Hopkins University Press, 1978), 118.

12. My argument assumes Stowe's familiarity with predominant literary modes and subgenres of antebellum culture. As a well-read professional writer who published in the periodical press, Stowe had both intellectual and pecuniary motives for intimately knowing her contemporaries' work. E. Bruce Kirkham provides the best analysis of Stowe as engaged professional writer in chap. 3, "Contributions to Periodicals," 41–57 in *The Building of Uncle Tom's Cabin* (Knoxville: University of Tennessee Press, 1977). I would also assert that like the slave narrators discussed in my chap. 3, Stowe had "read" many of the ideological claims of her society in material and popular culture surrounding her. To take an example pertinent to this chapter, as a woman immersed in evangelical religion, Stowe observed contrasting attitudes toward religion among males and females, a contrast that powers much of her novel.

13. Of course, Stowe's humor has not gone entirely unnoticed. Edmund Wilson refers to the "high comedy" of Ophelia's efforts to bring order to the St. Clare kitchen in *Patriotic Gore: Studies in the Literature of the American Civil War* (New York: Oxford University Press, 1962), 8. Kristen Herzog has discussed Stowe's use of humor and parody in *Women, Ethnics, and Exotics: Images of Power in Mid-Nineteenth-Century American Fiction* (Knoxville: University of Tennessee Press, 1983). Most importantly, in *Uncle Tom's Cabin and American Culture* (Dallas: Southern Methodist University Press, 1985), Thomas F. Gossett shows that Stowe uses humor to lighten an otherwise "dark" text, to show blacks in acts of psychological self-defense, and to make characters credible (98–99).

14. Forrest Wilson, *Crusader in Crinoline: The Life of Harriet Beecher Stowe* (New York: Lippincott, 1941), 484.

15. Letter to Lord Denmar, d. 20 January 1853, HM 24162, Huntington Library, 1.

16. *The Popular Book: A History of America's Literary Taste* (Berkeley and Los Angeles: University of California Press, 1963), 94.

17. *Shaftesbury's Philosophy of Religion and Ethics* (Athens: Ohio University Press, 1967), 120.

18. *Characteristics of Men, Manners, Opinions, Times*, 2nd ed., ca. 1714 (Reprint Farnborough, England: Gregg, 1968), 61, 65, 128, 134.

19. Elizabeth Ammons was perhaps the first scholar to develop this political kinship between the writings of Stowe and Beecher: "Like her sister Catharine Beecher, Harriet Beecher Stowe displays in *Uncle Tom's Cabin* a facility for converting essentially repressive concepts of femininity into a positive (and activist) alternative system of values in which a woman figures not merely as a moral superior of man, his inspirer, but as the model for him in the new millennium about to dawn" ("Heroines in *Uncle Tom's Cabin*," *American Literature* 49 [1977]: 163).

20. *A Treatise on Domestic Economy* (Boston: Marsh, Capen, Lyon, and Webb, 1841), 261.

21. *The Tradition of Women's Humor in America* (Huntington Beach, Calif.: American Studies, 1984), 14.

22. Here I am partially indebted to Fred G. See's suggestive analysis of desire in nineteenth-century American fiction. In *Desire and the Sign: Nineteenth-Century*

American Fiction (Baton Rouge: Louisiana State University Press, 1987), See analyzes *Uncle Tom's Cabin* in these terms:

> So sentimental fiction opens to its readers with the reminder that they are separated, by a gaze filled with longing beyond satisfaction, from the mystical body that once abided them. In this fictional mode we follow, and are distinct from, a beginning that was formerly immediate: coexistent, simultaneous, identical, but now lost to us. But more importantly, the rules of this fiction develop the possibility of a natural return, through maternal intervention, to that absent unity. (39)

23. "A Laughter of Their Own: Women's Humor in the United States," in *Critical Essays on American Humor,* ed. William Bedford Clark and W. Craig Turner (Boston: G. K. Hall, 1984), 201.

24. *Ruth Hall and Other Writings* (New Brunswick, N.J.: Rutgers University Press, 1986), 25, 17.

25. *The Curse of Clifton,* (Philadelphia: T. B. Peterson, 1852), 18, 27.

26. Annie Fields, *Life and Letters of Harriet Beecher Stowe* (Boston: Houghton Mifflin, 1897), 42.

27. "Uncle Lot," in *Regional Sketches, New England and Florida,* ed. John R. Adams (New Haven: College and University Press, 1972), 31. All further references will be cited in the text.

28. Mary Kelley, *Private Woman, Public Stage: Literary Domesticity in Nineteenth-Century America* (New York: Oxford University Press, 1984), 164.

29. *New England Local Color Literature: A Woman's Tradition* (New York: Ungar, 1983), 50.

30. *American Humor: A Study of the National Character* (New York: Doubleday, 1931). Rourke also discusses the vogue of burlesque comedy during the 1840s and 1850s, a fashion she relates to the revivalist culture of the period. However, that amorphous type of humor comprises not so much a distinguishable comic tradition as a general satiric style that influenced the three traditions discussed in this chapter.

31. *Anatomy of Criticism: Four Essays* (Princeton: Princeton University Press, 1957), 39–40, 172.

32. *A Very Serious Thing,* 24.

33. Stephen Railton, *Authorship and Audience: Literary Performance in the American Renaissance* (Princeton: Princeton University Press, 1991), 82.

34. Ronald Wallace, *God Be with the Clown: Humor in American Poetry* (Columbia: University of Missouri Press, 1984), 79.

35. Poem 401, *The Complete Poems,* ed. Thomas H. Johnson (Boston: Little, Brown, 1960), 191.

36. *Uncle Tom's Cabin; or, Life among the Lowly* (New York: Library of America, 1982), 185. All further references will be cited in the text.

37. "'Peacable Fruits': The Ministry of Harriet Beecher Stowe," *American Quarterly* 40 (1988): 319.

38. Ibid., 319–20.

39. Richard Yarborough argues in convincing terms that Sam and Andy conform to "darky" stereotypes and so cannot be treated as willful tricksters operating in opposition to the dominant slave ideology. "Strategies of Black Characterization in *Uncle Tom's Cabin* and the Early Afro-American Novel," in *New Essays on Uncle Tom's Cabin,* ed. Eric J. Sundquist (Cambridge, England: Cambridge University Press, 1986), 47. Leslie Fiedler argues more broadly that many of Stowe's characters are modeled on minstrel show stereotypes in *What Was Literature? Class, Culture and Mass Society* (New York: Simon and Schuster, 1982), 166. Christina Zwarg has as-

serted that Sam defies simple reduction to the "Sambo" stereotype, for "what Stowe toys with in her portrait of Sam is the way in which she . . . can take the stereotypes of the dominant culture, the 'myths' which empower its control, and use them effectively against it" ("Fathering and Blackface in *Uncle Tom's Cabin," Novel* 22 [1989]: 285). In my reading of Stowe's novel, the writer's "romantic racialism" is so pervasive, her unchallenged racist assumptions so consistent, that Zwarg's interpretation can only seem forced. See the concluding section of this chapter for an elaboration of my interpretation.

40. As Jean Fagan Yellin observes, "Against this throng [of black characters], we watch mulatto Eliza escape heroically with little Harry, and her mulatto husband George Harris defend his family with arms; in contrast to black Tom—the type of pious steady slave familiar in plantation fiction—who transcends his traditional acquiescent role and suffers martyrdom." *The Intricate Knot: Black Figures in American Literature, 1776–1863* (New York: New York University Press, 1972), 137.

41. *The Signifying Monkey: A Theory of Afro-American Literary Criticism* (New York: Oxford University Press, 1988).

42. Stowe was familiar with Douglass's *Narrative* prior to the writing of her novel. However, she did not become aware of Jacobs's story until the fugitive slave wrote her in 1852 to ask her help in composing her life story, a request that Stowe declined. For an account of this troubled relationship between slave narrator and female novelist, see Yellin, "Introduction" to *Incidents in the Life of a Slave Girl, Written by Herself,* ed. Jean Fagan Yellin (Cambridge: Harvard University Press, 1987), xviii–xix.

43. In "Gothic Imagination and Social Reform: The Haunted Houses of Lyman Beecher, Henry Ward Beecher, and Harriet Beecher Stowe," Karen Halttunen analyzes the writer's use of the Gothic: "Stowe's purpose in satirizing Gothic claptrap with this false haunting . . . was to highlight the true haunting of Simon Legree" (*New Essays on Uncle Tom's Cabin,* 124). In *Manhood and the American Renaissance* (Ithaca: Cornell University Press, 1989), David Leverenz presents this reading rather more bluntly: "Cassy's trickery, a piece of pure malice, climaxes Stowe's attack on manhood" (198).

44. Alfred Habegger has called attention to this clash of humorous styles in nineteenth-century culture in his analysis of the character "Mrs. Butterwell" in Elizabeth Stuart Phelps's *Doctor Zay:*

> There is a telling difference between Mrs. Butterwell's humor, and that of the Southwestern humorists or literary comedians. The men were funny because they were playing the fool in one way or another. But Mrs. Butterwell's humor is a function of her sagacity. She is a wise woman who has acquired a good deal of bitter and practical knowledge, and she utters it in a manner that is wry instead of foolish or self-parodying. Her voice is very close to that of the popular newspaper columnists, Gail Hamilton and Fanny Fern. Like these writers, Mrs. Butterwell is funny because of her superior and pungent insight. *Gender, Fantasy, and Realism in American Literature* (New York: Columbia University Press, 1982), 164.

If Habegger calls our attention to the mastery of male humor by female wit, Larzer Ziff tips the scale in the other direction when he writes of George Washington Harris's Sut Lovingood: "But the ferocious antisentimentalism of Harris's sadistic scenes provides a valuable, one might almost say a relieving, contrast to the unexamined pieties of even so accomplished a moralist as Stowe." *Literary Democracy: The Declaration of Cultural Independence in America* (New York: Penguin, 1982), 185. Railton argues that the male reader had powerful ideological motives for absorbing Southwestern humor: "If he felt impotent and even invisible in the home that he paid for but did not run, the gentleman could find vicarious compensation in the rough world of the humorists, where it is women who do not matter, except as occasional objects of unfrustrated resentment" (*Authorship and Audience*, 103–4).

45. *America's Humor from Poor Richard to Doonesbury* (New York: Oxford University Press, 1978), 199.

46. In *Beneath the American Renaissance: The Subversive Imagination in the Age of Emerson and Melville* (New York: Knopf, 1988), David S. Reynolds has written of this archetypal American confidence man, "Suggs is the first figure in American literature who fully manipulates Conventional values—piety, discretion, honesty, entrepreneurial shrewdness—for purely selfish ends" (454).

47. Chapel Hill: University of North Carolina Press, 1969, 8. All further references will be cited in the text.

48. As Gary Lindberg writes in his definitive *The Confidence Man in American Literature* (New York: Oxford University Press, 1982):

> A world in which everyone was assumed to be out to trick everyone else was not exactly a new phenomenon or perception after the Civil War. Such a situation, for example, is projected in the world of Southwestern Humor with its pranks, frauds, fights, and contests of boasting. And the hero of such a world—most engagingly represented in Simon Suggs and Sut Lovingood—frankly acknowledges the terms of it and exploits its fluidity with little inward pretension of goodness or piety. If Simon and Sut believe they are superior to others, it is simply because of skill in the game: bolder stratagems, more skillful impersonations, shrewder reading of motives and weaknesses, less befogging platitudes, more imagination and dexterity. (184)

49. *Domestic Manners of the Americans* (New York: Vintage, 1949), 75, 80–81.

50. *The Bonds of Womanhood: "Woman's Sphere" in New England, 1780–1835* (New Haven: Yale University Press, 1977), 132.

51. *A Shopkeeper's Millennium: Society and Revivals in Rochester, New York, 1815–1837* (New York: Hill and Wang, 1978), 98.

52. The term "Southwestern" seems geographically accurate for describing Haley since he refers often to conducting business from Natchez, Mississippi.

53. Loker, the drover, and Phineas Fletcher demonstrate Annette Kolodny's claim that nineteenth-century women's fiction recast an archetypal male figure: "At least part of that promise [of the West], these novelists also suggest, was the reconstitution of the American Adam. If, as R. W. B. Lewis argues, American fiction written by men often concerns itself with 'an Adamic person . . . at home only in the presence of nature and God,' the fiction composed by nineteenth-century American women stubbornly returned that figure to the human community." *The Land Before Her: Fantasy and Experience of the American Frontier, 1630–1860* (Chapel Hill: University of North Carolina Press, 1984), 203. Here Kolodny specifically alludes to fictions by E. D. E. N. Southworth and Maria Cummins.

54. Habegger, *Gender, Fantasy, and Realism*, 123.

55. "The Big Bear of Arkansas," in *The Mirth of a Nation: America's Great Dialect Humor*, ed. Walter Blair and Raven I. McDavid Jr. (Minneapolis: University of Minnesota Press, 1983), 58–59.

56. Blair and Hill, *America's Humor*, 252.

57. *The Great American Adventure* (Boston: Beacon, 1984), 6.

58. Ibid., 4.

59. *The Last of the Mohicans; A Narrative of 1757* (New York: Library of America, 1985), 824, 830–31.

60. As Michael D. Butler has commented in "Narrative Structure and Historical Process in *The Last of the Mohicans*," *American Literature* 48 (1976): "So at the end,

it would seem that in *The Last of the Mohicans* Cooper traced a historical process in which a physical, masculine, red culture embodied in the futureless bachelorhood of Uncas, Magua, and Chingatchgook gives way to a more spiritual, more feminine, white culture represented by the promising union of Alice and Duncan" (138).

61. Reynolds draws a distinction between two forms of adventure novel, the "moral" tradition represented by the narratives of Cooper, Sedgwick, Dana, and Parkman (184), and the "dark" tradition represented by *Nick of the Woods* (188). In my reading of antebellum adventure narratives, Reynolds overstates ideological differences between these two tendencies, a point I underline in the next paragraph by outlining the defining characteristics of antebellum male adventure.

62. *Nick of the Woods, or The Jibbenainosay, A Tale of Kentucky* (Philadelphia: Carey, Lea, and Blanchard, 1837), I, 42. As Dana D. Nelson comments in *The Word in Black and White: Reading "Race" in American Literature, 1638–1867* (New York: Oxford University Press, 1992), ". . . from the outset Bird assumes a universalized and unchanging Indian, one who is thoroughly debased and completely savage" (51).

63. *Nick of the Woods*, II, 234.

64. *The Adventurous Muse: The Poetics of American Fiction, 1789–1900* (New Haven: Yale University Press, 1977). In fairness to Spengemann, I must stress that his generic definition of "adventure narrative" differs in important ways from the one advanced here, for he traces a genealogy of adventure writing from the narratives of exploration to novels such as *Moby-Dick*. In fact, Spengemann categorizes Cooper's novels under the rubric "poetics of domesticity," along with picaresque narratives, an important form I shall discuss shortly.

65. For the definitive analysis of the captivity narrative, its political importance, and its influence on early national romance, see Richard Slotkin, *Regeneration through Violence: The Mythology of the American Frontier, 1600–1860* (Middletown, Conn.: Wesleyan University Press, 1973).

66. Lori Askeland, "Remodeling the Model Home in *Uncle Tom's Cabin* and *Beloved*," *American Literature* 64 (1992): 788.

67. In his study of *The Picaresque Hero in European Fiction* (Madison: University of Wisconsin Press, 1977), Richard Bjornson points out that the picaro has taken on diverse personalities, ranging from rogue to saint: "Variously described as a social conformist in avid pursuit of material possessions and a rebel who rejects society and its rewards, an optimist and a pessimist, a good-for-nothing without scruples and a wanderer with potentialities of sainthood, he has been called immoral, amoral, and highly moral. In actuality, picaresque heroes have at one time or another exhibited all these and many other characteristics; their fictional lives have served as vehicles for the expression of diametrically opposed ideologies and moral systems. . ." (5).

68. *Telling the Truth: The Theory and Practice of Documentary Fiction* (Ithaca: Cornell University Press, 1986), 244.

69. As Spengemann reminds us, the idealized home originated in a Christian trope that figured heaven as home (*The Adventurous Muse*, 70–71).

70. Kathryn Kish Sklar, *Catharine Beecher: A Study in American Domesticity* (New York: Norton, 1976), 158.

71. Kelley, *Private Woman, Public Stage*, 258.

72. *Gender, Fantasy, and Realism*, 21–33.

73. *Slavery, Race, and Violence in Melville's America* (Baton Rouge: Louisiana State University Press, 1980), 25. Gillian Brown has advanced a related argument in *Domestic Individualism: Imagining Self in Nineteenth-Century America* (Berkeley and Los Angeles: University of California Press, 1990): "In doing away with the

taints of the marketplace Stowe's purified domestic economy must ultimately do away with blackness, the mark of incongruity and exogamy" (59).

74. "Changing the Letter," 35.

75. *The Word in Black and White,* 132.

CHAPTER 5: TWIN PARODISTS

1. *Pierre or The Ambiguities* (Evanston: Northwestern-Newberry, 1971), 141. All further references will be cited in the text.

2. Richard Brodhead, *Hawthorne, Melville, and the Novel* (Chicago: University of Chicago Press, 1976), 163.

3. See Nancy Craig Simmons' "Why an Enthusiast? Melville's *Pierre* and the Problem of the Imagination," *ESQ* 33 (1987) for an examination of the gap between writer and antihero. Simmons demonstrates that Pierre's hapless career follows a pattern of "enthusiastic" religious behavior familiar to Melville and his audience, and furthermore, that "Melville uses Pierre's enthusiasm to explore the question of the validity of art . . . as a guide to action and a means to truth in an artificial world where habitual fictionalizing renders all 'Truth' suspect" (156).

4. *The Feminization of American Culture* (New York: Avon, 1977), 377. Douglas is probably following the suggestion of William Charvat in this regard, for Charvat remarked that "the language and dialogue [of *Pierre*], a combination of Shakespeare and Mrs. E. D. E. N. Southworth of the *Ledger,* are elevated right out of the realm of recognizable English speech." *The Profession of Authorship in America, 1800–1870. The Papers of William Charvat,* ed. Matthew J. Bruccoli (Columbus: Ohio State University Press, 1968), 276. I have found no conclusive evidence that Melville was familiar with Southworth's fictions. However, as Charvat suggests, there are striking verbal similarities between the female writer's fiction and Melville's novel, similarities that should become apparent in the course of this chapter. However, it is just as plausible that those correspondences resulted from influence by common sources on the two writers, especially Shakespeare and Gothic fiction.

5. I have confined my analysis to Southworth's novels composed up to and including *The Hidden Hand,* in part because that is her best known and probably best novel, but mainly because those narratives fall within the scope of this study of pre-Civil War culture.

6. Nina Baym, *Novels, Readers, and Reviewers: Responses to Fiction in Antebellum America* (Ithaca: Cornell University Press, 1984), 208.

7. Southworth was criticized by her contemporary reviewers for imitating the Brontë sisters too slavishly, perhaps because *Wuthering Heights* and *Jane Eyre* advance heterodox notions about Christianity and women's roles. For instance, in *Mrs. E. D. E. N. Southworth, Novelist* (Washington, D. C.: Catholic University of America Press, 1939), Regis Louise Boyle cites a review of *The Deserted Wife* published in *The New York Literary World* (Evert Duyckinck's journal) that notes the strong similarities between Hagar and Catherine Earnshaw and between minor characters and Rochester and Jane, and then takes Southworth to task for being too imitative (53).

8. *The Letters of Herman Melville,* ed. Merrell R. Davis and William H. Gilman (New Haven: Yale University Press, 1960), 128.

9. Ibid., 102.

10. The best discussions of Southworth's career are provided by Joanne Dobson in her introduction to *The Hidden Hand or, Capitola the Madcap* (New Brunswick,

N.J.: Rutgers University Press, 1988), xi–xlv; Mary Kelley, *Private Woman, Public Stage: Literary Domesticity in Nineteenth-Century America* (New York: Oxford University Press, 1984), which is especially cogent on Southworth's professional maneuverings following her husband's desertion; and Susan Coultrap-McQuin, *Doing Literary Business: American Women Writers in the Nineteenth Century* (Chapel Hill: University of North Carolina Press, 1990), esp. chap. 3, "The Place of Gender in Business: The Career of E. D. E. N. Southworth," 49–78. Boyle's *Mrs. E. D. E. N. Southworth, Novelist* places Southworth in context of the reviewing establishment and emphasizes the novelist's sense of humor, but Boyle does not seem sympathetic to Southworth's style nor the issues she raises in her fiction.

11. John S. Hart, *The Female Prose Writers of America*, rev. ed. (Philadelphia: E. H. Butler, 1855), 212.

12. Ibid., 213.

13. *Retribution; or, The Vale of Shadows. A Tale of Passion* (New York: Harper and Brothers, 1849), 85. All further references will be cited in the text.

14. Philadelphia: T. B. Peterson, 1854, 171–72. All further references will be cited in the text.

15. *Woman's Record; or, Sketches of all Distinguished Women, from the Creation to A. D. 1854*, 2nd, rev. ed. (New York: Harper and Brothers, 1860), 794.

16. Quoted in Baym, *Novels, Readers, and Reviewers*, 208.

17. Quoted in Dobson, "Introduction," xxvi.

18. Dating Southworth's novels is problematic, mainly because they were published in book form at varying durations following serialization. I date the texts by the initial serial publication, using the term "circa" to distinguish serial from book publication. I have relied on the datings provided by Dobson, Kelley, and Boyle.

19. Review of *The Curse of Clifton* (unsigned), *Godey's Lady's Book* 46 (1853): 371.

20. James D. Hart, *The Popular Book: A History of America's Literary Taste* (Berkeley and Los Angeles: University of California Press, 1963), 110.

21. For an excellent analysis of *India* as women's frontier fiction, see Annette Kolodny, *The Land Before Her: Fantasy and Experience of the American Frontier, 1630–1860* (Chapel Hill: University of North Carolina Press, 1984), 203–13.

22. "Hawthorne and His Mosses," in *Moby-Dick*, ed. Harrison Hayford and Hershel Parker (New York: Norton, 1967), 542.

23. *Representative Men* (Cambridge: Riverside Press, 1883), 193, 185.

24. Merton M. Sealts Jr., *Melville's Reading*, rev. ed. (Columbia: University of South Carolina Press, 1988), 176.

25. *Call Me Ishmael* (New York: Reynal and Hitchcock, 1947).

26. Boyle, *Mrs. E. D. E. N. Southworth*, 13.

27. In *Woman's Fiction: A Guide to Novels by and about Women in America, 1820–1870* (Ithaca: Cornell University Press, 1978), Nina Baym has discussed the ethical and political implications of "woman's fiction." Baym convincingly argues that female writers of the early to mid-nineteenth century depicted a heroine's movement from helplessness to mastery. "Mastery" in this genre has a typically mid-Victorian cast: the heroine finds fulfillment in a domestic setting. As Baym writes, "woman's fiction thus represented a protest against long-entrenched trivializing and contemptuous views of women that animated the fiction of Richardson and other later eighteenth-century fiction of sensibility. . ." (29).

28. Joanne Dobson analyzes Southworth's perverse twists upon the conventional heroine, as typified by Warner's Ellen Montgomery, in her "Introduction," xxviii–xxx.

29. "Introduction," xxi. See also David S. Reynolds' intelligent discussion of the

diversity of female types in antebellum fiction in *Beneath the American Renaissance: The Subversive Imagination in the Age of Emerson and Melville* (New York: Knopf, 1988), chap. 12, "Types of Womanhood," 337–67. Reynolds observes that this fiction openly represented female rage toward economic and social hardships.

30. In *Manhood and the American Renaissance* (Ithaca: Cornell University Press, 1989), David Leverenz makes a related point:

> Faced with the pervasive ascription of deviance, male and female writers tended to manage feelings of alienation, anger, and self-doubt in opposite ways. Men adopted intellectual strate-gies of self-splitting and reader disorientation—the false bottoms that academic critics love to expose. Women wrote impassioned and often duplicitous moral dramas, mirroring the values and conflicts of genteel evangelical women readers. Nevertheless, both men and women writers make the refashioning of self and reader a central process in their texts. (18)

In *19th-Century Women's Novels: Interpretive Strategies* (Cambridge, England: Cam-bridge University Press, 1990), Susan K. Harris provides a subtle, insightful analysis of "cover" plots in women's writing. Turning her attention to Southworth's *The Deserted Wife*, she remarks, "A writer committed to shifting popular images of women from the nineteenth century's valorization of the 'Angel of the House'—passive, obedient, and happy to be defined by others—to a recognition of women's talents for active self-determination, Southworth then fuses domestic imagery to a narrative framework evoking ancient Western regeneration myths" (130). I would only qualify Harris's theory by suggesting that the figure of a "cover" story misleads to the degree that Southworth openly represented oppositional (or subversive) desires. In other words, her countercultural ideals are shockingly on display in her most vivid prose, suggesting her confidence in a predominantly female readership or her assumption that readers would interpret the heterodoxy as sheer play.

31. *Letters*, 142.

32. *The Hidden Hand or, Capitola the Madcap*, ed. Joanne Dobson (New Bruns-wick, N.J.: Rutgers University Press, 1988), 121. All further references will be cited in the text.

33. The relationship between *Pierre* and the Littlepage Trilogy is indeed close, for as Samuel Otter has commented in "The Eden of Saddle Meadows: Landscape and Ideology in *Pierre*," *American Literature* 66 (1994): "We are further reminded of the violent struggle necessary for the appropriation and retention of land in America's first three centuries in the strangely oblique allusion to the fierce, prolonged Anti-Renter Wars in the Hudson River Valley from 1839 to 1846..." (69). In other words, Melville alludes to precisely the political crisis that fueled Cooper's writing in the 1840s.

34. *Letters*, 131.

35. *Subversive Genealogy: The Politics and Art of Herman Melville* (New York: Knopf, 1983), 161.

36. As Edward Halsey Foster comments, "... the landscape of Saddle Meadows, a landscape of 'uncommon loveliness,' has been purchased at an enormous cost; Saddle Meadows has associations with death and merciless slaughter. The family estate is far from being altogether the rural paradise that Pierre thinks it is." *The Civilized Wilderness: Backgrounds to American Romantic Literature, 1817–1860* (New York: The Free Press, 1975), 143. Otter amplifies this analysis when he remarks, "The landscape of Saddle Meadows ... is not merely embellished with images of Pierre's ancestors ... but saturated with reminders of those who were dispossessed" ("The Eden of Saddle Meadows," 72).

37. Edward H. Rosenberry is especially astute about the relationship between Pierre's sentimental upbringing and Melville's satiric purposes:

> . . . *Pierre* proves to be radically related to the central theme of American folk humor: Pierre is a dupe, a "sucker." He is not, however, the Yankee comic sucker, victimized by a fast-talking pitchman. He is "the fool of Truth, the fool of Virtue, the fool of Fate." As such he is what we are more likely to think of as the Cervantine or Meredithian comic sucker—the sentimentalist, whose exaggerated idealism provides the momentum for its own reduction to absurdity. In Melville as in Meredith, it is a comic absurdity only so long as the sucker fails to recognize his folly; the moment he comes face-to-face with it his absurdity becomes tragic. *Melville and the Comic Spirit* (Cambridge: Harvard University Press, 1955), 173.

38. *The Feminization of American Culture,* 355. In a provocative reading of Melville's complex text, Gillian Brown asserts, "In what is perhaps the nineteenth century's most negative portrayal of domestic values, Melville posits authorship as an annulment of the curriculum vitae supervised by sentimental motherhood and popularized by sentimental literature." *Domestic Individualism: Imagining Self in Nineteenth-Century America* (Berkeley and Los Angeles: University of California Press, 1990), 135.

39. *The Development of American Romance: The Sacrifice of Relation* (Chicago: University of Chicago Press, 1980), 228–29.

40. *The Discarded Daughter; or, The Children of the Isle. A Tale of the Chesapeake* (Philadelphia: Hart, 1852), I, 55–56. All further references will be cited in the text.

41. To garner some sense of Southworth's daring here, we should recall the degree to which Washington in particular was idolized by the early republic: "The new understanding of greatness as goodness reflected an essential theme of the antipatriarchal revolution that would replace patriarch with benefactor, precept with example, the authority of position with moral self-sufficiency, and static dichotomies with principles of growth: Sovereignty and power were no longer glorious in and of themselves. Rather, they were glorious, as Washington had demonstrated, only as opportunities to do good." Jay Fliegelman, *Prodigals and Pilgrims: The American Revolution against Patriarchal Authority, 1750–1800* (Cambridge, England: Cambridge University Press, 1982), 210–11.

42. *India: The Pearl of Pearl River* (Philadelphia: T. B. Peterson, 1856), 311–12.

43. Scholars have long noted Melville's use of the "light" and "dark" ladies of nineteenth-century romance. For example, in *The Romance in America* (Middletown, Conn.: Wesleyan University Press, 1969), Joel Porte has written that "[Lucy] is the representative of that prelapsarian world without darkness from which the fearful journey of Melville's Everyman inevitably begins" (172), while Isabel "is the dark lady made ten times darker" (173). We should also note the thematic correlation between Lucy/Isabel and Plotinus Plinlimmon's famous dichotomy of Chronometricals/Horologicals. In Melville's narrative logic, Lucy is associated with the former "Christ-like" ethical system, while Isabel embodies the latter. The writer probably intended an obscene pun upon the term (w)horological.

44. Critics have meticulously traced out the Freudian implications of Melville's novel, particularly Henry A. Murray in his introductory essay to *Pierre* (New York: Hendricks House, 1949), xiii-ciii, and Eric J. Sundquist in his witty chapter entitled "'At Home in his Words': Parody and Parricide in Melville's *Pierre*," *Home as Found: Authority and Genealogy in Nineteenth-Century American Literature* (Baltimore: Johns Hopkins University Press, 1979), 143–85.

45. *Hamlet and Oedipus* (Garden City, N.Y.: Doubleday, 1949), 97.

46. *The Feminization of American Culture,* 377.

47. Sandra M. Gilbert and Susan Gubar, *The Madwoman in the Attic: The Woman Writer and the Nineteenth-Century Literary Imagination* (New Haven: Yale University Press, 1979), 28.

48. In *Domestic Individualism*, Gillian Brown argues that Isabel embodies patriarchy, since she is the dark lady of romance who is associated with Glendinning père, and thus "the femme fatale whose appropriation reinforces masculine power" (156). I agree that this female character conforms to the "dark lady" stereotype, and thus manifests repressed desire in Mary, in the process providing powerful opposition to the false niceties of the domestic regime. Still, I would emphasize her vital role in ultimately discrediting the father.

49. See G. M. Goshgarian, *To Kiss the Chastening Rod: Domestic Fiction and Sexual Ideology in the American Renaissance* (Ithaca: Cornell University Press, 1992) for an analysis of the incestuous themes of *Pierre*, themes that this critic finds reproduced in the popular fiction of the 1850s.

50. Melville had almost certainly read *Frankenstein* prior to the writing of *Pierre*, for he received a copy from Richard Bentley during his visit to London in 1849 (Sealts, *Melville's Reading*, 214).

51. *Subversive Genealogy*, 167.

52. *What Was Literature? Class, Culture and Mass Society* (New York: Simon and Schuster, 1982), 169.

53. Southworth presents this same plot in comic form in the interpolated story of Mrs. Capitola Le Noir in *The Hidden Hand*. Cap's mother, narrating her attempt to gain freedom from her captors in the Hidden House, describes her nighttime encounter with one Colonel Eglen: "I entered his chamber, approached his bed to speak to him, when this hero of a hundred fields started up in a panic, and at the sight of the pale woman who drew his curtains in the dead of night, he shrieked, violently rang his bell, and fainted prone away!" (454).

54. *Literary Women* (Garden City, N.Y.: Doubleday, 1976), 126.

55. Alfred Habegger, "A Well-Hidden Hand," *Novel* 14 (1981): 199.

56. See Kelley 161–62 for a thoughtful analysis of Southworth's relationship with her male editors. Melville's relationship with Mrs. Morewood is intriguing, for she lent him a number of books, including Edward Bulwar-Lytton's *Zanoni*, that have been nominated as influences on *Pierre* and Melville's reading of popular novels in general. I am persuaded by Hershel Parker's argument that the male writer was quite literally writing for Mrs. Morewood as she represented the feminine reading public he needed in order to achieve a major popular success ("Why *Pierre* Went Wrong," *Studies in the Novel* 8 [1976]: 8).

57. *Sensational Designs: The Cultural Work of American Fiction, 1790–1860* (New York: Oxford University Press, 1985).

58. In "The Hidden Hand: Subversion of Cultural Ideology in Three Mid-Nineteenth-Century American Women's Novels," *American Quarterly* 38 (1986), Dobson has made a similar point about the rationalization of often unorthodox reading experience by antebellum women:

> Readers, as well as writers, were educated in the common ideology of femininity, and, on one level, they probably read for a literary experience that affirmed the ideology structuring their lives. In all of these novels, including *The Hidden Hand*, they were allowed such an affirmation, which may well have relieved latent anxieties regarding the nature of their lives. Individuals, however, are never completely constituted by the cultural ideal toward which they may well strive. Even conforming writers and readers must have brought to a text experiences and observations that lay beyond the purlieus of the conventional. (228)

59. *Reading the Romance: Women, Patriarchy, and Popular Literature* (Chapel Hill: University of North Carolina Press, 1984), 17.

60. "Introduction," xxxv.

61. See chap. 1, section 2, "Sibling Rivalry," for a fuller account of Beecher's influential presentation of familial relationships.

62. Review of *Pierre* (unsigned), *Godey's Lady's Book* 44 (1852): 390.

63. Here I take issue with Parker's overall argument in "Why *Pierre* Went Wrong," for he asserts that Melville's trip to New York City during the composition of the novel, a trip during which Melville read the mixed reviews for *Moby-Dick*, skewed the novel-in-progress by redirecting the writer's concerns from the bildungsroman of an American aristocrat to antebellum literary culture. However, I read the satire on Young America as a digression rather than a full-blown reorientation of the novel, for Pierre's tragic march toward self-immolation continues apace. His failed attempt to write a great book symbolizes his larger failure to mature toward an Ishmaelian complex understanding of a world of sweets and sours.

64. *Domestic Individualism*, 142.

65. *Manhood and the American Renaissance*, 74.

CONCLUSION: THE FALL OF THE HOUSE OF AMERICA

1. See Douglas Robinson's *American Apocalypses: The Image of the End of the World in American Literature* (Baltimore: Johns Hopkins University Press, 1985) for the now definitive treatment of American apocalyptic literature, including an extensive treatment of Poe as *the* American apocalyptic writer. I have not attempted to engage the voluminous critical commentary on "The Fall of the House of Usher." I am conscious of Robinson's influence on my interpretation of the narrative, especially in the critic's assertion that Roderick and Madeline "are . . . incarcerated . . . in selfhood, in a fearful, anticommunal individuality that, following Emerson, finds all presence inside but inexorably constricts into absence" (175).

2. *The Dispossessed Garden: Pastoral and History in Southern Literature* (Athens: University of Georgia Press, 1975), 67.

3. "Amorous Bondage: Poe, Ladies, and Slaves," *American Literature* 66 (1994): 252.

4. Ibid., 240.

5. "The Fall of the House of Usher," in *Edgar Allan Poe: Poetry and Tales* (New York: Library of America, 1984), 317. All further references will be cited in the text.

6. "'House Divided' Speech at Springfield, Illinois," *Speeches and Writings 1832–1858* (New York: Library of America, 1989), 426.

7. *Hawthorne* (New York: St. Martin's Press, 1967), 134–35.

8. *Literary Democracy: The Declaration of Cultural Independence in America* (New York: Penguin, 1982), 170.

9. In *Atlantic Double-Cross: American Literature and British Influence in the Age of Emerson* (Chicago: University of Chicago Press, 1986), Robert Weisbuch makes a related point when he analyzes the American anxiety of influence in relationship to British writing. He observes that "it is the contemporary or near-contemporary British writer who threatens his American counterpart: he who monopolizes the attention of the American reading public and proves in his every success the attraction of the British way. The more contemporary, the more threatening is the English writer" (16). No doubt Weisbuch is correct in emphasizing the professional and pecuniary motives for this intense transatlantic sibling rivalry, motives that hold for domestic

American sibling rivalry as well. We can also follow Weisbuch's lead in considering how contemporaries equally claim allegiance to the "great tradition" (be it the British literary tradition or the founding fathers and documents of America), asserting competing purity of interpretation, competing purity of filiopiety. In sum, contemporary or sibling writers pose a far more immediate and comprehensive threat than the deceased or "irrelevant" writer.

10. In a fascinating coincidence, Willis played a prominent role in the life of Harriet Jacobs as well, for he and his wife hired Jacobs as a nursemaid after her flight to New York City. However, Jacobs did not trust her male sponsor entirely, for she believed he remained pro-slavery. Jean Fagan Yellin, "Introduction" to *Incidents in the Life of a Slave Girl, Written by Herself,* ed. Jean Fagan Yellin (Cambridge: Harvard University Press, 1987), xviii.

11. "Why *Pierre* Went Wrong," *Studies in the Novel* 8 (1976): 8.

12. *Beneath the American Renaissance: The Subversive Imagination in the Age of Emerson and Melville* (New York: Knopf, 1988), 183.

13. "Introduction: The Country of the Blue," in *American Realism: New Essays,* ed. Eric J. Sundquist (Baltimore: Johns Hopkins University Press, 1982), 5.

14. *The Incorporation of America: Culture and Society in the Gilded Age* (New York: Hill and Wang, 1982), 3–4.

15. Michael Paul Rogin, *Subversive Genealogy: The Politics and Art of Herman Melville* (New York: Knopf, 1983), 164.

16. *Hard Facts: Setting and Form in the American Novel* (New York: Oxford University Press, 1985), 131.

17. *The Education of Henry Adams* (Boston: Houghton Mifflin, 1961), 7. All further references will be cited in the text.

18. *The Incorporation of America,* 209.

19. Quoted in Trachtenberg, *The Incorporation of America,* 220.

Bibliography

Adams, Henry. *The Education of Henry Adams.* Boston: Houghton Mifflin, 1961.

Ammons, Elizabeth. "Heroines in *Uncle Tom's Cabin.*" *American Literature* 49 (1977): 161–79.

Andrews, William L. *To Tell a Free Story: The First Century of Afro-American Autobiography, 1760–1865.* Urbana: University of Illinois Press, 1986.

Ashton, Jean W. *Harriet Beecher Stowe: A Reference Guide.* Boston: G. K. Hall, 1977.

Askeland, Lori. "Remodeling the Model Home in *Uncle Tom's Cabin* and *Beloved.*" *American Literature* 64 (1992): 785–805.

Axelrad, Allan M. *History and Utopia: A Study of the World View of James Fenimore Cooper.* Norwood, Penn.: Norwood Editions, 1978.

Baker Jr., Houston A. *The Journey Back: Issues in Black Literature and Criticism.* Chicago: University of Chicago Press, 1980.

Bakhtin, Mikhail. "Discourse in the Novel." In *The Dialogic Imagination: Four Essays.* Ed. Michael Holquist. Trans. Caryl Emerson and Michael Holquist. Austin: University of Texas Press, 1981. 259–422.

———. "Epic and Novel: Toward a Methodology for the Study of the Novel." In *The Dialogic Imagination.* 3–40.

———. *Problems of Dostoevsky's Poetics.* Ed. and Trans. Caryl Emerson. Minneapolis: University of Minnesota Press, 1984.

Bakker, Jan. "Time and Timelessness in Images of the Old South: Pastoral in John Pendleton Kennedy's *Swallow Barn* and *Horse-shoe Robinson.*" *Tennessee Studies in Literature* 26 (1981): 75–88.

Barnum, P. T. *Struggles and Triumphs Or, Forty Years' Recollections.* New York: Penguin, 1981.

Baym, Nina. *Novels, Readers, and Reviewers: Responses to Fiction in Antebellum America.* Ithaca: Cornell University Press, 1984.

———. *Woman's Fiction: A Guide to Novels by and about Women in America, 1820–1870.* Ithaca: Cornell University Press, 1978.

Beecher, Catharine E. *A Treatise on Domestic Economy, for the Use of Young Ladies at Home and at School.* Boston: Marsh, Capen, Lyon, and Webb, 1841.

Bell, Michael Davitt. *The Development of American Romance: The Sacrifice of Relation.* Chicago: University of Chicago Press, 1980.

Bird, Robert Montgomery. *Nick of the Woods, or The Jibbenainosay, A Tale of Kentucky.* Philadelphia: Carey, Lea, and Blanchard, 1837.

Bjornson, Richard. *The Picaresque Hero in European Fiction.* Madison: University of Wisconsin Press, 1977.

Blair, Walter, and Hamlin Hill. *America's Humor from Poor Richard to Doonesbury.* New York: Oxford University Press, 1978.

Blassingame, John W. *The Slave Community: Plantation Life in the Ante-bellum South*. New York: Oxford University Press, 1972.

Bloom, Harold. *The Anxiety of Influence: A Theory of Poetry*. New York: Oxford University Press, 1973.

Bohner, Charles H. *John Pendleton Kennedy: Gentleman from Baltimore*. Baltimore: Johns Hopkins University Press, 1961.

Boyle, Regis Louise. *Mrs. E. D. E. N. Southworth, Novelist*. Washington, D. C.: Catholic University of America Press, 1939.

Bradfield, Scott. *Dreaming Revolution: Transgression in the Development of American Romance*. Iowa City: University of Iowa Press, 1993.

Brodhead, Richard. *Hawthorne, Melville, and the Novel*. Chicago: University of Chicago Press, 1976.

Brown, Gillian. *Domestic Individualism: Imagining Self in Nineteenth-Century America*. Berkeley and Los Angeles: University of California Press, 1990.

Butler, Michael D. "Narrative Structure and Historical Process in *The Last of the Mohicans*." *American Literature* 48 (1976): 117–39.

Butterfield, Stephen. *Black Autobiography in America*. Amherst: University of Massachusetts Press, 1974.

Byerman, Keith. "We Wear the Mask: Deceit as Theme and Style in Slave Narratives." In *The Art of the Slave Narrative*. Ed. John Sekora and Darwin T. Turner. Carbondale: Western Illinois University Press, 1982. 70–82.

Chandler, Marilyn R. *Dwelling in the Text: Houses in American Fiction*. Berkeley and Los Angeles: University of California Press, 1991.

Charvat, William. *The Profession of Authorship in America, 1800–1870. The Papers of William Charvat*. Ed. Matthew J. Bruccoli. Columbus: Ohio State University Press, 1968.

Clark Jr., Clifford Edward. *The American Family Home, 1800–1960*. Chapel Hill: University of North Carolina Press, 1986.

Cooke, John Esten. *The Virginia Comedians: or, Old Days in the Old Dominion. Edited from the MSS. of C. Effingham, Esq.* New York: D. Appleton, 1854.

Cooper, James Fenimore. *The American Democrat*. New York: Penguin, 1969.

——. *The Chainbearer or The Littlepage Manuscripts*. Boston: Houghton Mifflin, n. d.

——. *The Last of the Mohicans; A Narrative of 1757*. In *The Leatherstocking Tales*, Vol. 1. New York: Library of America, 1985.

——. *The Letters and Journals of James Fenimore Cooper*, Vol. 5, 1845–1849. Ed. James Franklin Beard. Cambridge: Belknap, 1968.

——. *The Pioneers, or the Sources of the Susquehanna; A Descriptive Tale*. In *The Leatherstocking Tales*, Vol. 1. New York: Library of America, 1985.

——. *The Redskins or Indian and Injin, being the conclusion of the Littlepage Manuscripts*. Boston: Houghton Mifflin, n. d.

——. *Satanstoe or The Littlepage Manuscripts, A Tale of the Colony*. Boston: Houghton Mifflin, n. d.

Cosgrove, William. "Family Lineage and Narrative Pattern in Cooper's Littlepage Trilogy." *Forum* 12 (1974): 2–8.

Cott, Nancy F. *The Bonds of Womanhood: "Woman's Sphere" in New England, 1780–1835*. New Haven: Yale University Press, 1977.

Coultrap-McQuin, Susan. *Doing Literary Business: American Women Writers in the Nineteenth Century.* Chapel Hill: University of North Carolina Press, 1990.

Cowie, Alexander. *The Rise of the American Novel.* New York: American Book Company, 1946.

Crozier, Alice C. *The Novels of Harriet Beecher Stowe.* New York: Oxford University Press, 1969.

Davidson, Cathy N. *Revolution and the Word: The Rise of the Novel in America.* New York: Oxford University Press, 1986.

Davis, Charles T., and Henry Louis Gates Jr. "Introduction." In *The Slave's Narrative.* Ed. Charles T. Davis and Henry Louis Gates Jr. New York: Oxford University Press, 1985. xi–xxxiv.

Dawley, Alan. *Class and Community: The Industrial Revolution in Lynn.* Cambridge: Harvard University Press, 1976.

Dayan, Joan. "Amorous Bondage: Poe, Ladies, and Slaves." *American Literature* 66 (1994): 239–73.

Dekker, George. *The American Historical Romance.* Cambridge, England: Cambridge University Press, 1987.

———. *James Fenimore Cooper: The American Scott.* New York: Barnes and Noble, 1967.

Dickinson, Emily. *The Complete Poems.* Ed. Thomas H. Johnson. Boston: Little, Brown, 1960.

Dobson, Joanne. "The Hidden Hand: Subversion of Cultural Ideology in Three Mid-Nineteenth-Century American Women's Novels." *American Quarterly* 38 (1986): 223–42.

———. "Introduction." *The Hidden Hand or, Capitola the Madcap.* New Brunswick, N.J.: Rutgers University Press, 1988. xi–xlv.

Doherty, Robert. *Society and Power: Five New England Towns, 1800–1860.* Amherst: University of Massachusetts Press, 1977.

Donovan, Josephine. *New England Local Color Literature: A Woman's Tradition.* New York: Ungar, 1983.

Douglas, Ann. *The Feminization of American Culture.* New York: Avon, 1977.

Douglass, Frederick. *My Bondage and My Freedom.* New York: Dover, 1969.

———. *Narrative of the Life of Frederick Douglass, an American Slave, Written by Himself.* Boston: Anti-Slavery Office, 1845.

Dowling, William C. *Jameson, Althusser, Marx: An Introduction to The Political Unconscious.* Ithaca: Cornell University Press, 1984.

Downing, Andrew Jackson. *The Architecture of Country Houses.* New York: D. Appleton, 1850.

Eliade, Mircea. *The Sacred and the Profane: The Nature of Religion.* New York: Harper, 1959.

Elliot, Emory. *Revolutionary Writers: Literature and Authority in the New Republic, 1775–1810.* New York: Oxford University Press, 1982.

Emerson, Ralph Waldo. *Representative Men.* Cambridge: Riverside Press, 1883.

Fern, Fanny. *Ruth Hall and Other Writings.* New Brunswick, N.J.: Rutgers University Press, 1986.

Fiedler, Leslie. *What Was Literature? Class, Culture and Mass Society.* New York: Simon and Schuster, 1982.

Fields, Annie. *Life and Letters of Harriet Beecher Stowe.* Boston: Houghton Mifflin, 1897.

Fisher, Philip. *Hard Facts: Setting and Form in the American Novel.* New York: Oxford University Press, 1985.

Fliegelman, Jay. *Prodigals and Pilgrims: The American Revolution against Patriarchal Authority, 1750–1800.* Cambridge, England: Cambridge University Press, 1982.

Foley, Barbara. *Telling the Truth: The Theory and Practice of Documentary Fiction.* Ithaca: Cornell University Press, 1986.

Foster, Edward Halsey. *The Civilized Wilderness: Backgrounds to American Romantic Literature, 1817–1860.* New York: The Free Press, 1975.

Foster, Frances Smith. "'In Respect to Females' . . .: Differences in the Portrayals of Women by Male and Female Narrators." *Black American Literature Forum* 15 (1981): 66–70.

———. *Witnessing Slavery: The Development of Ante-bellum Slave Narratives.* Westport, Conn.: Greenwood, 1979.

Fox-Genovese, Elizabeth. *Within the Plantation Household: Black and White Women of the Old South.* Chapel Hill: University of North Carolina Press, 1988.

Franklin, H. Bruce. *The Victim as Criminal and Artist: Literature from the American Prison.* New York: Oxford University Press, 1978.

Freud, Sigmund. *Beyond the Pleasure Principle.* Trans. James Strachey. New York: Norton, 1961.

———. "The Uncanny." Trans. Alix Strachey. In *On Creativity and the Unconscious: Papers on the Psychology of Art, Literature, Love, and Religion.* New York: Harper and Row, 1958. 122–61.

Frye, Northrop. *Anatomy of Criticism: Four Essays.* Princeton: Princeton University Press, 1957.

———. *The Secular Scripture: A Study of the Structure of Romance.* Cambridge: Harvard University Press, 1976.

Garrett, Peter K. *The Victorian Multiplot Novel: Studies in Dialogical Form.* New Haven: Yale University Press, 1980.

Gates Jr., Henry Louis. "Binary Oppositions in Chapter One of *Narrative of the Life of Frederick Douglass an American Slave Written by Himself.*" In *Afro-American Literature: The Reconstruction of Instruction.* Ed. Dexter Fisher and Robert B. Stepto. New York: MLA, 1979. 212–32.

———. *The Signifying Monkey: A Theory of Afro-American Literary Criticism.* New York: Oxford University Press, 1988.

Genovese, Eugene D. *Roll, Jordan, Roll: The World the Slaves Made.* New York: Pantheon, 1974.

Gilbert, Sandra M., and Susan Gubar. *The Madwoman in the Attic: The Woman Writer and the Nineteenth-Century Literary Imagination.* New Haven: Yale University Press, 1979.

Gilligan, Carol. *In a Different Voice: Psychological Theory and Women's Development.* Cambridge: Harvard University Press, 1982.

Godden, Richard. "Pioneer Properties, or 'What's in a Hut?'" In *James Fenimore Cooper: New Critical Essays.* Ed. Robert Clark. London: Vision and Barnes and Noble, 1985. 121–42.

Goshgarian, G. M. *To Kiss the Chastening Rod: Domestic Fiction and Sexual Ideology in the American Renaissance.* Ithaca: Cornell University Press, 1992.

Gossett, Thomas F. *Uncle Tom's Cabin and American Culture*. Dallas: Southern Methodist University Press, 1985.

Grean, Stanley. *Shaftesbury's Philosophy of Religion and Ethics*. Athens: Ohio University Press, 1967.

Green, Martin. *The Great American Adventure*. Boston: Beacon, 1984.

Habegger, Alfred. *Gender, Fantasy, and Realism in American Literature*. New York: Columbia University Press, 1982.

———. "A Well-Hidden Hand." *Novel* 14 (1981): 197–12.

Hale, Sarah Josepha. *Woman's Record; or, Sketches of all Distinguished Women, from the Creation to A. D. 1854*. 2nd, rev. ed. New York: Harper and Brothers, 1860.

Halttunen, Karen. *Confidence Men and Painted Women: A Study of Middle-Class Culture in America, 1830–1870*. New Haven: Yale University Press, 1982.

———. "Gothic Imagination and Social Reform: The Haunted Houses of Lyman Beecher, Henry Ward Beecher, and Harriet Beecher Stowe." In *New Essays on Uncle Tom's Cabin*. Ed. Eric J. Sundquist. Cambridge, England: Cambridge University Press, 1986. 107–34.

Harris, Susan K. *19th-Century American Women's Novels: Interpretive Strategies*. Cambridge, England: Cambridge University Press, 1990.

Hart, James D. *The Popular Book: A History of America's Literary Taste*. Berkeley and Los Angeles: University of California Press, 1963.

Hart, John S. *The Female Prose Writers of America*. Rev. ed. Philadelphia: E. H. Butler, 1855.

Hawthorne, Nathaniel. *The Blithedale Romance*. New York: Norton, 1978.

Hedin, Raymond. "The American Slave Narrative: The Justification of the Picaro." *American Literature* 53 (1982): 630–45.

Hedrick, Joan D. "'Peacable Fruits': The Ministry of Harriet Beecher Stowe." *American Quarterly* 40 (1988): 307–32.

Henderson III, Harry B. *Versions of the Past: The Historical Imagination in American Fiction*. New York: Oxford University Press, 1974.

Hentz, Caroline Lee. *The Planter's Northern Bride*. Chapel Hill: University of North Carolina Press, 1970.

Herbert Jr., T. Walter. *Dearest Beloved: The Hawthornes and the Making of the Middle-Class Family*. Berkeley and Los Angeles: University of California Press, 1993.

Herzog, Kristen. *Women, Ethnics, and Exotics: Images of Power in Mid-Nineteenth-Century American Fiction*. Knoxville: University of Tennessee Press, 1983.

Hooper, Johnson Jones. *Adventures of Captain Simon Suggs, Late of the Tallapoosa Volunteers*. Chapel Hill: University of North Carolina Press, 1969.

Hubbell, Jay B. *The South in American Literature, 1607–1900*. Durham, N.C.: Duke University Press, 1954.

Ickstadt, Heinz. "Instructing the American Democrat: Cooper and the Concept of Popular Fiction in Jacksonian America." In *James Fenimore Cooper: New Critical Essays*. Ed. Robert Clark. London: Vision and Barnes and Noble, 1985. 15–37.

Irving, Washington. *A History of New York*. New Haven: College and University Press, 1964.

Iser, Wolfgang. *The Act of Reading: A Theory of Aesthetic Response*. Baltimore: Johns Hopkins University Press, 1978.

Jacobs, Harriet A. *Incidents in the Life of a Slave Girl, Written by Herself.* Ed. Jean Fagan Yellin. Cambridge: Harvard University Press, 1987.

James, Henry. *Hawthorne.* New York: St. Martin's Press, 1967.

Jameson, Fredric. *The Political Unconscious: Narrative as a Socially Symbolic Act.* Ithaca: Cornell University Press, 1981.

Johnson, Paul E. *A Shopkeeper's Millennium: Society and Revivals in Rochester, New York, 1815–1837.* New York: Hill and Wang, 1978.

Jones, Ernest. *Hamlet and Oedipus.* Garden City, N.Y.: Doubleday, 1949.

Jones, Howard Mumford. *The Pursuit of Happiness.* Ithaca: Cornell University Press, 1953.

Karcher, Carolyn L. *Slavery, Race, and Violence in Melville's America.* Baton Rouge: Louisiana State University Press, 1980.

Kelley, Mary. *Private Woman, Public Stage: Literary Domesticity in Nineteenth-Century America.* New York: Oxford University Press, 1984.

Kennedy, John Pendleton. *Swallow Barn, or A Sojourn in the Old Dominion.* Philadelphia: Carey and Lea, 1832.

———. *Swallow Barn, or A Sojourn in the Old Dominion.* Rev. ed. New York: George P. Putnam, 1851.

Kermode, Frank. *The Sense of an Ending: Studies in the Theory of Fiction.* New York: Oxford University Press, 1967.

Kirkham, E. Bruce. *The Building of Uncle Tom's Cabin.* Knoxville: University of Tennessee Press, 1977.

Kolodny, Annette. *The Land Before Her: Fantasy and Experience of the American Frontier, 1630–1860.* Chapel Hill: University of North Carolina Press, 1984.

Leverenz, David. *Manhood and the American Renaissance.* Ithaca: Cornell University Press, 1989.

Lewis, Paul. "Mysterious Laughter: Humor and Fear in Gothic Fiction." *Genre* 14 (1981): 309–27.

Lincoln, Abraham. "'House Divided' Speech at Springfield, Illinois." In *Speeches and Writings 1832–1858.* New York: Library of America, 1989. 426–34.

Lindberg, Gary. *The Confidence Man in American Literature.* New York: Oxford University Press, 1982.

Lynn, Kenneth S. "Introduction." *Uncle Tom's Cabin or Life among the Lowly.* Cambridge: Belknap, 1962. vii–xxiv.

MacKethan, Lucinda. "Introduction." *Swallow Barn, or, A Sojourn in the Old Dominion.* Baton Rouge: Louisiana State University Press, 1986. xi–xxxiii.

McDowell, Deborah E. "In the First Place: Making Frederick Douglass and the Afro-American Narrative Tradition." Paper presented at "'Looking Back with Pleasure': A Bicentennial Commemoration of Equiano's *Narrative.*" University of Utah, 28 October 1989.

McWilliams Jr., John P. *The American Epic: Transforming a Genre, 1770–1860.* Cambridge, England: Cambridge University Press, 1989.

———. *Political Justice in a Republic: James Fenimore Cooper's America.* Berkeley and Los Angeles: University of California Press, 1972.

Melville, Herman. "Hawthorne and His Mosses." In *Moby-Dick.* Ed. Harrison Hayford and Hershel Parker. New York: Norton, 1967. 535–51.

———. *The Letters of Herman Melville.* Ed. Merrell R. Davis and William H. Gilman. New Haven: Yale University Press, 1960.

———. *Pierre or The Ambiguities.* Evanston: Northwestern-Newberry, 1971.

Meyers, Marvin. *The Jacksonian Persuasion: Politics and Belief.* Stanford: Stanford University Press, 1957.

Moers, Ellen. *Literary Women.* Garden City, N.Y.: Doubleday, 1976.

Morrison, Toni. "An Interview conducted by Nellie McKay." *Contemporary Literature* 24 (1983): 413–29.

Murray, Henry A. "Introduction." *Pierre or, The Ambiguities.* New York: Hendricks House, 1949. xiii-ciii.

Nelson, Dana D. *The Word in Black and White: Reading "Race" in American Literature, 1638–1867.* New York: Oxford University Press, 1992.

Niemtzow, Annette. "The Problematic of Self in Autobiography: The Example of the Slave Narrative." In *The Art of the Slave Narrative.* Ed. John Sekora and Darwin T. Turner. Carbondale: Western Illinois University Press, 1982. 96–109.

Olsen, Charles. *Call Me Ishmael.* New York: Reynal and Hitchcock, 1947.

Osborne, William S. "An Introduction." *Swallow Barn, or A Sojourn in the Old Dominion.* New York: Hafner, 1962. xiii–xliii.

Otter, Samuel. "The Eden of Saddle Meadows: Landscape and Ideology in *Pierre.*" *American Literature* 66 (1994): 55–81.

Parker, Hershel. "Why *Pierre* Went Wrong." *Studies in the Novel* 8 (1976): 7–23.

Patterson, Mark R. *Authority, Autonomy, and Representation in American Literature, 1776–1865.* Princeton: Princeton University Press, 1988.

Paulding, James Kirke. *The Dutchman's Fireside.* New Haven: College and University Press, 1966.

Peck, H. Daniel. *A World By Itself: The Pastoral Moment in Cooper's Fiction.* New Haven: Yale University Press, 1977.

Poe, Edgar Allan. *Edgar Allan Poe: Poetry and Tales.* New York: Library of America, 1984.

Porte, Joel. *The Romance in America.* Middletown, Conn.: Wesleyan University Press, 1969.

Radway, Janice. *Reading the Romance: Women, Patriarchy, and Popular Literature.* Chapel Hill: University of North Carolina Press, 1984.

Railton, Stephen. *Authorship and Audience: Literary Performance in the American Renaissance.* Princeton: Princeton University Press, 1991.

———. *Fenimore Cooper: A Study of his Life and Imagination.* Princeton: Princeton University Press, 1978.

Review of *The Curse of Clifton* (unsigned). *Godey's Lady's Book* 46 (1853): 371.

Review of *Pierre* (unsigned). *Godey's Lady's Book* 44 (1852): 390.

Reynolds, David S. *Beneath the American Renaissance: The Subversive Imagination in the Age of Emerson and Melville.* New York: Knopf, 1988.

Ridgely, J. V. *John Pendleton Kennedy.* New York: Twayne, 1966.

Ringe, Donald A. "Cooper's Littlepage Novels: Change and Stability in American Society." *American Literature* 32 (1960): 280–90.

Roberts, David. "Introduction" to "Parody's Pretexts." In *Comic Relations: Studies in the Comic, Satire, and Parody.* Ed. Pavel Petr, David Roberts, and Philip Thomson. Frankfurt am Main: Verlag Peter Lang, 1985. 183–85.

Robinson, Douglas. *American Apocalypses: The Image of the End of the World in American Literature.* Baltimore: Johns Hopkins University Press, 1985.

Rogin, Michael Paul. *Subversive Genealogy: The Politics and Art of Herman Melville.* New York: Knopf, 1983.

Rosenberry, Edward H. *Melville and the Comic Spirit.* Cambridge: Harvard University Press, 1955.

Rourke, Constance. *American Humor: A Study of the National Character.* New York: Doubleday, 1931.

Ryan, Mary P. *Cradle of the Middle Class: The Family in Oneida County, New York, 1790–1865.* Cambridge, England: Cambridge University Press, 1981.

Rybczynski, Witold. *Home: A Short History of an Idea.* New York: Penguin, 1986.

Sale, Maggie. "Critiques from Within: Antebellum Projects of Resistance." *American Literature* 64 (1992): 695–718.

Scott, Sir Walter. *Waverley.* New York: Harper and Brothers, n. d.

Sealts Jr., Merton M. *Melville's Reading.* Rev. ed. Columbia: University of South Carolina Press, 1988.

See, Fred G. *Desire and the Sign: Nineteenth-Century American Fiction.* Baton Rouge: Louisiana State University Press, 1987.

Shaftesbury, Anthony, Earl of. *Characteristics of Men, Manners, Opinions, Times.* 2nd ed. Ca. 1714. Reprint Farnborough, England: Gregg, 1968.

Shi, David E. *The Simple Life: Plain Living and High Thinking in American Culture.* New York: Oxford University Press, 1985.

Silverman, Kenneth. *Edgar A. Poe: Mournful and Never-Ending Remembrance.* New York: HarperCollins, 1991.

Simmons, Nancy Craig. "Why an Enthusiast? Melville's *Pierre* and the Problem of the Imagination." *ESQ* 33 (1987): 146–67.

Simms, William Gilmore. *Woodcraft or, Hawks about the Dovecoat: A Story of the South at the Close of the Revolution.* New York: Norton, 1961.

Simpson, Lewis P. *The Dispossessed Garden: Pastoral and History in Southern Literature.* Athens: University of Georgia Press, 1975.

Sklar, Kathryn Kish. *Catharine Beecher: A Study in American Domesticity.* New York: Norton, 1976.

Slotkin, Richard. *Regeneration through Violence: The Mythology of the American Frontier, 1600–1860.* Middletown, Conn.: Wesleyan University Press, 1973.

Southworth, E. D. E. N. *The Curse of Clifton.* Philadelphia: T. B. Peterson, 1852.

——. *The Deserted Wife.* New York: D. Appleton, 1850.

——. *The Discarded Daughter; or, The Children of the Isle. A Tale of the Chesapeake.* Philadelphia: Hart, 1852.

——. *The Hidden Hand or, Capitola the Madcap.* Ed. Joanne Dobson. New Brunswick, N.J.: Rutgers University Press, 1988.

——. *India: The Pearl of Pearl River.* Philadelphia: T. B. Peterson, 1856.

——. *The Lost Heiress, A Novel.* Philadelphia: T. B. Peterson, 1854.

——. *Retribution; or, The Vale of Shadows. A Tale of Passion.* New York: Harper and Brothers, 1849.

Spengemann, William C. *The Adventurous Muse: The Poetics of American Fiction, 1789–1900.* New Haven: Yale University Press, 1977.

Spillers, Hortense J. "Changing the Letter: The Yokes, the Jokes of Discourse, or, Mrs. Stowe, Mr. Reed." In *Slavery and the Literary Imagination*. Ed. Deborah E. McDowell and Arnold Rampersad. Baltimore: Johns Hopkins University Press, 1989. 25–61.

Stampp, Kenneth M. *The Peculiar Institution: Slavery in the Ante-bellum South*. New York: Vintage, 1956.

Stone, Albert E. "Identity and Art in Frederick Douglass's *Narrative*." *CLA Journal* 17 (1973): 192–213.

Stowe, Harriet Beecher. Letter to Lord Denmar, d. 20 January 1853. HM 24162, Huntington Library.

———. "Uncle Lot." In *Regional Sketches, New England and Florida*. Ed. John R. Adams. New Haven: College and University Press, 1972. 31–55.

———. *Uncle Tom's Cabin; or, Life among the Lowly*. In *Harriet Beecher Stowe: Three Novels*. New York: Library of America, 1982.

Sundquist, Eric J. *Home as Found: Authority and Genealogy in Nineteenth-Century American Literature*. Baltimore: Johns Hopkins University Press, 1979.

———. "Introduction: The Country of the Blue." In *American Realism: New Essays*. Ed. Eric J. Sundquist. Baltimore: Johns Hopkins University Press, 1982. 3–24.

———. "Introduction." In *New Essays on Uncle Tom's Cabin*. Ed. Eric J. Sundquist. Cambridge, England: Cambridge University Press, 1986. 1–44.

———. "Slavery, Revolution, and the American Renaissance." In *The American Renaissance Reconsidered*. Ed. Walter Benn Michaels and Donald E. Pease. Baltimore: Johns Hopkins University Press, 1985. 1–33.

Tanner, Laura E. "Self-Conscious Representation in the Slave Narrative." *Black American Literature Forum* 21 (1987): 415–24.

Thorpe, T. B. "The Big Bear of Arkansas." In *The Mirth of a Nation: America's Great Dialect Humor*. Ed. Walter Blair and Raven I. McDavid Jr. Minneapolis: University of Minnesota Press, 1983. 48–59.

Tocqueville, Alexis de. *Democracy in America*. Ed. Richard D. Heffner. New York: Mentor, 1956.

Tompkins, Jane P. *Sensational Designs: The Cultural Work of American Fiction, 1790–1860*. New York: Oxford University Press, 1985.

Toth, Emily. "A Laughter of Their Own: Women's Humor in the United States." In *Critical Essays on American Humor*. Ed. William Bedford Clark and W. Craig Turner. Boston: G. K. Hall, 1984. 199–215.

Trachtenberg, Alan. *The Incorporation of America: Culture and Society in the Gilded Age*. New York: Hill and Wang, 1982.

Trollope, Frances. *Domestic Manners of the Americans*. New York: Vintage, 1949.

Walker, Nancy. *A Very Serious Thing: Women's Humor and American Culture*. Minneapolis: University of Minnesota Press, 1988.

———. *The Tradition of Women's Humor in America*. Huntington Beach, Calif.: American Studies, 1984.

Wallace, Ronald. *God Be with the Clown: Humor in American Poetry*. Columbia: University of Missouri Press, 1984.

Warner, Susan. *The Wide, Wide World*. New York: Feminist Press, 1987.

Watson Jr., Ritchie Devon. *The Cavalier in Virginia Fiction*. Baton Rouge: Louisiana State University Press, 1985.

Weisbuch, Robert. *Atlantic Double-Cross: American Literature and British Influence in the Age of Emerson*. Chicago: University of Chicago Press, 1986.

Werner, Craig. "The Old South, 1815–1840." In *The History of Southern Literature*. Baton Rouge: Louisiana State University Press, 1985. 81–91.

Willis, Susan. *Specifying: Black Women Writing the American Experience*. Madison: University of Wisconsin Press, 1987.

Wilson, Edmund. *Patriotic Gore: Studies in the Literature of the American Civil War*. New York: Oxford University Press, 1962.

Wilson, Forrest. *Crusader in Crinoline: The Life of Harriet Beecher Stowe*. New York: Lippincott, 1941.

Yacovone, Donald. "Abolitionists and the 'Language of Fraternal Love.'" In *Meanings for Manhood: Constructions of Masculinity in Victorian America*. Ed. Mark C. Carnes and Clyde Griffen. Chicago: University of Chicago Press, 1992. 85–95.

Yarborough, Richard. "Strategies of Black Characterization in *Uncle Tom's Cabin* and the Early Afro-American Novel." In *New Essays on Uncle Tom's Cabin*. Ed. Eric J. Sundquist. Cambridge, England: Cambridge University Press, 1986. 45–84.

Yellin, Jean Fagan. *The Intricate Knot: Black Figures in American Literature, 1776–1863*. New York: New York University Press, 1972.

———. "Introduction." *Incidents in the Life of a Slave Girl, Written by Herself*. Ed. Jean Fagan Yellin. Cambridge: Harvard University Press, 1987. xiii–xxxiv.

Young, Robert. "Back to Bakhtin." *Cultural Critique* 2 (1985–86): 71–92.

Ziff, Larzer. *Literary Democracy: The Declaration of Cultural Independence in America*. New York: Penguin, 1982.

———. *Writing in the New Nation: Prose, Print, and Politics in the Early United States*. New Haven: Yale University Press, 1991.

Zwarg, Christina. "Fathering and Blackface in *Uncle Tom's Cabin*." *Novel* 22 (1989): 274–87.

Index